NARRATIVE MAGIC IN THE FICTION OF ISABEL ALLENDE

NARRATIVE MAGIC IN THE FICTION OF ISABEL ALLENDE

Patricia Hart

Rutherford • Madison • Teaneck
Fairleigh Dickinson University Press
London and Toronto: Associated University Presses

This work grew out of a dissertation of the same title at the University of North Carolina at Chapel Hill, © 1987 by Patricia Hart.

Associated University Presses
440 Forsgate Drive
Cranbury, NJ 08512

Associated University Presses
25 Sicilian Avenue
London WC1A 2QH, England

Associated University Presses
P.O. Box 488, Port Credit
Mississauga, Ontario
Canada L5G 4M2

The paper used in this publication meets the requirements of the American National Standard for Permanence of Paper for Printed Library Materials Z39.48-1984.

Library of Congress Cataloging-in-Publication Data

Hart, Patricia, 1954–
Narrative magic in the fiction of Isabel Allende / Patricia Hart.
p. cm.
Originally presented as the author's thesis (University of North Carolina at Chapel Hill) with same title.
Bibliography: p.
Includes index.
ISBN 0-8386-3351-X (alk. paper)
1. Allende, Isabel—Criticism and interpretation. 2. Magic in literature. I. Title.
PQ8098.1.L54Z69 1989 88-46152
CIP

PRINTED IN THE UNITED STATES OF AMERICA

CONTENTS

ACKNOWLEDGMENTS

Many thanks—

—to Alicia Martí of Plaza y Janés Editores for kindly sending me much valuable information not available in this country regarding all three Isabel Allende novels;

—to María Salgado, for her invaluable help;

—to Frank A. Domínguez, George B. Daniel, and Frederick W. Vogler, for helpful suggestions;

—to Lauren Lepow for much-appreciated help with the editing;

—to Manuel López for the hours he spent discussing my book and his Chile;

—to Teresa Huerta, for sharing with me the poetry of Raúl Zurita

And most of all, thanks to Josef, to whom this book is dedicated.

NARRATIVE MAGIC IN THE FICTION OF ISABEL ALLENDE

1
INTRODUCTION

Os amo, idealismo y realismo
como agua y piedra
sois
partes del mundo
luz y raíz del árbol de la vida.
—Pablo Neruda, "La verdad"

There is magic at the heart of Isabel Allende's 1982 novel, *La casa de los espíritus*. Readers sense it, and virtually every critic or reviewer mentions it—frequently applying ready-made labels like *magical realism* or *Garciamarquian*. But despite this magic, the book's climax is based on a starkly real historical event, the military coup that ended the government of Salvador Allende in 1973 and its bloody aftermath. Allende's 1985 book, *De amor y de sombra*, also has touches of magic, of hyperbole, of tall tale, but it is based largely on a somber true occurrence, the discovery of fifteen unidentified bodies in a clandestine grave near the Chilean locale of Lonquén. In Allende's 1983 children's book, *La gorda de porcelana*, reality and fantasy again vie for prominence, and even in the author's 1974 book, *Civilice a su troglodita* (a compilation of satirical pieces on the war of the sexes published originally in the magazine *Paula*), whimsy, hyperbole, and a sometimes literal expression of figurative truths make reality and the fanciful difficult to separate. Isabel Allende's newest novel at this writing, *Eva Luna*, contains a mixture of marvel and hyperbole in settings that range from lush jungles to unnamed metropolises. Again in this novel the real coexists with the unlikely, and the plausible with the fantastic. Does all this mean that Isabel Allende is a new practitioner of that amorphous Latin American tendency, magical realism? Or has she by her politics, her commitment to women's issues, her liberal, liberated female characters, and even her gender forged a new category that we might call *magical feminism*? Has Allende developed her own, individual style of combining the magical and the real, or is her work a slavish imitation of the master, Gabriel García Márquez? Did she begin under the Colombian's shadow but then grow more independent with *De amor y de sombra,* or was the second novel a comedown from the first? And what about her most recent novel at the date of this writing, *Eva Luna?* Is it magically real, magically feminist, *Garciamarquian,* or something else entirely? Most importantly, do the realistic and magical currents flow together harmoniously in the three novels, or are they at odds with each other? This study will examine in depth the role of magic in the fiction of Isabel Allende in an attempt to suggest answers to the above questions.

MAGIC, REALISM, AND MAGICAL REALISM

Before one can begin to say anything about magic, realism, or magical realism in the novels of Isabel Allende, it is necessary to define the terms—not an easy task, despite their simple appearance. Let us begin with *realism.* Realism initially sounds straightforward enough—of or relating to that which is real. But what is real and what is not turns out to be a distinction philosophers have debated for centuries. Even when the term is reduced to its literary dimensions, historical background weighs heavily on a simple definition.

In this simplest form, most literary definitions of realism come eventually to the idea of an imitation of nature. For example, according to the *Diccionario enciclopédico Espasa,* "realismo" is defined as:

> sistema estético que asigna como fin a las obras artísticas o literarias la imitación fiel de la naturaleza.[1]

The *Diccionario Enciclopédico Salvat* repeats these words virtually verbatim, and adds:

> realmente, lo que se encuentra en la base de todo arte realista es el viejo concepto aristotélico de mímesis.

From the earliest novels written as the genre emerged in Europe, one can find examples of books that attempted to hold up a mirror to life and reflect it honestly, for example first in Defoe and Richardson and later in Dickens and Balzac. But when one speaks of realism as a literary movement, the term gains the weight of its particular historical moment. As C. Hugh Holman put it in his *Handbook to Literature:*

> Realism in the broadest sense is simple fidelity to actuality in its representation in literature . . . [but] . . . in order to give it a more precise definition, one needs to [consider] the movement which arose in the nineteenth century, at least partially in reaction against romanticism, and which was centered on the novel. . . . In this latter sense, realism defines a literary method, a philosophical and political attitude, and a particular kind of subject matter.[2]

So as the so-called realistic novel developed, it was in part a political reaction to what had gone before. Holman recognized the force of this political element on the genre and pointed out that although one person's idea of truth and reality may not be another's, still the great practitioners of the form had a common set of values:

> Generally, the realist is a believer in democracy, and the materials he elects to describe are the common, the average, the everyday. Furthermore, realism can be thought of as the ultimate middle-class art, and it finds its subject in bourgeois life and manners.[3]

If the realistic novel is the ultimate expression of the middle class and its cornerstone bourgeois manners and values, then it is not difficult to begin to postulate why the form could not remain indefinitely the most apt means of expression for Latin America. In England and the United States most of the prizewinning novels continue to be essentially realistic and essentially middle-class. But Latin America in general has never really seen the emergence of a large middle class on the scale that occurred in the United States and Europe. Moreover, the realistic novel developed late in Spain and later still in Latin America, so that other considerations were already competing with the desire for pure realism by the time the first important novels appeared there. To illustrate this, I will begin by noting that many definers of realism as a literary mode see it as the opposite of idealism or subjectivity. Consider the definition given by *Webster's Third New International Dictionary,* for example:

> Preoccupation with fact or reality. Objective procedure not influenced by idealism, speculation, or sentimentalism; disposition to

> think or act unemotionally and to reject what is impractical or visionary.[4]

Reflection on the Latin-American novel at its beginnings will show that an objective desire to mirror reality without editorial comment was rarely the purpose. Although many novels contained some realistic descriptions, from the beginning, a desire to use fiction as a means to social change is common. Examples range from *Los de abajo*, *La vorágine*, and *Doña Barbara* to *Huasipungo*, to include most of the early Latin-American novels. Realistic as passages sometimes were, these novels were all essentially novels of thesis that attempted to prove a point, whether about the role of the Indian, the importance of progress, the chaos of revolution, or the voracity of the jungle. George Eliot, one of the foremost early practitioners of the realistic novel, expressed in an aside in chapter 17 of *Adam Bede*, her opinion as to why an idealistic purpose defeats the practice of pure realism:

> Certainly . . . if I held the highest vocation of the novelist to represent things as they never have been and never will be . . . then . . . I might refashion life and character after my own liking. . . . But it happens, on the contrary, that my strongest effort is to avoid any such arbitrary picture. . . . Perhaps you will say, "Do improve the facts a little; make them more accordant with those correct views which it is our privilege to possess. . . . But, my good friend . . . these fellow mortals . . . must be accepted as they are: you can neither straighten their noses nor brighten their wit. . . . So I am content to tell my simple story . . . dreading nothing but falsity, which, despite one's best efforts, there is reason to dread.[5]

To say that the early Latin-American novels were not totally realistic because many were written in the pursuit of an ideal is not to detract from their merit, for I know of no divine decree that has determined that realism is the highest form of fiction. Rather it is meant to show that from the earliest pages, there was an important consideration competing in Latin America with the bourgeois novel's desire to hold up a mirror to life. Any novel that wishes to make a point is by definition unrealistic, for life, in general, has no point. As Holman put it:

> Life [the realist felt] lacked symmetry and plot; fiction which truthfully reflected it should, therefore, avoid symmetry and plot. Simple, clear, direct prose was the vehicle.[6]

As the novel develops in Latin America there are of course instances of realistic novels of bourgeois mores. In José Donoso's beautifully written 1966 novel, *Coronación*, for example, one senses the author's longing to be a Chilean Henry James. But Donoso longs to be many other things as well, and his later production, including *El obsceno pájaro de la noche, La misteriosa desaparición de la marquesita de Loria, Casa de campo,* and *El jardín de al lado* cover a wide range of techniques for interpreting or expressing reality that defy labeling. Later, that quintessentially elite member of the *haute bourgeoisie*, Jorge Luis Borges, goes far beyond the frustrated Englishman in his soul to combine the magical, the fantastic, and the real.

When the "Boom" brought novelists from Latin America their first international acclaim, it is interesting to note that virtually none of their work was limited to strict realism. If realism is characterized by middle-class values and a desire for objective presentation, and it is no surprise that the "Boom" writers were not strict realists, for as José Donoso himself points out in his 1972 book, *Historia personal del "Boom"*, initially virtually all the writers included were committed leftists:

> El entusiasmo de . . . [Carlos Fuentes] por la figura de Fidel Castro en esa primera etapa, su fe en la revolución, enardecía a todos. . . . Creo que esta fe y unanimidad política—o casi unanimidad—fue entonces, y siguió siendo hasta que estalló el asunto Padilla en 1971, uno de los grandes factores en la internalización de la novela hispanoamericana, unifiacando miras y metas, proporcionando una estructura ideológica de la cual se podía estar más o menos cerca—rara vez totalmente contrario—y dando por un tiempo la sensación de coherencia continental.[7]

An artistic mode that ran counter to the expression of leftist ideals could hardly be the perfect tool for authors who believed that they had not only an artistic calling, but a social one as well. Yet returning to the excesses of romanticism can hardly have appealed to these men of the late twentieth century. What solution was there, then, for writers who would express the quality life had as it reached their senses honestly yet at the same time wanted to build their narrative structures on the foundation of an idealistic philosophy such as Marxism? Of course each of the very different writers usually labeled as part of the "Boom" found an individual answer to the above question. No one with common sense would pretend that Julio Cortázar, Gabriel García

Márquez, Juan Rulfo, Mario Vargas Llosa, or Carlos Fuentes belong to a "school" with one set of values and rules, and with interchangeable techniques. Each writer finds his own solution to the dilemma of presenting Latin-American life realistically and at the same time "correctly" according to his personal philosophy. What these solutions have in common is that each of them from time to time strays from what most of us generally understand as natural law. Thus, all of these writers have at one time or another been grouped within that shifting protean heading of "magical realism."

Exactly what is magical realism? In the simplest possible terms, it is realism that is juxtaposed with magic. If realism implies an objective narrative, then magic sometimes implies just the opposite—a subjective touch, an idealistic brushstroke. In the phrase *magical realism,* two contradictory terms vie for prominence, for in the literal mind, what is realistic cannot contain magic, and what is magical cannot be called realistic. But even to understand this dichotomy, one needs a clear definition of *magic*—again, something not easy to find. The *Diccionario Enciclopédico Espasa,* for example, begins immediately to emit value judgments in its definition of "magia":

> ciencia o arte que enseña a hacer cosas extraordinarias y admirables. Tómase por lo común en mala parte.[8]

The *Oxford English Dictionary* is similarly disdainful and feels impelled to stress from the beginning the *pretended* existence of such a thing as magic, calling it:

> the pretended art of influencing the course of events, and of producing marvellous physical phenomena, by processes supposed to owe their efficacy to their power of compelling the intervention of spiritual beings, or bringing into operation some occult controlling principle of nature.[9]

The *Salvat* also stresses that such effects are only apparent, not real:

> arte de ejecutar obras aparentemente extraordinarias y admirables.[10]

And *Webster's* reduces anything denominated magic to simple sleight of hand:

> The art of producing unusual illusions by legerdemain.[11]

Anyone who thinks of the insomnia plague in Gabriel García Márquez's *Cien años de soledad*, the stalled vehicles in Cortázar's "La autopista del sur," the half-dead characters in Rulfo's *Pedro Páramo*, or the chameleon quality of Pantaleón in Vargas Llosa's *Pantaleón y las visitadoras* will realize that such a narrow definition of magic as sleight of hand or deception is likely to be of no use at all. A more helpful definition of the term comes from *The American Heritage Dictionary* (a work whose admirable attempt to avoid value judgments and to include terms from all levels of usage without prejudice has caused it to be banned from many schools in Texas). In that worthy tome, magic is defined as:

> the art . . . that attempts to produce supernatural effects or to control events in nature.[12]

Magic, then, most simply stated, is anything supernatural, and the supernatural, says the *American Heritage*, is

> . . . a power that seems to violate or go beyond natural laws.[13]

But how sufficient are these modern dictionary definitions, so useful in other contexts (for example, in trying to get a general idea of what people today may mean by a certain word) when trying to get closer to the implications of a word as old and charged with connotation as magic?

Sixteenth-century celebrated physician, theologian, and occultist Heinrich Cornelius Agrippa penned a famous treatise, *The Philosophy of Natural Magic*, which came to be known simply as *White Magic*. In it he included an entire chapter titled, "What magic is, what are the parts thereof, and how the professors thereof must be qualified." Going back to Agrippa thus reveals that the idea that magic violates natural law is a modern one, and is in fact directly opposed to his more primitive belief that magic is at the heart of nature:

> Magic is a faculty of wonderful virtue, full of most high mysteries, containing the most profound contemplation of most secret things, together with the nature, power, quality, substance and virtue thereof, as also the knowledge of whole Nature, and it doth instruct us. . . . This is the most perfect and chief Science, that sacred and sublimer kind of philosophy. . . .[14]

This view of magic as a part of science and nature reminds one of the naturalness with which medieval Spanish philosopher-king

Alfonso el Sabio juxtaposed numerology with optics, history with mythology, astrology with astronomy, and lapidary superstitions with medical knowledge of his times. Clearly, then, what seems "unnatural" may change from generation to generation, along with prevailing tastes and philosophical bents. An example within our own century would be pendular swings in what is considered "natural" or "unnatural" human sexual behavior.

Nevertheless, there is an inevitable return to the notion that magic can only be defined by contrast with natural law. In *The Golden Bough*, the classic 1890 work by Sir James George Frazer,

> In short, magic is a spurious system of natural law as well as a fallacious guide of conduct; it is a false science as well as an abortive art.[15]

The only problem with accepting Frazer's definition, so similar in fact to the simple one proposed by the *American Heritage Dictionary*, is that it implies rather optimistically an individual knowing what natural law is in a given case. As citizens of the twentieth century we believe in general that we know natural law; still, who is to say that in two decades some of our most cherished beliefs on the subject might not be proved worthless superstitions? For the primitive person, whose worldview included many "nonscientific" superstitions, the idea that magic contradicted nature was unthinkable, for he believed nature to be full of magic. By contrast, even the most modern scientist among us cannot honestly claim to fully comprehend all natural law. More to the point for this study, many of the characters in Latin-American "magically real" fiction, along with many of their readers, fall somewhere between the primitive tribesman and the modern scientist in their views of what constitutes "nature," "law," and "natural law." Moreover, it seems to me that all of these definitions leave out an important element, though perhaps they hint at it. I think that what a person tends to call "magic" produces a sense of wonder, a wonder that cannot be dispelled by rational explanation as can, say, initial marvel at some new electronic gadget. If the sense of wonder is missing, "magic" is devalued to "trickery." For example, I cannot explain the physical process through which Uri Geller bends spoons, but I do not wonder at it, because I am sure it is a conjuring trick.[16]

For these reasons, I would like to propose my own working definition of magic to be used in this study, a thoughtful one arrived at after considering the ones presented here and a dozen others:

> Any phenomenon which produces a sense of wonder in us that cannot be dispelled by what we think we know or what we assume *somebody* knows of natural law.

Ultimately, this seems the most useful definition for magic within "magical realism," any phenomenon in the narrative that goes beyond what we understand as natural law. Thus in the phrase *magical realism* a fascinating conflict of both terms and literary traditions exists, with the attempt to truthfully mirror the workings of a quotidian world vying with an idealistic desire to use literature for change, or to find in it something that transcends the banal and the mundane. That such a dichotomous mode of expression should develop in Latin America is not surprising—consider for example José Enrique Rodó's landmark work, *Ariel*, which contrasts spirit and matter, and in which materialism is synonymous with imperialism, while higher spiritual values must shy away from an overly mechanized, specialized world. From Rodó's time on, much of Latin-American literature is a body of works well aware of the threat of cultural imperialism from the north, wrestling with a desire to write like the great European and North American masters (notably Faulkner) and at the same time having something of their own, something unique.

For decades in the early twentieth century, this quest for uniqueness took the thematic form of the presence in many novels of a pitiless, overwhelming nature. It was as if there were some sort of unspoken agreement that man versus domineering nature was an "acceptable" topic. Consider Horacio Quiroga's "monte," José Eustasio Rivera's "selva," Rómulo Gallegos's "llano," or Ricardo Güiraldes's "pampas." As Carlos Fuentes put it in *La nueva novela hispanoamericana:*

> "¡Se los tragó la selva!", dice la frase final de *La Vorágine* de José Eustasio Rivera. La exclamación es algo más que la lápida de Arturo Cova y sus compañeros: podría ser el comentario a un largo siglo de novelas latinoamericanas: se los tragó la montaña, se los trago la pampa, se los tragó la mina, se los tragó el río.[17]

Moreover, not only does the role of nature dominate the thematic side of Latin-American fiction; it also controls the interpersonal relations. Says Fuentes:

Y lo que refuerza absolutamente este poder protagonista de la naturaleza es que las relaciones personales que se dan dentro de ella o en sus márgenes, son acaso más negativas y destructoras que la pura voracidad natural. La sucessión de males e injusticias en la novela hispanoamericana tradicional hace pensar que, en efecto, más vale ser tragado por la selva que sufrir la muerte lenta en una sociedad esclavista, cruel y sanguinaria.[18]

But after World War II, a realistic or even naturalistic description of the inevitability of nature seemed sadly lacking. As Hispanic America continued largely under totalitarian dictators, even after the victory in Europe of "democratic" nations, a wave of experimentation swept Latin-American novelists. Some sought to go beyond realism into surrealism, others to transcend the realists' lack of symmetry to find total absurdity in the human condition through existentialism. Enrique Anderson Imbert describes the years from 1940–55 as "Babel years" and says of the plethora of styles and techniques:

Surrealism had just burst into flame . . . combined with existential philosophies. Style strove to be essentially lyric, to express the truth of being. In addition there were stylizations of the popular element (like those of García Lorca in the preceeding generation). Between personalism and populism surged neo-romantic and neo-naturalistic tendencies. They wrote "gratuitous literature" and "committed literature," with spiritualisms and materialisms, with the beautiful and the ugly, with hopeless anguish and revolutionary ire. . . . It was as though an earthquake had unearthed all the geological strata and had juxtaposed them.[19]

One of the most important things this shake-up unearthed was the work of an exciting new multicultural author, Cuban Alejo Carpentier, who found in his new continent a way to escape the clichés that had begun to invade European fantastic literature, something he described as "lo real maravilloso." In his prologue to *El reino de este mundo* (1954), he describes this marvelous reality thus:

. . . lo maravilloso comienza a serlo de manera inequívoca cuando surge de una inesperada alteración de la realidad (el milagro), da una revelación privilegiada de la realidad de una iluminación inhabitual o singularmente favorecedora de las inadvertidas riquezas de la realidad, de una ampliación de las escalas y categorías de la realidad, percibidas con particular intensidad en virtud de una exaltación de espíritu que lo conduce a un modo de "estado límite."[20]

To believe that these marvelous events occur, one cannot take the coldly skeptical attitude toward miracles and magic that one glimpsed in the earlier definitions cited of magic. No, to really experience the kind of "marvelous realism" of which Carpentier speaks, one cannot be coldly realistic, but must be able to look beyond the quotidian. Says Carpentier:

> Para empezar, la sensación de lo maravilloso presupone una fe. Los que no creen en santos no pueden curarse con milagros de santos, ni los que no son Quijotes pueden meterse en cuerpo, alma y bienes en el mundo de Amadís de Gaula o Tirante el Blanco.[21]

Moreover, although Carpentier claims that his own initial first-hand experience with a sensation of "lo real maravilloso" occurred in Haiti, he goes on to insist that in general the phenomenon is something particular to Latin America:

> Pensaba . . . que . . . lo real maravilloso no era privilegio único de Haití, sino patrimonio de la América entera, donde todavía no se ha terminado de establecer, por ejemplo, un recuento de cosmogonías. Lo real maravilloso se encuentra a cada paso en las vidas de hombres que inscribieron fechas en la historia del continente y dejaron apellidos aún llevados: desde los buscadores de la Fuente de la Eterna Juventud, de la áurea ciudad. . . . Siempre me ha parecido significativo el hecho de que en 1780, unos cuerdos españoles, salidos de Angostura, se lanzaran todavía a la busca de El Dorado, y que, en días de la Revolución Francesa—¡vivan la Razón y el Ser Supremo!—el compostelano Francisco Menéndez anduviera por tierras de Patagonia buscando la ciudad encantada de los Césares.[22]

But perhaps the most important thing that Carpentier adds is the notion that marvelous reality is not fantastic, based from the beginning on a nature with laws different from our own, but rather the events related weave a miraculous occurrence into a rigorously everyday reality:

> dejando que lo maravilloso fluya libremente de una realidad estrictamente seguida en todos sus detalles.[23]

Other Latin American writers of about the same time were similarly concerned with expressing the juxtaposition of the supernatural and the real, and borrowing a term German critic Franz Roh introduced in 1925 to describe postexpressionist painting in Europe—*magical realism.* Dramatist Rodolfo Usigli penned "Realismo moderno y realismo mágico" in 1940 to discuss the way modern themes could be treated with "magic" or idealistic touches mainly in the language, the dialogue, and the selection of events.[24] In a landmark article, "Magical Realism in Spanish American Fiction," published in 1955, literature professor Angel Flores claimed that magical realism was a tendency in modern Latin American fiction headed by Jorge Luis Borges, with his 1935 publication of *Historia universal de la infamia*.[25] He even lists magical realists, including María Luisa Bombal, Silvina Ocampo, Adolfo Bioy Casares, Eduardo Mallea, Juan José Arreola, Juan Rulfo, Juan Carlos Onetti, Enrique Anderson Imbert, Julio Cortázar, and Ernesto Sábato. As main characteristics of the mode he lists:

> interés en transformar lo común y cotidiano en tremendo e irreal; lo irreal acaece como parte de la realidad; el tiempo existe en una especie de fluidez temporal; y gran preocupación estilística.[26]

It is interesting to note that Flores does not include in his classification Miguel Angel Asturias or Alejo Carpentier, both of whom had already published well-known works. In his book *"Realismo mágico" y "lo real maravilloso,"* Juan Barroso suggests a possible explanation:

> es posible que . . . sean excluídos a propósito debido a las "innecesarias descripciones barrocas" peculiares de su estilo, que el profesor rechaza específicamente.[27]

Since Angel Flores's authoritarian list of 1955, rivers of ink have flowed attempting to define magical realism and to say who practiced it and who did not. Attempting to enumerate all the opinions expressed would be both time-consuming and beside the point. For the reader who wishes to read in depth about the evolution of the term, a number of excellent books exist, including Amaryll Beatrice Chanady's *Magical Realism and the Fantastic* (1985), and Barroso's above-mentioned work. But for the goal here of forging a working definition of magical realism for the purpose of seeing how such a label applies to the fiction of Isabel Allende, perhaps it is enough to summarize the definitions that some detailed critical works have reached.

To begin with, Chanady concludes that fantastic literature and magical realism have three common elements: the natural juxtaposed with the supernatural, the emphasis on the resolution of antinomy in the fictional world, and authorial reticence. What differentiates the two, she says, is the reliability of the narrator:

> The narrator in the fantastic, for example, must be reliable in order to produce the desired effect on the reader. If he shares our conventional perception of reality, we are more inclined to accept his testimony than if his world view differs from our own.[28]

Nineteenth-century fantastic tales, she asserts, succeeded because the narrator's adherence to a scrupulously exact, realistic description enhanced the reader's belief in reason and logic, which seemed contradicted by a disquietingly illogical event.[29] By contrast, she says, in magical realism, the narrator's unreliability or eccentricity dramatically changes the way one sees the narrative:

> Since the magico-realist narrator adopts a point of view that differs from our own, we cannot identify with him to the same extent as in the fantastic. While the reader accepts the unconventional world view, he does so only within the context of the fictitious world, and does not integrate it in his own perception of reality.[30]

By contrast, Juan Barroso, after an exhaustive study of existing terms, suggests the following, much simpler definitions, which distinguish between "realismo mágico" and "lo real maravilloso":

> El realismo mágico es la combinación de temas que reflejan la realidad dentro de una exactitud y hondura detallística con técnicas que aunque rompen con las leyes de causalidad, acoplan apropiadamente con temas dentro de la unidad total de la obra. Cuando los temas tratados son americanos, se ofrece la variante de "lo real maravilloso."[31]

Barroso's definition comes back to what is suggested on the surface by the words themselves—a juxtaposition of magic and realism—but adds that the magic must not be casual, but rather should express a deeper "truth" or reality within the world of the work. His insistence that "lo real maravilloso" is the American variant of this technique is problematic, however, if for no other reason than the horde of practicing critics who today see magical realism as an intensely American product, and do not hesitate at all to apply it to García Márquez and the rest.

A less dogmatic definition is suggested by David Young in his introduction to *Magical Realist Fiction: An Anthology* (1984):

> One way to understand "magical realism" is as a kind of pleasant joke on "realism," suggesting as it does a new kind of fiction pro-

> duced in reaction to the confining assumption of realism, a hybrid that somehow manages to combine the "truthful" with the "magical." . . . A crucial feature of the term, then, lies in its duality. It is a centaur, an easy or uneasy "amalgamation" as Flores called it. . . . Normal notions about time, place, identity, matter, and the like are challenged. . . .[32]

Importantly, Young also suggests that not only is the narrator's attitude toward the magic important (i.e., is he bemused or matter-of-fact?), but also important is how the presentation of the magical event changes the reader's initially rigid concepts of what is real and what is not:

> After seeing ice through the entranced eyes of the natives of Macondo in García Márquez's *One Hundred Years of Solitude*, we will never take it quite for granted again, and the relativity of "reality" as we know it will have been made clear to us in yet another way.[33]

He also returns to a historical consideration mentioned earlier, pointing out that he has

> taken the term to imply a reaction to literary realism.[34]

Scores of other definitions of magical realism could be presented, so perhaps a few more of different slant would be in order. In 1969 critic Angel Valbuena Briones insisted on the *Americanness* of "realismo mágico" in general, and gave the following definition that is specific in the importance of locale, though perhaps otherwise vague:

> Se trata de una expresión rica en posibilidades y sugerencias, las cuales se alimentan en una bifurcación mental del término. Este indica una inquietante dualidad contradictoria que descabala la ordenación. Ofrece una visión imaginaria de sorpresas y misterios.[35]

Obvious in Valbuena Briones's definition is an insistence on the duality present in the term, and the struggle between contradictory elements. This fits in well with the idea developed above that magical realism essentially represents a conflict between realism and idealism.

Critic Seymour Menton, who has produced an important body of criticism about magical realism, offers this concise definition:

> Magical Realism may be defined as the unobtrusive, matter-of-fact insertion by the precise, objective artist or author of an unexpected or

> improbable (but not impossible) element in a predominantly realistic work which creates a strange or eery effect that leaves the viewer or reader disconcerted, bewildered, or delightfully amazed. . . . In certain stories . . . everyday, banal occurrencences are invested with a magical quality because of the author's apparently objective, precise, low-key approach.[36]

When Menton's promised, in-depth examination of magical realism appears, it will certainly add much to our understanding of the term. In the meantime, other opinions should be considered.

Teresinha Pereira, in her short book, *El realismo mágico, y otras herencias de Julio Cortázar,* by contrast insists that magical realism is the expression of a desire to go beyond vanguardism, which she defines as "un movimiento intelectual de carácter burgués."[37] This suggestion fits in well with the notion that Latin American authors of magical realist fiction initially had leftist ideals (although many would disagree with her assertion that all vanguardists were bourgeois). Curiously enough, she cites as the ultimate example of magical realism Julio Cortázar's *Rayuela,* saying it shows a refusal to adopt the sentimental posture she associates with surrealism:

> [La novela] sólo acepta el mundo aparentemente real de los objetos, descrito con minucias. Su filosofía consiste en que la vida es un enorme desorden en el cual el azar, la pesadilla, la irracionalidad y la locura son los muebles que funcionan.[38]

Although Pereira's *description* applies to much of what the other critics cited consider magical realism, on the other hand, it is not clear whether her understanding of the term does or not, since *Rayuela* is not a book particularly abundant in examples of magic as defined as acts contrary to natural law. Indeed, its protagonist, Horacio Oliveira, is practically a monument to rationalistic thought, and the individual scenes are painted with careful realism. On the other hand, chronology does exist in a state of flux in the novel, there is experimentation with the idea of narrator and with a text, that seems to be writing itself as we watch, and most importantly of all, Oliveira himself embodies the conflict of realism and idealism from which magical realism springs. As a man who tries to excise all irrational sentimentality from his being and behave according to strict logic, he follows the results of such a course through degradation and madness, perhaps eventually to arrive at death—or something worse. Ultimately, Pereira's definition returns to the notion that magical realism is based on a vital conflict between idealism and pragmatic reality.

It should be pointed out that not all observers of the development of magical realism in Latin America have been totally enthusiastic. The success of the Americans provoked a certain amount of jealousy, particularly in Spain. For example, to Sevillan novelist Alfonso Grosso, the term magical realism suggests something third-worldly and primitive:

> En América se puede decir, por lo menos en la América que yo conozco, que hay un burro que vuela y los ojos miran porque pueden esperar que un burro vuela. Naturalmente hay una tradición indigenista en América que está llena de la imagen del fenómeno de la magia.[39]

Grosso attributes much of the "Boom" authors' success to a well-developed "maquinaria publicitaria."[40] But his definition puts a finger on one reason for the popularity of *Cien años* and other classics of magical realism in Europe and the United States—a feeling by those distant readers that they were reading something possible in a distant Latin American setting. Later I will examine the implications of such a reception for future Latin American authors, but for now, it is important to summarize the definitions of magical realism.

On first glance, all of the explanations of what magical realism is and even opinions as to what it is worth seem so varied that reconciling them might be impossible. But on closer examination, many of these apparently contradictory notions may actually be able to coexist within a working definition the way the supernatural and the real live side by side in a story by García Márquez. For example, both Chanady and Barroso agree that in magical realism, the realistic and the magical are juxtaposed. Chanady points out that unlike in fantastic literature, magical strokes generally cause no surprise to the narrator or characters but are narrated matter-of-factly; Barroso adds that the apparently "magical" element, while strictly "untrue" to natural laws in the outside world the reader knows, leads the reader to deeper truths that hold absolutely within the ethics of the novel, and resonate in the outside world as well. Over and over, the idea of a struggle between the idealistic and the realistic recurs—what Chanady calls "resolution of antimony"[41] and Valbuena Briones refers to as the "inquietante dualidad contradictora."[42] Young completes the picture by showing that in magical realism, conventional notions of time, place, identity, and matter may be challenged, and that often the narration may actually cause the reader to reevaluate what he has previously held to be real.

For purposes of this study, then, *magic* will refer to events counter (or apparently counter) to natural law; *realism* will refer to narrative that attempts to mirror nature; and *magical realism* will be defined as narration in which:

1. the real and the magic are juxtaposed;
2. this juxtaposition is narrated matter-of-factly;
3. the apparently impossible event leads to a deeper truth that holds outside the novel;
4. conventional notions of time, place, matter, and identity are challenged; and
5. the effect of reading the fiction may be to change the reader's prejudices about what reality is.

To clarify what is meant by each of the above five conditions, here are some concrete examples of each:

(1) A juxtaposition of the magic and the real would be for example, the insomnia plague that strikes Macondo in *Cien años de soledad*—apparently impossible, yet described in minute realistic detail such as the inhabitants' labeling of everyday objects in order to remember their names. Another example would be the way the nameless drivers in Cortázar's "La autopista del sur" face with total pragmatism the impossibly extended traffic jam that keeps them for days, months, or possibly years from reaching their destinations.

(2) The above two examples also illustrate a matter-of-fact narration of magical intrusions. Other examples of this can be seen in the way the protagonists of Cortázar's "Casa tomada" never question the existence of a supernatural force taking over their dwelling little by little, or the fact that the protagonist of Rulfo's *Pedro Páramo* never seems to react with surprise on discovering that his interlocutors are in fact dead.

(3) We can see the way impossible events lead to a deeper truth for example in the aging of Ursula in *Cien años*. Her shrinkage to the size of a football is at the very least hyperbolic, yet when her great-grandchildren play with her like a doll, forgetting her in drawers and corners, the "magical" event is really no more than a literal expression of a figurative truth about aging—that descendents of the elderly sometimes drag them around like dolls or inanimate objects, treating them like even

less than children. Another good example of this use of magic to express a deeper truth is Juan José Arreola's story, "El guardagujas," in which the magically impossible frustration of an anonymous train traveler is nothing more than a literal representation of the unfortunate complaint that Mexican trains never seem to arrive on time.

(4) Examples of how conventional notions of time are changed in magical realism are myriad—in Carpentier's "Viaje a la semilla" a man's life is lived backwards; in "La noche boca arriba," by Cortázar the space between history and the present is eliminated in the blink of an eye, while in his "Todos los fuegos el fuego" different historical moments flow into each other, joined by unchanging human similarities. In Borges's El milagro secreto" a man facing a firing squad is miraculously granted a year before the bullets reach his body in which to finish mentally composing his magnum opus, a drama that, ironically, "observaba las unidades de tiempo, lugar y de acción" (21), and in José Donoso's *Casa de Campo*, children left behind when their parents take an afternoon outing find that months or years go by before the elders return. The notion of space is questioned in stories like Cortázar's "Las babas del diablo," in which a photograph becomes the stage for an endlessly repeated drama. Other stories reduce space as if to seal the magic inside, as in Carlos Fuentes's *Aura* or in the Borgesian labyrinths. Identity switches between man and amphibian in Cortázar's "Axolotl," or between men in Borges's "La muerte y la brújula."

(5) As an example of how magical realism can change the reader's perception of external reality, a reading of Jorge Amado's *Dona Flor and her Two Husbands* might prompt a woman to wonder how she ever survived years with only one man. A hospital patient with the bad luck to read Cortázar's "La noche boca arriba," or "Señorita Cora" might grow to fear taking the nightly sleeping medication. One might also acquire a new way of looking at lapdogs after reading Donoso's "Paseo" or at jungle cats after perusing his "Santelices."

Ultimately, very little of Chanady or Barroso's definitions need be eliminated to make them compatible. Only Barroso's insistence on using the term "lo real maravilloso" for magical realism as practiced on American themes seems less convincing, if for no other reason than the widespread critical use of the term on American authors, and a general tendency to reserve the term "lo real maravilloso" specifically for Alejo Carpentier. Moreover, if Barroso were to take his distinction seriously, it would exclude

Los pasos perdidos from this definition of "lo real maravilloso," since nothing actually contrary to natural law occurs in the book, and the sensation of the "marvelous" is, rather, produced by the unexpected juxtapositions of civilizations.

The hybrid definition given here, of course, also excludes some things that many call magical realism. For example, Enrique Anderson Imbert's short story, "El leve Pedro," would not meet the requirements of an externally resonating deeper truth. Pedro becomes ill and floats ceilingward, and this is accepted pragmatically by his wife, but the event does not unsettle our vision of reality or represent literally a profound truth, except perhaps the cliché of a sick person being "light enough to float away." But the definition I have given generally includes the body of fiction usually referred to as magical realism, along with its major authors. Moreover, as we shall see later, it proves a useful tool in the examination of the fiction of Isabel Allende.

Alfonso Grosso's offhand suggestion that magical realism is appropriate only in an America with primitive traditions and a "backward" culture is also useful, for it brings to mind another important question: Carlos Fuentes, as mentioned earlier, observed that the early twentieth-century novel in Latin America was swallowed up by telluric themes deemed "appropriate" for Latin American writers by literary establishments on both sides of the ocean. Could it be that magical realism is in danger of swallowing the novel of the later part of the same century? Has the enthusiastic international reception of Latin American magical realism limited the development and propagation of other forms? Has a worldview of Latin America that is strong on entertaining descriptions of mystical rural regions where marvels occur discouraged discussion of the problems and realities of its modern urbs? Not all present-day Colombia is Macondo, and the Mexico City that serves as a painted backdrop for *Aura* has little to do with the troubled capital's pressing problems.

In seeking to measure the fiction of Isabel Allende against the definition given above, then, I will address a number of questions: Not only will this study look at whether or not Isabel Allende's fiction fits within magical realism, but it will also look at whether there ought to be a subdivision of magical realism called "magical feminism," If so, does Isabel Allende's fiction fit into it? To what extent?

Since I am the coiner of the phrase, "magical feminism," I will take the neologician's right to define it myself. I define "magical feminism" as magical realism employed in a femino-centric work, or one that is especially insightful into the status or condition of women in the context described in the work. Note that I avoid using the word *feminism* in my definition. This is deliberate. In a broad social sense, the term *feminism* has as many acceptations as people, and these vary widely. Some see it in terms of equal opportunities in the workplace, while others believe it implies special considerations for women at home raising children, and indeed how these children (male and female) might best be raised. Some define it in terms of strict equality between the sexes, while others think in terms of affirmative action to correct past inequalities, or speak of special "feminine" insight, intuition, or other traits. Some think it means new opportunities for women, and others see in it a breakdown of traditional values and the destruction of the family. Then there are those who simply think it is about who has to wash the dishes on a given night. In view of this, a dictionary definition is not likely to be much help at all, and we cannot be satisfied with one like the *American Heritage Dictionary* offers:

> A doctrine that advocates or demands for women the same rights granted men, as in political or economic status.[43]

Such a definition ignores the vast emotional charge that accompanies the word, evoking freedom of choice to some, while terrifying others with spectres of what they consider morally unacceptable alternatives such as lesbian lifestyles and abortion on demand.

Even when we begin to attempt to narrow feminism down to a literary definition, it remains many faceted and often elusive. Is feminism to be found in Sappho's love lyrics, defined by her "pure" verse? Or is it that which seeks to prepare the way for Virginia Woolf's imagined Judith Shakespeare? Is it that which listens to Woolf's exhortation?:

> I maintain that she would come if we worked for her, and that so to work, even in poverty and obscurity, is worth while.[44]

Or is it something that women must wait for men to grant them, as Simone de Beauvoir seems to imply in the following lines from *The Second Sex*?:

> It is for man to establish the reign of liberty in the midst of the world of the given. To gain the supreme victory, it is necessary, for one

> thing, that by and through their natural differentiation men and women unequivocally affirm their brotherhood.[45]

It should be noted that these two pillars of feminist criticism, Woolf and Beauvoir, do not seem to agree even on whether "equality" is necessarily a part of feminist literature, and if so, when, why, how, and how much. Notes Stimpson:

> . . . De Beauvoir's language of "brotherhood" repeats the pattern she otherwise so greatly disdains: blowing up men's experience until it becomes all experience, a universal happening; ballooning towards "brotherhood" while jettisoning "sisterhood." Massive though it is, *The Second Sex* erases women from history. In contrast, *A Room of One's Own* helps to create an archeology of women, a dig for the literary artifacts that women have deposited.[46]

Clearly, the difficulties of defining a feminist perspective (to say nothing of defining feminism) are many and complex within the tradition of English letters.

But how much more complicated this becomes when we add to the equation of feminism=X another element, feminism x Latin American=X! Practically speaking, feminism in many Latin American countries is in its infancy, and to expect a dialectical sophistication is absurd from women who are still struggling to achieve basic rights taken for granted in the United States and much of Europe. Even if we were to base a definition of Latin American feminism on study of the works of authors to whom that label has been applied, we would find that they are widely different from each other. Both Luisa Valenzuela and Elena Poniatowska are called feminists by many, yet how unlike each other they are! Valenzuela's consciousness is complex and refined. By contrast, the pragmatic Poniatowska sees day-to-day issues and describes the strong Jesusa so eloquently in *Hasta no verte Jesús mío*, yet at the same time, inexplicably, thinks her monument to female masochism, *Querido Diego, te abraza Quiela*, is a love story about a "good woman."[47]

Because of all of these difficulties in defining "feminism" adequately, I have chosen instead to define "magical feminism" as a phrase, a literary concept of my own creation, and one that I want to define without making invidious value judgments about the "correctness" of woman A's feminism over woman B's brand by forcing a comparison with some supposed ideal of feminism possibly concocted in a culture far different from the women's own (in other words, I wanted a definition that would not indulge in femino-cultural imperialism).

If "magical feminism," then, is "magical realism" employed in a femino-centric work, or one that is especially insightful into the condition of women, nonetheless, this definition (sans magic) is very close to what Ellen Morgan, in *Humanbecoming: Forms and Focus in the Neo-Feminist Novel,* suggests as a definition for the neo-feminist novel. She insists that it should show the condition of women from old to new forms, and that the way this is shown should at all times seek to be authentic.[48]

As more evidence of the appropriateness of this definition of "magical feminism" that I have coined as a tool to deal with the fiction of Isabel Allende, I would like to point out that in his thoughtful discussion of feminism in *La casa de los espíritus,* Mario A. Rojas calls the book both femino-centric and also neo-feminist, according to Morgan's definition.[49]

Juan Manuel Marcos also points out in "Isabel viendo llover en Barataria" that within the novel:

> Sus mujeres evolucionan de manera natural, sin desligarse psicológicamente de su context histórico.[50]

With this understanding of how I define my own term, and of how I have limited its use to the three novels at hand, I propose to examine whether the fiction of Isabel Allende can be called "magically feminist" either because it is plainly "magical realism" used to make points about the female condition, or because in certain specific instances it uses magic to demonstrate a truth about the female condition.

In addition to addressing the questions of whether Allende practices "magical realism" or "magical feminism", the study will also examine the possibility that Allende uses "magical realism" at times, and uses it to advantage to score feminist points, but then subtly calls the whole literary tradition into question, asking if at the present time "magical realism" is really the appropriate vehicle for her continent at all, or whether magic may at times be the opiate of the oppressed.

In sharp contrast to the cautious way the term "magical realism" has been approached in this study, in the "real" world of literary criticism, it is thrown about with a great deal more freedom. Book reviewers, in particular, seem to feel no hesitation about applying it right and left, or about using it as a synonym for "Garciamarquian." In fact, one of the most frequent criticisms of

La casa de los espíritus is that it begins with magical realism a la Garcíca Márquez only to abandon the technique to tell a harsh reality in a style that verges on pamphleteerism. Paul West in *The Nation* for example, writes:

> As *The House of the Spirits* advances, it calms down into the book Allende probably wanted to write and would have if she had not felt obliged to toe the line of magical realism.[51]

The *New Statesman*'s Marion Glastonbury was even less kind:

> No doubt necrophily [*sic*] and necromancy sell well, but they are not what Isabel Allende does best.[52]

And D. A. N. Jones of the *London Review of Books* writes with thinly disguised contempt:

> The bizarre little fantasies come sputtering out with an inconsequential brevity, like ideas thrown up at a script conference for a Latin-American soap opera or horror film. Some of the ideas, if properly developed, might make a film story: directors could introduce a sense of place and actors could put some flesh on the bones of the characters. But it would be as well to keep real-life politics out of it.[53]

He sums Allende up with the label, "magically unrealistic."

Among Spanish-speaking critics, the book has generally been received with enthusiasm, particularly in Spain. But one hears the same insistence on the label *Garciamarquian* and some of the same objections are voiced, though to a lesser degree. Allende's compatriot, Jorge Edwards, writes:

> *La casa de los espíritus* . . . es un libro para mi gusto irregular. Porque comienza siendo excesivamente garcia-marquiano y a la mitad del libro parece olvidarse de García Márquez. Y termina apareciendo una crónica rápida.[54]

Fellow Chilean novelist, José Donoso also insists on this influence, saying,

> también hay gente como Isabel Allende, que está influída por García Márquez.

While the Spanish critics were warmer in their praise, similar phrases cropped up. Javier Goñi wrote in *Informaciones:*

> El lector se adentra en las primeras páginas de *La casa de los espíritus* y la primera impresión que le sale al paso es que hay indudables ecos—las mismas voces, los mismos ámbitos—de *Cien años de soledad* de García Márquez . . . todo lo que al lector europeo le parece mágico todo lo que le sobresalta por irreal, puede tener cabida en esta historia.[56]

But the magical side is only half of the story, as Goñi points out:

> Pero Latinoamérica no es eso únicamente: lo mágico, lo sorprendente, no logra ocultar una realidad trágica e injusta, y la sangre derramada, es bien sabido, es una realidad cotidiana . . . *La casa de los espíritus* se convierte a partir de [un día de septiembre de 1973] en un relato escalofriantemente real; la represión brutal, los primeros días del golpe, están contados con una frialdad admirable.[57]

Unlike some of the North American critics, Goñi finds no problem with these variances of tone:

> La tortura, el fusilamiento, no tienen nada de grandioso ni de mágico. Son más bien brutalmente reales. Realismo y magia. Realismo mágico. En pocas novelas como ésta la grandeza y la tragedia de Latinoamérica están tan dura y claramente narradas.[58]

Luis Suñén also prefers Allende's realistic prose over her magic touches:

> La escritura no es, desde luego, deslumbrante, pero hay un buen tono, suficientemente personal, y, desde leugo, una eficacia narradora de primerísimo orden, que hace, por ejemplo, que la presencia de lo sobrenatural no moleste.[59]

Juan José Armas Marcelo by contrast, minimizes the similarity to García Márquez and Vargas Llosa, and stresses instead Allende's continuity with great novelists of the past in general:

> Introducir el pico rapaz en la historia cercana, y casi inmediata, y relatar las impresiones reales traspuestas por el talento creador en categoría literaria, es la más vieja tradición de la novela universal.[60]

But many more thought the labels magical realism and Garciamarquian inevitable. As the *Comercio-Gijón* put it:

> Quizás la novela ha nacido un poco apegada a las lecturas del Nobel García Márquez y su realismo mágico, ya que para Isabel Allende, "en América Latina, lo que parece magia es verdad."[61]

Maruja Torres went even further, insisting after an interview with Allende:

> Viciosa de los escritores del "Boom," confiesa que vivirá un momento muy feliz cuando, por fin, pueda colocar a su propia novela junto a aquellas de sus más admirados autores.[62]

Juby Bustamante in *Diario 16* called the book, in fact,

> el mejor heredero de *Cien años de soledad*.[63]

Here is a good place to point out that the last person who would deny the influence of García Márquez on *La casa de los espíritus* would be Allende herself, for she has frequently referred to him with reverence. In 1982 she told the newspaper *ABC:*

> Todos los escritores latinoamericanos estamos profundamente influídos por García Márquez. Es el auténtico padre del realismo mágico. Por eso, al escribir esta novela, traté de evitar esta gran influencia que ha ejercido sobre mí el escritor colombiano. Aún más: eliminé capítulos enteros de la novela por temor a que se pareciera demasiado a algo.[64]

Yet some go even further than to speak of "influence" of García Márquez. The West German magazine, *Der Spiegel*, with charateristic bluntness, went so far as to suggest that plagiarism of style might be a better term, to which Allende responded:

> Das ehrt mich! Das ist ja, als ob Sie mir sagen würden, ich tanze wie die Pawlowa. Das wäre phantastisch![65]
>
> (That flatters me. It's as if you told me I dance like Pavlova. That would be fantastic!)

To counter all of these facile assumptions, one of the most eloquent responses to date has been given by Juan Manuel Marcos in his article, "Isabel viendo llover en Barataria":

> A pesar de . . . semejanzas superficiales . . . confundir a Isabel Allende con García Márquez consistiría en incurrir en el mismo error que considerar a Cervantes un continuador de las novelas de caballería. Don Quijote no es una imitación del Amadís, sino su sepulturero paródico.[66]

Marcos gives a lengthy enumeration of differences between the two, not the least of which is, interestingly, Allende's

> lucidez crítica respecto a la condición social de la mujer latinoamericana.[67]

Marcos's contribution will be further discussed in chapter 1. In this chapter, as in the other six dealing with *La casa de los espíritus*, the thread of comparison to *Cien años de soledad* will be maintained in an attempt to show whether what Allende writes is simply a servile imitation of the master, or whether she integrates magic on its own terms in ways especially appropriate to the themes presented. In analysis of the three novels, an additional question addressed will be whether the magical elements are smoothly integrated into the works or are sharply set off from the more realistic portions of the narrative.

In order to answer all of these questions about Isabel Allende's narrative magic, we must first identify it and mark out its scope. The next seven chapters will each deal with a specific magic element in *La casa de los espíritus*, and each will be a component in defining the magical world view within the novel, then of suggesting answers to the above questions. Chapter 9 will examine the role of magic in Allende's second novel, *De amor y de sombra;* chapter 10 will do the same for the author's children's book, *La gorda de procelana*, and Chapter 11 will look at narrative magic in Allende's most recent book to date, *Eva Luna*.

To begin, then, where should one start in looking for magic in *La casa de los espíritus*? One might be guided by Samuel Johnson's simple definition of "magick" from his dictionary as "the art of putting into action the power of the spirits." No one in *La casa de los espíritus* has more art at putting the power of the spirits into action than Clara del Valle, so let us begin with that figure around whom all magic in the novel revolves: Clara, *clarividente*.

2
CLARA/CLARIVIDENTE

We do not know very much about the future,
Only that from generation to generation
The same things happen again and again.
Men learn little from other's experience,
But in the life of one man, never
The same time returns. . . .

—T. S. Eliot, *Murder in the Cathedral*

"True," said Poirot thoughtfully. "That much-vaunted possession, a woman's intuition—it does not seem to have been working."

—Agatha Christie, *The Mystery of the Bagdad Chest*

If magic is that which contradicts natural law, then certainly one of the most prominent of the magical elements in *La casa de los espíritus* is the prescience of Clara del Valle, who gives the name to the first chapter of the book—"Clara, clarividente." According to the author's own definition, then, Clara is clairvoyant. But what exactly is clairvoyance, and if it is magic, what are the natural laws it contravenes? Once again, the search for a clear definition is not as easy as first might appear. The *Diccionario Enciclopédico Salvat* calls "clarividencia" "la facultad de comprender y discernir claramente las cosas," and then adds as an afterthought, "penetración, perspicacia."[1] One cannot help noting that there is nothing magic implied by this definition at all; no characteristics are listed that even the average newspaper reporter might not claim to possess. Yet surely they are not what we mean generally when we talk of clairvoyants? The *Diccionario Enciclopédico Espasa* adds weight to the *Salvat*'s definition by repeating it word for word.[2] However, they both also point out that the term was borrowed from the French, "clairvoyant," so the next logical place to look for a definition seems to be the *Grand Larousse Encyclopédique*. The *Larousse* begins with much the same words as its Spanish counterparts, calling clairvoyance, "la faculté de voir avec clarté, sagacité, pénétration."[3] But it goes beyond this, suggesting something a bit more unusual, vaguely hinted at under the general heading of "magnétisme":

> Faculté attribuée aux personnes soumises a une influence magnétique de voir à distance et à travers les corps opaques, de pénétrer la pensée, etc.[4]

This definition hints at parlor tricks, but again, curiously, does not even mention what most people *mean* when they say, "clairvoyance," i.e., the ability to see the future or to read minds, unless one is supposed to "see" such activities in the abbreviation "etc." After all, it does not say *whose* "pensée" is being penetrated.

The idea of seeing concealed objects is again the extent of the "magic" that the *O.E.D.* attributes to "clairvoyance," and once again, it is expressed with proper British skepticism:

> A supposed faculty attributed to certain persons, or to persons under certain mesmeric conditions, consisting in mental perception of objects at a distance or concealed from sight.[5]

Again, according to this definition, "clairvoyance" sounds like little more than a card trick.

Once more it is the *American Heritage Dictionary* that gives a more useful definition, although its characteristic concision seems here to have been superseded by a desire to be all-inclusive:

> 1) The power to perceive things that are out of the natural range of human senses. 2) Acute insight or perceptiveness.[6]

In making a working definition of "clairvoyance" as used in *La casa de los espíritus*, this last entry seems the most helpful. Allende calls her character "Clara, clarividente." Clara is able to see the future, to read the minds or auras of those near her, and to envision scenes and objects at a distance. She is also possessed at times of acute insights and perceptions. To Allende, then, it would seem that a clairvoyant is one who can see with equal ease the past, present, and future—the obvious and the concealed. Moreover, in her novelistic world, this power is not "supuesto," "attribué," or "supposed," but rather, as is appropriate to magical realism, taken as literally real. To understand how Allende's use of clairvoyance as here defined contributes to her overall narrative magic, it is necessary to start at the beginning and examine Clara's powers in detail.

The early pages of *La casa de los espíritus* reveal that Clara del Valle has enjoyed certain unusual powers from childhood. When her mind wanders, so do the saltcellars, and as soon as she learns to talk, she begins announcing events to come:

> Ella anunciaba los temblores con alguna anticipación, lo que resultaba muy conveniente en este país de catástrofes, porque daba tiempo para salir arrancando en la noche.[7]

On the surface, this statement fits neatly into the definition of magical realism given in the first chapter. There is the unnatural event (prediction of the future) and its matter-of-fact acceptance by the family, seen in the humorous juxtaposition of magic and mundane reality (in the way the family takes advantage of Clara's magic to the prosaic end of avoiding broken crockery and cold feet). But below the surface, one can glimpse a trend beginning, the way the real is used to undercut the magical. In fact, this is the beginning of a continuous campaign during this novel and the author's second work to place magical realism in trivial settings, ones that do little to affect the larger problems of contemporary Latin America.

As has been stated, the subject of Clara's clairvoyance is treated lightheartedly at the beginning. The child's nurse reassures her mother thus:

> Hay muchos niños que vuelan como las moscas, que adivinan los sueños y hablan con las ánimas, pero a todos se les pasa cuando pierden la inocencia. (15)

But very quickly this playful attitude toward clairvoyance disappears. At the age of six Clara predicts that a horse will throw her brother Luis, but he ignores her warning:

> Desde entonces tenía una cadera desviada. Con el tiempo se le acortó la pierna izquierda y tuvo que usar un zapato especial con una gran plataforma que él mismo se fabricaba. (15)

Suddenly the gift of seeing the future does not seem so funny anymore. Along with Luis's accident comes an unexpressed sense of responsibility. If someone can see the future, should he not, then, be able to prevent bad things from happening with this foreknowledge? Is not forewarned forearmed? Greek mythology, of course, is full of figures who had similar bad luck in seeing the future accurately, but not being believed, and the ancients sensed that the gift of soothsaying could be a curse, frequently accompanied by blindness (Tiresias, for example) or at the very least, unpopularity (like Cassandra, whose family and friends believed her to be crazy, and whose name, according to J. E. Zimmerman, "has become synonymous with prophets of doom whose warnings are heeded too late."[8] Similarly, although Allende delights the reader with the magical powers of Clara del Valle, from the beginning she plants small seeds of ambivalence about the value of Clara's gift.

The playfulness returns, however, with a visit by Clara's flamboyant Uncle Marcos, an adventurer and explorer who brings with him a trunk laden with "libros mágicos." Marcos, with a convenient blend of mysticism and capitalistic chutzpah, sees in the girl's inclination commercial possibilities:

> Marcos sostenía que la rara virtud de su sobrina podía ser una fuente de ingresos y una buena oportunidad para desarrollar su propia clarividencia. (21)

With these goals in mind, uncle and niece set themselves up in the carriage house of the family manse with a crystal ball and saffron robes, ready to tell the fortunes of all the maids and cleaning women in the area. The business prospers, as Clara really *can* tell not only of events to come, but also of unseen happenings in the past, like lost rings that have rolled under dressers. From all of these examples it is again clear that Allende's definition of clairvoyance is most nearly in accordance with the one borrowed from the *American Heritage Dictionary* for use in this chapter.

But before long, although Clara's fame has spread and her predictions have come true, the magical aspect is undercut by the introduction of a competing reality. We discover that the crystal ball is "sólo un flotador de bote pesquero" (21) and moreover, uncle and niece gradually come to realize that their cosmic meddling may be a dangerous thing:

> Los adivinos, al darse cuenta de que sus aciertos podían modificar el destino de la clientela, que seguían al pie de la letra sus palabras, se atemorizaron y decidieron que ése era un oficio de tramposos. (22)

It is all very well to be able to see into the future or the past in a way that an ordinary person cannot, and the thought of such magic powers delights the reader. But after Allende has shown us that she knows how to conjure up such magic, she also shows us that she knows its scope; even in a hermetic setting like the large upper-middle class del Valle manse where life's realities seem remote, they cannot be forever denied.

Clara's next major prophecy has catastrophic results for the entire family. In the midst of a stir over father Severo's announced candidacy with the Liberal Party in the parliamentary elections, Clara announces that there will be another death in the family. "Pero será un muerto por equivocación," she adds. When her words come graphically true, and her older sister, la bella Rosa, is poisoned by some brandy given as an anonymous gift to her father and clearly intended for him, the effect on Clara is devastating:

> Tenía la terrible duda de que su hermana había muerto porque ella lo había dicho. Creía que así como la fuerza de su mente podía mover el salero, igualmente podía ser la causa de las muertes, de los temblores de tierra, y otras desgracias mayores. En vano le había explicado su madre que ella no podía provocar los acontecimientos, sólo verlos con alguna anticipación. Se sentía desolada y culpable. . . . (39)

At this point, Clara's clairvoyance strangely fails her. When she goes to look for her sister's body, she finds the family doctor and his assistant in the process of performing an improvised autopsy on her in the middle of the kitchen table. Here, what Clara sees is not a clear "truth" brought to her by supernatural power of vision, a concealed reality, or an acute insight or perception. Rather, she sees a fantastic tableau constructed from a blend of reality and her childish imagination, which has been colored by her readings:

> El Doctor Cuevas, hombre bonachón y dulce . . . que la ayudó a nacer y que la atendió en todas sus pequeñas enfermedades de la niñez . . . se había transformado en un vampiro gordo y oscuro como los de las ilustraciones de los libros de su tío Marcos. (40)

Here, as in practically every crucial moment in Clara's life, clairvoyance is of no real help to her. Instead of being able to see beyond the horrible appearances to the dutiful reality of Dr. Cuevas's intent, she perceives the scene at face value, influenced as any child could be by the fantastic books her Uncle Marcos has left behind. These "libros mágicos" will be the subject of individual scrutiny in a later chapter, but for now it is enough to note that Clara's childish imagination, inflamed by her readings, takes over and distorts what she sees, producing a trauma so great that she does not speak a word for the next nine years. It is as if the text would remind us that magic has very little power in the matters of real importance in this harsh business called mortality.

During Clara's adolescent silence, she nevertheless continues predicting the future, moving small objects, and interpreting dreams. These abilities on the surface seem sympathetic, humorous. However, when we examine them more closely we see that the text systematically undermines their importance. For example, although Clara can play the piano with the lid closed, the description of this activity deliberately trivializes it:

> . . . Podía mover las teclas del piano con la tapa cerrada, aunque nunca pudo desplazar el instrumento por la sala, como era su deseo. (74)

Although Clara possesses a magic, telekinetic ability that delights the reader, the stress on limitations to this ability suggests that it has, after all, slight practical application.

Clara's ability to see the future has similar limitations. In minor matters, her prescience can bring about limited gain; for example, through interpreting a dream she enables the gardener to win eighty pesos in an illegal gambling game, with the following results:

> Se los gastó en un traje nuevo, una borrachera memorable con todos sus amigos y una muñeca de loza para Clara. (73)

Here, the very human reaction of the gardener helps to undercut the magic of the event. On this small scale, Clara's powers have brought a brief, temporary benefit. But even this benefit is reduced when it is remembered that Clara does not even like dolls, considering them a monstrous adult invention. In matters of more importance, by contrast, she has no effect. Her vision cannot prevent earthquakes or her father's hernia, and in both cases the forewarnings are of little or no help. This is even more clear in the case of her godfather's suicide. Clara's announcement of the death of don Simón Valdés comes only in time to facilitate the finding of the body:

> . . . Era corredor de la Bolsa de Comercio . . . que creyendo haberlo perdido todo, se colgó de la lámpara en su elegante oficina. Allí lo

> encontraron, por insistencia de Clara, con el aspecto de carnero mustio, tal como ella lo describió en la pizarra. (74)

Clara's vision did not, for example predict her godfather's suicidal intentions in time for someone to help him. After the body has been found and the tragedy faced, what difference does it really make to anyone that Clara predicted the event a little before it happened? The reality of the disaster is the same, and in retrospect, chronology becomes meaningless. Moreover, there is a slight suggestion that the suicide was unwarranted, brought on by the godfather's possibly false attempts to see his own future. We are told that the man killed himself, "creyendo haberlo perdido todo." This wording suggests that the belief may in fact have been incorrect. If this is so, again we are faced with a practical failure of Clara's clairvoyance. If she had used her powers to see that her godfather's situation was not as bleak as he believed it to be, perhaps she could have warned him, but in such practical situations, Clara's prescience scarcely ever manifests itself.

In another instance, Clara tries to use the fruits of her vision to warn her father of a impending business disaster, but Severo del Valle refuses to believe her:

> Clara se dio cuenta a la primera mirada que Getulio Armando iba a estafar a su padre con el negocio de las ovejas australianas, porque se lo leyó en el color del aura. Se lo escribió a su padre, pero éste no le hizo caso, y cuando vino a acordarse de las predicciones de su hija menor, había perdido la mitad de su fortuna y su socio andaba por el Caribe, convertido en un hombre rico, con un serrallo de negras culonas y un barco propio para tomar el sol. (74)

Like Cassandra, Clara again sees the future but is unable to convince others of it.

When Clara ends her nine years of silence, it is to announce her forthcoming marriage to Esteban Trueba, much as she has announced other natural disasters: "Ella había visto su propio destino, por eso . . . estaba dispuesta a casarse sin amor" (85).

In a way, this explanation recalls that popular Greek device for introducing a bit of magic into the stage world of otherwise mortal behavior—the *deus ex machina*. For the plot to proceed, Esteban Trueba and Clara del Valle must marry, yet in the eyes of the narrator (young Alba, as one discovers in the end), there is no real reason for Clara to willingly take such a step. The bride's parents—so often the villains in cases of this sort—here do not seem about to force the girl into this union. If anything, they do their best to discourage it. When Esteban Trueba appears on the scene seeking a wife, they seem hesitant to offer Clara:

> Le informaron . . . que . . . Clara era una criatura algo estrafalaria, poco apta para las responsabilidades matrimoniales y la vida doméstica. Con toda honestidad, le contaron las rarezas de su hija menor, sin omitir el hecho de que había permanecido sin hablar durante la mitad de su existencia. (83)

Why, then, should Clara enter into a marriage with someone of a temperament so different from her own (and so different, as well, from the other men in her life, such as the understanding Severo and the carefree Uncle Marcos)? The answer once more seems to be a devaluation of prescience. Once more, the ability allows Clara to see her future (a marriage that is hardly an unqualified success) but not to change it, opting, perhaps, for someone whose love she could return, like Pedro Segundo. Why, for example, does she not see that she will later fall in love with Pedro Segundo, and he with her? Or is Clara too aristocratic to seriously consider marrying someone who could not give her a mansion to fill with friendly spirits? In fact, the belief in clairvoyance implies a certain belief in determinism in human events. After all, if one can read the future, does that not mean that the events cannot be changed by human volition? This idea of determinism will be discussed in depth in the next chapter. Here, however, it is sufficient to note that Clara's prescience is of little help in avoiding a problematic situation. Even in the trivial details pertaining to this marraige, the relative uselessness of Clara's gift is stressed. For example, her vision fails before her first meeting with her future husband, although she claims to have summoned him with her mind.

> La joven . . . había estado ayudando al jardinero . . . y en esta ocasión le falló la clarividencia para esperar al futuro novio con un arreglo más esmerado. (84).

Other interesting failures of prescience can be cataloged throughout the portion of the novel in which Clara appears. Being able to predict the sex of her children before they are born, she mixes into the prediction of the inherent (gender) the selective factor of names, and uses this, knowingly or un, to irritate her husband. On the occasion of her first pregnancy we read:

> Esteban quería un hijo que llevara su nombre y le pasara a su descendencia el apellido de los Trueba.
>
> —Es una niña y se llama Blanca—dijo Clara desde el primer día que anunció su embarazo.
>
> Y así fue. (94)

With Clara's next pregnancy, Esteban Trueba tells us he repeated his wish:

> —Espero que esta vez sea hombre, para que lleve mi nombre—bromeé.
>
> —No es uno, son dos—replicó Clara—. Los mellizos se llamarán Jaime y Nicolás.
>
> Eso fue demasiado para mí. . . . Me puse furioso. Alegué que ésos eran nombres de comerciantes extranjeros, que nadie se llamaba así en mi familia ni en la suya . . . pero Clara explicó que los nombres repetidos crean confusiones en los cuadernos de anotar la vida y se mantuvo inflexible en su decisión. . . . Salí dando un portazo y me fui al Club. (107)

Once again, foreknowledge has little practical application, except perhaps to permit the women of the househould to knit the correct color of booties. By contrast, it does serve once more to show how Esteban Trueba is excluded from intimate family decisions, such as choosing the babies' names, and made to feel an outsider. At the same time, it pokes gentle fun at *Cien años de soledad*, with its tangle of uncountable Aurelianos and José Arcadios. By prophesying both her babies' names and their sexes, however, Clara makes a kind of statement of belief in determinism. For if even such factors as a baby's *name* can be seen before the baby is born, then there can be no free will, even in factors where humans normally believe they are exercising their own choices. By mixing the foreordained (the baby's sex, which is quite literally ordained before birth) with that which humans can choose (the baby's name), Clara unconsciously states her disbelief in the freedom of the will. This idea of determinism is crucial in a novel about an important historical event (the Chilean coup of 1973) because one of the most important questions political scientists ask even today is whether or not the event was inevitable, given the circumstances. The Chilean coup is a textbook example for some of modern political determinism—that is, a type of political psychology that sees an individual state as controlled entirely by its history. This doctrine is opposed to the principle of emergence, which states that truly novel and unpredictable events may emerge from the composite forces of a situation. The next chapter will examine the implications of this question in detail, but for now it is important to point out that the question of determinism versus free will is clearly and frequently posed in the character of Clara del Valle and her ability to see in the future not only "natural" events (such as earthquakes) but also those which depend, theoretically, on human choice.

But the catalog of Clara's failures of prescience does not end here. When her parents are killed in a motoring accident just before she is due to deliver the twins, once more her gift is useless to save her loved ones. Apparently she had no actual forewarning of the event but rather, as in the case of her godfather's death, learned of the event through a dream after the fact.

Literally, then, we cannot speak of prescience here, although according to the definition of clairvoyance, she is seeing things normally hidden. By contrast, it was not Clara who predicted the accident before it occurred, but rather Clara's mother, Nívea. The matriarch, "había anunciado a menudo en broma que morirían" (111). In this case, the prognostication is part joke and part practical observation of the way Severo drives, added to a minor mechanical defect in the car itself, that makes an accident practically inevitable: "nunca funcionaron bien los frenos" (111). Once more, it is as if the text would remind us that in certain cases anyone can see the future; and the real magic lies in what a person does with that foreknowledge (i.e., Severo could have repaired the brakes or bought a more modern vehicle).

In the next domestic drama of the Trueba household, Clara's clairvoyance is again good for nothing. For a long time a jealousy has been developing between Esteban and his sister Férula, who lives with the couple. "El amor desmedido de Esteban por Clara" (119) crashes headlong into "el amor desmesurado" of Férula (102). With two worshipping and only one being worshipped, it is inevitable that competition should develop, just as it is inevitable that Esteban Trueba should be the winner in a clash of wills. But Clara does not seem to have any special "penetrations" or "insights" into this situation, but rather contentedly ignores both of them for the most part, though she generously allows both to wait on her hand and foot. In the final buildup before disaster, curiously, everyone sees the situation clearly *except* Clara, who does not in this case see clearly at all:

> La atmósfera de la casa se hizo irrespirable, densa y sombría y hasta la Nana andaba como espirituada. La única que permanecía ajena por completo a lo que estaba sucediendo, era Clara, que en su distracción e inocencia, no se daba cuenta de nada. (120)

Here, strangely, it is Clara's failure of prescience that allows a tragic mistake to remove from her side the closest thing to a friend that she has ever had. In this case, the excuses "inocencia" and "distracción" ring strangely hollow. By contrast, it is Esteban Trueba who comes home unannounced, "con un presentimiento atroz, con un deseo inconfessado," to find Férula in bed with his wife. Férula never has time to explain that she has crept there in the night frightened by an earthquake, "buscando un poco de compañía y calor" (120). Clara's usual knack for predicting tremors sleeps through both the physical and the psychical ones here that upset the household. What is more, in Esteban Trueba's mingling of "presentimiento" and "deseo," perhaps there is a truth concealed about all the foreknowledge in the book—that through "visions" wishes are sometimes fulfilled, and companions manipulated.

Once more, the ability to see the future has failed Clara at a crucial moment, and the author has clearly shown prescience to be of little use against life's serious problems. When Clara (a blessedly sound sleeper) discovers the following morning that Esteban has expelled Férula, she employs all the psychic tools and powers at her disposal to try to locate the woman—her pendulum, the ouija board, her friendly spirits. But once again, at a critical moment, the magic breaks down.

> Entonces decidió recurrir a los métodos tradicionales y comenzó a buscarla entre las amigas . . . los proveedores y . . . todos los que tenían trato con ella, pero nadie la había vuelto a ver. (122)

When the priest finally tells Clara that Férula does not want to be found, Clara reacts passively, quoting from her spiritual gurus, the Mora sisters, "no se puede encontrar a quien no quiere ser encontrado" (122), a bit of homey wisdom that comfortably ignores, among other things, all the major principles of modern police work. With that, Clara gives up the search. Again, the ability to "see" the hidden has failed, and the ability to "see" the future (i.e., the futility of a search), provides Clara with a pretext for inaction: when one has seen the future, after all, one cannot fight for a better version of it. Even when Férula dies, Clara sees the event only after it occurs, not before. Her gift does not even enable her to offer the lonely spinster any deathbed consolation.

The next major disaster in the Trueba family occurs away from the city, at the ranch Las Tres Marías, when an earthquake buries Esteban Trueba under a pile of rubble, breaking, "tantos . . . huesos . . . que no se podía contar" (145). Although the text has repeatedly insisted on Clara's power to foresee earthquakes with exactitude, this time her timing mechanism is off, and she does not predict an exact night for the catastrophe, but rather limits herself to saying over and over, "la tierra va a temblar," until her husband responds, annoyed, "¡siempre tiembla, Clara, por Dios!" (143). Moreover, once more Clara's ability to see the future is totally undermined by the stronger forces of situation and character. In Esteban's case, the warnings fall on deaf ears because of his bold and insensitive nature. When Clara announces that this earthquake will be different because it will cause ten thousand deaths, he jokes, "no hay tanta gente en todo el país" (143). Clara's daughter Blanca has other reasons for ignoring the warnings. Her childhood love of Pedro Tercero García has just blossomed with adolescence into a consuming passion:

> Los últimos días antes de volver [Blanca] a la ciudad . . . ante la inminiencia de una nueva separacion, los jóvenes aprovechaban todos los momentos posibles para amarse con desenfreno. (143)

There is another possibility lying just below the surface here. Could it be that Clara's predictions do not always come true? This is not the first time we have been told of their being ignored (by Severo, by Luis, and now by Blanca and Esteban). If Clara's predictions were totally accurate, would they be so lightly laughed off? The question is never posed directly in the text, but given these situations, the reader begins to wonder if he is actually meant to take Clara's prescience completely literally. Or could it rather be a metaphor of the narrator, Alba, recounting many years later a story in which her grandmother played a strongly intuitive role? Whatever reading one chooses, this scene serves to accentuate both Esteban's stubbornness and the strength of Blanca's attraction to Pedro Tercero García.

In any case, once more Clara's prescience serves not to predict and prevent tragedy, but rather as a remedial device after the disaster has occurred. Just as her powers helped her to locate her godfather's body and her mother's severed head, in this instance it aids Clara in locating Esteban Trueba's crushed form under the rubble. "¡Hay que sacarlo! ¡Está vivo y nos escucha!" she assures the rest (144).

Once Esteban Trueba has been recovered, it is another character with clairvoyant powers—this time the blind soothsayer, old Pedro García—who makes the key prediction, "si lo mueven, se muere" (143). This time the prediction is based on experience and literally palpable evidence as much as on any magic ability.

Another example of Clara's failure of clairvoyance comes at the time of Blanca's marriage to Jean de Satigny. First of all, Clara has not been able to see the events transpiring with Pedro Tercero García, and perhaps to predict some method of birth control for the pair. Neither does she warn them when Jean de Satigny denounces their nocturnal meetings to Esteban Trueba. Later, she does not warn Blanca about her marriage to Jean de Satigny. Once more, as in Clara's own case, the marriage is not forced on the woman but is something she freely agrees to:

> Blanca nunca pudo explicar a su madre las razones por las cuales había aceptado casarse, porque ni ella misma las sabía. Analizando el pasado, cuando ya era una mujer madura, llegó a la conclusión que la causa principal fue el miedo que sentía por su padre. . . . Su embarazo y la noticia de que Pedro Tercero estaba muerto terminaron por decidirla. (219)

If Clara were truly clairvoyant, would not she have known both that Pedro Tercero was still alive and also that Jean de Satigny's sexual inclinations started at pederasty and then ventured into realms so exotic that photos of them which Blanca later discovers fill her not so much with disgust as confusion? One suspects that such pieces of information might have changed Blanca's passive acceptance of a wedding that she spent, "sentada en una silla observando la torta con expresión alelada" (193). The marriage serves only to deplete Blanca's dowry and thus to eliminate any possibility of later economic independence from her father, while the absent Jean de Satigny becomes the stuff of nightmares for his stepdaughter, Alba.

But Clara neither sees the truth nor discourages Blanca from the wedding; instead she reacts with total passivity: "decidió no asistir a la fiesta" (192). In fact, the only magic to the wedding at all is that performed by the tailor who designs Blanca's wedding dress, "quien hizo milagros para disimular el vientre prominente de la novia con chorreras de flores y pliegues greco-romanos" (192).

Nor does Clara try to tell the truth about Jean de Satigny to her husband. Of course, by this time she is not speaking to him, nor will she ever again speak to him in their married life—the height of passive punishment within a marriage! Once more, Clara accepts the information about the future as evidence that any human action is useless to change destiny, so she simply settles down to wait:

> Clara pudo adivinar que la separación con Blanca no sería por mucho tiempo. Sin decirle a nadie, arregló una de las más asoleadas y amplias habitaciones de la casa, para esperarla. (219)

Both Clara and Blanca now indulge in passive behavior, although they have opposite excuses, letting life carry them wherever it will. Clara reasons that because she has seen the future, there is no point in struggling against the inevitable. Blanca, by contrast, argues later that since she saw the future imperfectly (believing Pedro Tercero to be dead) she cannot be blamed for passively drifting into marriage with a person whom she neither specially liked nor disliked. Both attitudes add up to women who seldom face the problems of their lives directly. Remember that it is Alba, the product of a different generation and education, who recounts this behavior to us, and the young Alba who is finally able to inherit her grandmother's intuitive sensitivity, without her bovine passivity.

At numerous points in the novel it has been stressed that Blanca did not inherit her mother's psychic abilities, but an examination of her marriage to Jean de Satigny makes it clear that she inherited a deeper and more central trait of her mother's character—passivity. Later, after she discovers that Pedro Tercero is still alive, Blanca is again passive, responding to his passion, but never being quite able to make the decision to live with him and totally share the realities of adult life and cohabitation. It is useful to recall that Blanca's reactions are being recounted by Alba, the first woman in the line of descendance to take full responsibility for her body and actions. Unlike her mother and grandmother, Alba would certainly never allow herself to be forced into a marriage against her will. Alba has only the green hair of a previous generation, but not the magical beauty and especially not the prescience, which more and more we come to see as a metaphor for passivity.

Clara's passivity is vividly illustrated in another case, when, even though she foresees an earth tremor, she actually forgets to announce it, with the result that Jaime is buried under a mountain of books in his room, in an ironic echo of the earthquake that injured his father (another catastrophe that Clara's powers were useless to prevent):

> Durante un temblor de tierra que Clara olvidó predecir, se sintió un estrépito de tren descarrilado y cuando pudieron abrir la puerta vieron que . . . [Jaime] estaba enterrado debajo de una montaña de libros. . . . Mientras Clara quitaba libros, se acordaba del terremoto y pensaba que ese momento ya lo había vivido. (97)

Now, after looking at the way Clara's prescience has been presented in the novel, one begins to wonder if it is not a metaphor for that very passivity with which Blanca struggles and with which Alba must finally come to terms in the novel's final pages. If this can be shown, then it would seem that the accusation of some critics—that the novel begins with magic such as clairvoyance in order to get our attention, and then abandons it—would begin to crumble.

Evidence that Clara's magical powers are not to be taken totally at face value has already been presented. Most obvious is the fact that frequently characters who have long experience with Clara tend to ignore her predictions, suggesting that perhaps the trivial, dilettantish nature of some of her pastimes discourages them from taking her seriously. But stronger evidence for this can be obtained by trying several metaphorical readings to see how they stand up.

In the account of Clara's childhood, clairvoyance functions well as a metaphor for sensitivity. In this reading, little Clara is the sensitive child who is misunderstood by most adults in control, like Padre Restrepo, who accuses her of being possessed by a demon, or the well-meaning Nana, who dresses up in horrible costumes to frighten the child out of muteness. In such a reading, Clara's childhood is a fantasy of permissiveness in which she is left to develop her creativity (represented by psychic powers) without the strictures of a normally repressive education. Nívea is wonderfully, almost magically understanding, never pressing the child to talk but rather accepting her silence while feeding her fantasies with talk of the family mythology. Nana waits on her hand and foot, fulfilling her physical needs to a hyperbolic degree. Already there is a suggestion that the "magic" surrounding Clara could be a metaphor for or even a product of her imagination, and of the imagination of those who obsessively love and care for her:

> Clara habitaba un universo inventado para ella, protegida de las inclemencias de la vida, donde se confundía la verdad prosaica de las cosas materiales con la verdad tumultosa de los sueños. . . . (79)

These words hint that the adults see in Clara magic of their own invention, just as any doting parents imagine extraordinary talents and sensibilities in their offspring.

The wonderfully, totally impractical education Clara receives in her mother's sewing room leaves her with few practical skills for life, either within the home or outside of it. The only thing it really serves to develop is her clairvoyance. Clairvoyance is, in the final analsyis, that which Clara has instead of practical abilities or power over her life, and this point is essential to an understanding of how "magic" functions metaphorically in Clara's adult life.

At first glance, the adult Clara's prescience could almost be a synonym for that old myth of feminine intuition. After all, it is a quality that stubbornly evades the men in the family. Moreover, Clara often uses it as a tool to get her own way, as when she "predicts" the names of her unborn babies, refusing to name either son after her husband. Her annual dinner-table prognosticiations on elections ("van a ganar los de siempre") also begin to sound like the words of a woman trying to appear important by intuiting something that everyone else already knows through observation. On one level, then, it is perfectly possible to read "clairvoyance" as "intuitution" and to see Clara as a woman who functions completely intuitively—at least in part because she has not the slightest training in behaving practically, and in fact has no need to do so during much of the novel, with the bourgeois accompaniment of servants and maiden aunts who do most of the practical work for her. In support of this reading is the fact that when Clara is forced by Esteban Trueba's accident to assume the management of Las Tres Marías with Pedro Segundo García, her psychic activity diminishes drastically, as she is forced to maintain a "delicado equilibrio . . . entre los espíritus del Más Allá y las almas necesitadas del Más Acá" (148).

But an even deeper metaphorical reading for Clara's prescience has already been suggested. Clara, wonderfully magical and lovable as she is—adored unconditionally by at least three characters in the novel—is an essentially passive human being, and her passivity in a metaphorical sense is closely related to and excused by her clairvoyance. As I have demonstrated, throughout the novel Clara uses her clairvoyance as an excuse for nonaction. It can also be seen as a metaphor for passivity itself. If this is true, then perhaps the "magic" element of clairvoyance is not simply introduced for fun and then abandoned arbitrarily. If clairvoyance is a metaphor for female passivity, then it is *essential* that this magic diminish gradually and finally be replaced by something better in Alba's generation, when she and women like Ana Díaz begin to accept responsibility for the world in which they live.

The carefully controlled use of a supernatural phenomenon as a metaphor that makes a point about sex-role conditioning is a prime example of what I like to call Allende's magical feminism. In other words, she has used magical realism to make a feminist point. Much more about this will be said later.

Several metaphorical synonyms for Clara's "clairvoyance" have thus been suggested: sensitivity, intuition, and lastly, passivity. It is this last interpretation that provides the key to the inevitable submergence of magic in the latter part of this novel. Perhaps Allende does not share Clara del Valle's determinism but wants, rather, to show how it functions. If Clara believes in determinism, then it is real for her—to the extent that she believes she is about to die, her will is strong enough to make her prediction come true. But the novel itself undercuts this psychological determinism in the succession of female characters from Clara to Blanca to Alba. Clara is never able to shed her belief in an unchangeable future: For her, clairvoyance is nothing more than an excuse for letting the future come to her instead of going to meet it. Because she has forseen her role in life, Clara never makes any attempt to leave her husband and seek a love she could return with someone, for example, like Pedro Segundo. In fact, she does quite the contrary—preserves the status quo with Esteban Trueba so that she will not be forced to make any such decision. She does this by manipulating Esteban sexually and emotionally, avoiding a complete break with him at all costs:

> Un día Clara hizo poner un pestillo a la puerta de su habitación y no volvió a aceptarme en su cama, excepto en aquellas ocasiones en que yo forzaba la situación, que negarse habría significado una ruptura definitiva. (161–62)

Here we see that Clara uses sex to prevent a separation from Esteban, even when she finds it distasteful. The subterranean explanation seems to be that much as Clara likes to detest Esteban for his crass materialism and his lack of spirituality, she cannot live from the spirits alone. Clara seems very comfortable in the *gran casa de la esquina,* and does not appear anxious to leave it, even though she does not care to speak to the man who pays the expenses.

Blanca is less passive than her mother in love. After all, she is in love with Pedro Tercero. Still, she uses sex subtly to keep him dancing, refusing either to break with him or to make the final move of full commitment to him year after year, decade after decade. When events finally push them, Blanca is at last able to make the decision to escape with Pedro Tercero, but it takes a genuine cataclysm to force her into this decision.

Alba is the product of a new generation and education. In her at last we have a Trueba woman who chooses her man for love and does not hesitate to take any risks such a decision may entail. It is up to Alba to break the chain of passivity that has kept the women in her family from meeting life fully for so long. Moreover, whatever one can say against Esteban Trueba, at least he is fiercely loyal to Clara, trying by every means he knows to win the love and companionship of his beloved. In love, then, Alba actually owes more to the example of devotion shown by her grandfather than to the watery crush that Clara has for Pedro Segundo but never acts on. Thus it is no surprise that by Alba's time the "magical" clairvoyance of her grandmother's days should have gone underground. In terms of personal psychology, it is essential that the apparent magic of Clara should submerge and be replaced by Alba's more practical, direct attitude. Alba has inherited the best of both grandparents, not just some vague feminine characteristics from Clara. It would seem no accident then, that the magic of clairvoyance figures more prominently in the passive generation of Clara, in a time when economic, social and educational factors combined to pressure women into compensating for their lack of real power with indirect manipulations, pretended intuitions, and a serenity that was sometimes all but indistinguishable from a low I.Q.

Such use of the magic of clairvoyance is another example of what I call Allende's magical feminism. Magic is alternately used or withheld to make a point about the economic and emotional dependence of women at certain time periods. The fact that Blanca and Clara are unable to liberate themselves from passivity and manipulation is hardly a criticism of Allende's own feminism; rather it is a tribute to her honesty as a novelist. Juan Manuel Marcos makes precisely this point, saying:

> Sus mujeres evolucionan de manera natural, sin desligarse psicológicamente de su contexto histórico.[9]

He goes on to say that this "lucidez crítica respecto a la condición social de la mujer en Latinoamérica" is precisely one of many characteristics that distinguish her from García Márquez.[10]

Mario A. Rojas also speaks insightfully on feminism in the novel, concluding that for all the characters' imperfections with regard to their own liberation, the novel itself can be called feminist on many grounds:

> *La casa de los espíritus* es una novela femino-céntrica en que los personajes femeninos ya no son el *pre-texto* tradicional de la escritura masculina, sino que constituyen centros de energía pulsores y propulsores del dinamismo narrativo, sino fuerzas que desafían el despotismo patriarcal, los prejuicios sociosexuales, la dictadura y la represión política.[11]

He calls the novel "neofeminista," with the following explanation:

> A través de Nívea, Clara, Blanca y Alba, Isabel Allende va registrando el curso de viejas a nuevas formas de participación de la mujer en su lucha por los derechos de su propio sexo y por los de las clases sociales desposeídas.[12]

This sampling of critical opinion as to the feminist quality of Allende's first novel, along with the possible metaphorical readings I have suggested, all go to support the idea of her use of "magical feminism."

All of these suggestions about possible metaphorical readings for *La casa de los espíritus* are just that: suggestions. At this point, it should be said in all fairness that author Isabel Allende's attitude toward the clairvoyance of Clara del Valle *outside* of the novel has been one of arguing for a literal reading. In many interviews she has insisted that her own grandmother, the model, so she says, for the character of Clara, really possessed telekinetic and soothsaying powers. For example, she told Marcelo Intili of Argentina's *La Prensa* in 1985:

> Mi madre . . . al separarse de mi padre, fue a vivir a la casa de los abuelos, y yo me crié allí . . . con . . . una abuela clarividente que movía objetos con el poder de la mente, y que es el personaje de Clara en *La casa de los espíritus*.[13]

She has repeated the insistence often, from the earliest interviews on the publication of the novel. In 1982 she told *El País:*

> *La casa de los espíritus* es básicamente la historia de mi familia. Esteban Trueba es mi abuelo, Clara es mi abuela, Blanca es mi madre, y todo es real, hasta el perro que acaba convertido en alfombra.[14]

As recently as 1986 she repeated the assertion to the Puerto Rican newspaper, *El Mundo:*

> El personaje de Esteban Trueba es mi abuelo, y Clara del Valle es mi abuela.[15]

Later that year she went even further, telling *Der Spiegel* in an interview that not only was her grandmother psychic, but she and her mother (who stayed behind in Chile) communicate telepathically every evening at eleven:

> Wir . . . [haben] . . . da noch ein besonderes System: Jede Nacht um elf denken wir ganz intensiv aneinander. Ich sage nicht, dass wir Kochrezepte austauschen, aber ich fühle ganz deutlich die Nähe meiner Mutter.[16]

> (We have for this a special system. Every night at eleven we think very intensively of each other. I'm not saying we exchange cooking recipes, but I feel very clearly the nearness of my mother.)

In public then, at least, Allende argues strongly for a literal acceptance of Clara's clairvoyance. But, as Wimsatt and Beardsley pointed out in their important essay, "The Intentional Fallacy," the author is just one witness to the meaning of a work, a witness whose testimony is secondary to the evidence presented by the text itself.[17] Here, a careful examination of the text has shown that with regard to Clara's clarivoyance, the displacement of that magic from a literal to a more figurative level of the text responds to a very logical schema, one that seems to refute the notion that the author began with the magic of clairvoyance and then abandoned it as the story got underway. The next chapter will study the way clairvoyance becomes an obsessive theme of the novel, one that reaches an explosion not in the early part but precisely at the novel's climax. It will also examine the broader implications of such an obsession, both literary and political.

3
VISIONS AND REVISIONS

> Gracias a la vida que me ha dado tanto
> me dio dos luceros que cuando los abro
> perfecto distingo lo negro de lo blanco
> y en el alto cielo su fondo estrellado
> y entre las multitudes al hombre que yo amo.
>
> —Violeta Parra, "Gracias a la vida"

The question of clairvoyance, prefiguration, and prediction of the future in *La casa de los espíritus* does not end with the character of Clara del Valle. On the contrary, it is a motif that recurs frequently and in many forms, and is actually seen more often at the end than at the beginning. This chapter will examine the uses of foreseeing the future that do not involve Clara and will then suggest how this recurrent thread functions thematically in the work as a whole.

First of all, it should be noted that Clara is far from being the only character in the book who predicts the future. Other characters frequently engage in speculation, prediction, and outright statement of things to come. Moreover, the frequency of these other predictions increases as the book progresses. It has been pointed out in the previous chapter that with Clara's death, actual clairvoyance seems to disappear, but in its place occurs a kind of explosion of false or confused predictions that come to a head in the chaos surrounding the military coup.

By the end of this chapter, it will be shown that the book has a virtual obsession with the knowing of future events, and the purpose of these pages will be to attempt to explain how this obsession functions.

One purpose of the many prognostications is that they reveal much about the characters who make them. For example, when Clara's French nanny is impregnated by brother Luis, and Severo summarily orders them to marry, we are told, "contra todos los pronósticos de Nívea y sus amigas, fueron muy felices" (73). This detail serves not only to remind us of the literal impossibility of knowing the future, but also to characterize to some extent Nívea and her friends. Within the context of the novel, we understand clearly from these few words that the ladies predict marital failure because the bride is a foreigner (and French at that!), and this reveals a kind of gossipy provincialism in them, or even a mild xenophobia. The event also serves as a contrast to Clara's developing clairvoyance with its reportedly infallible correctness.

Nívea's predictions are not always false, however. For example, in deciding not to educate her daughter Rosa in housewifely arts, she relies on foreshadowing:

> Ella prefería, no atormentar a su hija con exigencias terrenales, pues presentía que Rosa era un ser celestial, que no estaba hecho para durar mucho tiempo . . . en . . . este mundo. . . . (13)

Later, when she shows Clara the poplar stump in the yard and tells her the story of the family tree-climbing contest in which blind cousin Jerónimo was killed, she tells how she had the tree cut down to avoid future tragedy. "Yo sabía que algún día mis hijos tendrían que continuar esa bárbara tradición," she says (referring to the contest) in the tone of a woman who has seen the future clearly without need of clairvoyance (77). "Por eso lo hice cortar" (77). Later, as has been discussed, she correctly predicts her own death with husband Severo in an automobile accident. In this case Nívea and Clara's predictions coincide:

> Los esposos del Valle murieron tal como Clara lo soñó y tal como Nívea había anunciado que morirían.
>
> —Cualquier día nos vamos a matar en esta máquina infernal— decía Nívea señalando al viejo automóvil de su marido. (111)

In this case, as in the previous one, Nívea's experience and common sense enable her to predict the future without need of magic. That Nívea can arrive by reason at the same conclusion that Clara does by magic also serves to undercut the importance of Clara's gift.

La Nana also shows a moment of prescience in a key scene, the death of la bella Rosa. When she knocks on the girl's door on the fateful morning, she hesitates, "golpeada por la fuerza de un presentimiento" (30).

Férula too makes several interesting predictions of the future that reveal much about her and those around her. For example, when Clara decides to take baby Blanca along with Esteban Trueba to Las Tres Marías, Férula correctly predicts that the trip will be "agobiante." Clara's reaction heightens the contrast between her highly impractical nature and Férula's intensely practical one:

> . . . Clara estaba entusiasmada. El campo le parecía una idea romántica, porque nunca había estado dentro de un establo, como decía Férula. (97)

Later, when Férula curses Esteban Trueba, it is in the form of a prediction:

> —¡Te maldigo, Esteban! . . . ¡Siempre estarás solo, se te encogerá el alma y el cuerpo, y te morirás como un perro! (121)

But this prediction is only partially fulfilled. Although Esteban does shrink literally and figuratively, and although he is terribly alone for much of his life, at the end he has the company of Alba, he manages to rehabilitate his soul to some extent by facing the past squarely, and lastly, Alba assures us:

> No murió como un perro, como él temía, sino apaciblemente en mis brazos . . . consciente y sereno, más lúcido que nunca y feliz. (372)

The partial incorrectness of Férula's prediction stresses both that her prescience has been marred by bitterness, the repression of her passions, and an abysmal education. It also suggests that there is hope even for a cursed man like Esteban Trueba to regenerate himself if he will face his own past and try to see it clearly.

Early on, Esteban Trueba has an important failure of prescience that helps to substantiate the claim that seeing the future is an obsession with the characters of *La casa de los espíritus*. When Esteban learns of Rosa's death, he finds most pain in the fact that he had failed to foresee the catastrophe:

> Nunca [contemplé] la muerte de Rosa, a pesar de mi proverbial pesimismo, que me hace siempre esperar lo peor. (35)

Later he reproaches himself at her graveside for failing to see her future, and by seeing it, forcing it to change:

> Le dije . . . que si yo hubiera sabido que iba a durar tan poco en este mundo, habría robado el dinero necesario para casarme con ella y construir un palacio . . . donde la habría mantenido secuestrada y

> donde sólo yo tuviera acceso. La habría amado ininterrumpidamente por un tiempo casi infinito, porque estaba seguro que si hubiera estado conmigo, no habría bebido el veneno destinado a su padre y habría durado mil años. (38–39)

Like most mortals, Trueba has been unable to see the future. The interesting thing here is his conviction that he *should* have been able to foresee the tragedy. This obsession is one shared by most of the characters in the book, and it becomes an important metaphor in both human and political terms.

Another character who is imperfectly clairvoyant is old Pedro García. Although his magic succeeds in leading off the plague of ants (104) and although he both predicts and brings about Esteban Trueba's cure after the earthquake, Pedro García fails dramatically to save the life of his own daughter when she falls victim to "la lipiria calambre" (127). Instead of taking her to a hospital, he feeds her cow dung and horse droppings and then wraps her up to "sudar el mal." It is not until she is dying that her father seeks help:

> Pancha se fue en una diarrea interminable que le estrujó las carnes y la hizo padecer una sed insaciable. . . . El médico del hospital . . . dijo al viejo que estaba perdida, que si la hubiera llevado antes y no le hubiera provocado esa sudadera, habría podido hacer algo por ella. . . . Pedro García se ofendió y siguió negando su fracaso aun cuando regresó con el cadáver de su hija envuelto en una manta. . . . (127)

Once more magic fails to prevent life's brutal realities. What is more, an essential underpinning of magic is revealed here: ignorance and superstition. A novelistic technique that depends on magic, such as magical realism, is then called into question as an appropriate vehicle for chronicling the problems of Latin America, for the technique itself participates to some extent in these very problems.

Another character with vision is Tránsito Soto, the young prostitute from Las Tres Marías who becomes a madam of one of the most successful brothels in the capital. With the creation of her "cooperativa de putas y maricones," Tránsito shows what Esteban Trueba calls "visión comercial" (365). She pairs this vision with practical observation to make an admonitory prediction to Esteban Trueba, one that comes true later—if only temporarily:

Váyase con cuidado, mire que si sus inquilinos le forman una cooperativa en el campo, usted se jodió. (109)

When Tránsito sets out to make her fortune she predicts that she will become rich, and this prediction comes true, as she reminds Esteban Trueba. Moreover, she too operates on an ability to see the magical side of things, manipulating the décor of her brothel like a magician to match the fantasies of her clientele:

. . . Todos los años ella renovaba algunos decorados, cambiando naufragios en islas polinésicas por severos claustros monacales y columpios barrocos por potros de tormento, según la moda, pudiendo introducir tanta cosa en una residencia de proporciones relativamente normales, gracias al artilugio de los espejos y las luces, que podían multiplicar el espacio, engañar al clima, crear el infinito y suspender el tiempo. (366)

But Tránsito Soto's magic is, after all, a trick of mirrors, a deception in the last pages of the novel, at a time when the airy magic of Clara has gone underground and been replaced by the demonic agents of the satanic dictator who makes people like Alba disappear "por obra de magia" (367). Tránsito Soto's vision of the military hierarchy, which enables her to negotiate Alba's release, is based on cold-eyed observation of their past behavior and commonsense estimations of the future, aided by her secret vision—"su conocimiento del lado más secreto de los hombres que están en el poder . . ." (369).

But the tightest knot of predictions in the novel centers on the events relative to the brief government of "el Presidente" and the military coup that ends it. With this observation, in fact, one draws nearer to understanding the central function of clairvoyance in the novel.

The character with the most direct use of prediction is el Presidente himself. El Presidente is not at all clairvoyant in the sense that Clara is, but in certain key moments he allows himself to predict the future, using a combination of experience, idealism, and even perhaps wishful thinking. His first prediction comes when he announces in advance his long-overdue electoral victory:

Su larga experiencia en la derrota y su conocimiento del pueblo, permitieron al candidato darse cuenta antes que nadie que en esa ocasión iba a ganar. (297)

El Presidente's prediction emerges through a haze of false or contradictory predictions by other characters. Esteban Trueba, for example, is interviewed about the elections on television: " 'Ganaremos los de siempre,' dijo soberbiamente . . ." (302). By contrast, Trueba's son, now a doctor and a close friend of el Presidente, predicts victory for the socialists, "pero como hacía veinte años que pronosticaba lo mismo, nadie lo creyó" (296). Alba, parroting the words of her fiery young revolutionary boyfriend, Miguel, scoffs at her uncle's prediction:

> Eso no ha ocurrido nunca, tío, no seas ingenuo. . . . ¡Jamás dejarán que ganen tus socialistas! (295)

As the novel nears its climax, predictions, prognostications, foreshadowings, and oracular statements become more and more frequent until a chaotic state is reached, leaving Clara dead and no Delphic voice remaining that can be relied upon.

Fear of future events is manipulated by Senator Trueba, who organizes a smear campaign against el Candidato, predicting that if he wins, the country will be run by the Russians. One day Jaime wakes up to find the city papered with posters graphically predicting this catastrophe:

> . . . Aparecía una madre barrigona y desolada, que intentaba inútilmente arrebatar a su hijo a un soldado comunista que se lo llevaba a Moscú. (297)

Out of all of this confusion and contradiction, el Candidato's prediction prevails, and he indeed becomes el Presidente. But almost immediately a netherworldly magic emanating from the conservative camp begins to overshadow the victory, and we are told ominously.

> Pronto fue evidente para todos que sólo un milagro cambiaría el resultado. . . . (302)

Esteban Trueba begins to personify this shadowy spirit, with predictions of his own, which, when joined to intentions, gradually evolve from prognostications into threats:

> —Una cosa es ganar la elección y otra muy distinta es ser Presidente—dijo misteriosamente a sus llorosos correligionarios. (303)

He soon joins forces with "otros políticos, algunos militares, y con los gringos enviados por el servicio de inteligencia," and begins to form plans for overthrowing the president (303). The gringos have a plan, based on long-term predictions of the effect such an event will have outside the country:

> Queremos que el marxismo fracase estrepitosamente y caiga solo, para quitar esa idea de la cabeza a otros países del continente. (304)

But the plan the gringos suggest involves bribing some senators, prompting Trueba to explode with another prediction:

> ¡Sáquese esa idea de la cabeza, míster!. . . . ¡Aquí no va a poder sobornar a nadie! El congreso y las Fuerzas Armadas son incorruptibles. (304)

Here the prediction is a bitter mixture of vision and blindness. As Trueba predicts, the parliamentary members are incorruptible. By contrast, the armed forces within the world of the novel are not incorruptible, as Esteban Trueba naïvely believes, but rather an almost demonic essence of corruption, as we see in Alba's torture.

But Esteban Trueba's predictions do not even stop here. Again he bases his plan to regain control on his prognostications of how el Presidente will behave:

> Yo conozco este país. Nunca acabarán con la libertad de prensa. Por lo demás, está en su programa de gobierno, ha jurado respetar las libertades democráticas. Lo cazaremos en su propia trampa. (304)

The prediction is charged with irony, first because Trueba seeks to use el Presidente's very sense of honor against him in buying up the press, and second because it is not el Presidente but rather the military junta that Trueba helps to power which disposes of freedom of the press in this novel.

Another character who contributes to the babel of predictions is Miguel, who has been a lone, cynical voice throughout. We recall that earlier when Alba joined him and other students in occupying part of the university, he was a voice of skeptical prediction, refuting the naïvely hopeful predictions of Professor Sebastián Gómez. "Se plegarán los estudiantes de todo el país, los sindicatos, los colegios profesionales. Tal vez caiga el gobierno," Gómez opines optimistically (285). "No lo creo," Miguel denies the prediction based on his own experience (285).

A bit later Gómez and Miguel disagree again about whether the *carabineros* would dare to enter. Once again, Gómez utters the optimistic prediction, "el gobierno . . . no va a meterse con nosotros" (286). And once again, Miguel refutes the prophecy based on history, "no sería la primera vez que carga contra los estudiantes." (286)

Once more Gómez tries to answer with an optimistic prognostication, to which Miguel again responds with a learned cynicism that is in its own way another prediction of the future:

> —Esta es una democracia. No es una dictadura y nunca lo será.
> —Uno siempre piensa que esas cosas pasan en otra parte—dijo Miguel—. Hasta que también nos pasa a nosotros. (286)

After the socialist victory at the polls, the confusion of predictions continues, and Miguel once more predicts events to come with practiced cynicism. "¡Te dije que ganaríamos por las buenas, Miguel!" Alba tells her boyfriend, conveniently forgetting her dire predictions—uttered to her uncle—to the contrary (303). "Ganamos, pero ahora hay que defender el triunfo," Miguel replies, unconvinced (303).

Not only individual characters but also entire classes of people dispense predictions and rely on them to determine their behavior as well. The bourgeoisie, believing the myths they themselves have invented, assault the banks with withdrawals and in many cases even flee the country, thus forcing some of their direst predictions to come true:

> En veinticuatro horas, el valor de la propiedad disminuyó a menos de la mitad y todos los pasajes aéreos se agotaron en la locura de salir del país antes de que llegasen los soviéticos a poner alambre de púas en las fronteras. (303)

Meanwhile the socialists are equally culpable, according to the novel, believing their own predictions for the future and ignoring the dire warnings of people like Miguel, who try to incite them to arms:

> Pero nadie le hacía caso. Estaban convencidos que si habían llegado al poder por vía legal y democrática, nadie se lo podía quitar, al menos hasta las próximas elecciones presidenciales.
> —¡Son unos imbéciles, no se dan cuenta de que la derecha se está armando! dijo Miguel a Alba. . . . (311)

At the height of all this chaos of contradictory prediction, an oracular figure comes to the Trueba household, and we note that this is well into the so-called "realistic" stage of the novel. The visitor is Luisa Mora, who cuts through the confusion with a straightforward and unequivocal prediction:

> Vengo a anunciarle desgracias, Esteban. Se avecinan tiempos atroces. Habrá tantos muertos que no se podrán contar. Usted estará en el bando de los ganadores, pero el triunfo no le traerá más que sufrimiento y soledad. (322).

Then Luisa Mora pauses, and adds ironically, "pero no he venido a molestarles con noticias que escapan de su control." (322) Instead, she claims to bring a message for Alba from her dead grandmother, Clara, warning her to leave the country for a time. Again, even while presenting us with a "magical" prediction, the text undercuts the overall force of the supernatural in natural events, and Luisa Mora warns:

> Tu abuela Clara te proteje [sic] desde el Más Allá, pero me mandó decirte que los espíritus protectores son ineficaces en los cataclismos mayores. (322)

But once more, as in the time of Clara, the prediction turns out to be useless. Esteban Trueba refuses to believe it out of characteristic insensitivity and skepticism, "y estaba seguro de que se encontraba frente a una anciana demente" (322). Alba, for her part, chooses not to believe the prediction, or at least not to act on it, because as was the case with her mother years before on the night of the great earthquake, the fear of danger is less than the force of young love, and Alba wants to remain near her lover Miguel, whatever the cost.

Chapter 13 is, appropriately enough, a compendium of evil luck titled, "El terror." It begins with the coup, and it is at this moment that el Presidente makes his last great prediction. In his radio farewell speech, broadcast just before the bombing of the presidential palace, the fictional leader sends his final message, couched in the tragically heroic terms of one who would transcend present defeat with the promise of future victory:

> Me dirijo a aquellos que serán perseguidos, para decirles que yo no voy a renunciar: pagaré con mi vida la lealtad del pueblo. Siempre estaré junto a ustedes. Tengo fe en la patria y su destino. Otros

> hombres superarán este momento y mucho más temprano que tarde se abrirán las grandes alamedas por donde pasará el hombre libre para construir una sociedad mejor. . . . Estas serán mis últimas palabras. Tengo la certeza de que mi sacrificio no será en vano. (325)

Note that nearly all verbs are in the future tense, and that the message seeks to inspire the hearers with the vision of a better future. Of all the book's predictions, this is surely the most important. But is it true or false? Within the context of this novel one cannot know, for the story ends with the dictatorship still in place, although the character of Alba, with her love for the new life within her, and her compassion, offers some hope for the future. But should consideration of this prediction be kept, within the confines of the novel? Or is it legitimate to step outside the text when the text itself invites us to do so? It is hardly a coincidence that the farewell speech of el Presidente is nearly identical to that of Salvador Allende, and therefore, as we examine this most-important prophecy, perhaps in order to make sense of it we must look briefly outside the book.

But even if we look beyond the world of the book to the specific case of Chile, the accuracy of el Presidente's prophecy still remains to be seen. At the time of this writing free elections have still to be held there, and a military general still runs the country. The prediction of el Presidente, then, reverberates in an empty space that has yet to be filled with a future that either confirms or denies it. This raises an important point, however. After Isabel Allende has taken such pains throughout her novel to show how prophecies can sometimes fulfill themselves, is it not logical to suggest that perhaps a primary purpose of her work was to make el Presidente's prophecy stand as an incentive to the very human reader who holds the book in his hands to make use of this prediction and transform it into reality?

Within the world of *La casa de los espíritus* the Left torments itself over failure to foresee the coup d'état, while the Right continues to use clairvoyant arguments to justify brutality (i.e., the coup was necessary because without it el Presidente would have declared himself President-For-Life and a civil war would have erupted). It is the role of a political scientist, not a student of literature, to assess whether such obsessions with future vision exist in real-life Chile. What a reader of Allende's novel *can* point out, however, is that her use of clairvoyance as a political symbol is extremely appropriate to her perception of the political situation in her novelistic world and probably to the way she perceives the actual situation in Chile. What is more, her use of this symbol is so specifically tailored to her peceptions of the Chilean situation that this would seem to refute the notion of many critics that her use of magical realism is a facile imitation of García Márquez's *Cien años de soledad* (1967) for if the magic of clairvoyance is specifically fitted to the Chilean coup, then it can hardly be an imitation of a book written a decade before Salvador Allende was elected president.

American and British reviewers have been quite harsh on the book's political content and on its similarity to the work of García Márquez. Critic Paul West notes disparagingly:

> If you recall the opening of *One Hundred Years of Solitude* . . . you may hear echoes of it in this book. . . . Such echoes are bows, perhaps, but a book of bows becomes a bow-wow.[1]

Time's Patricia Blake is even more forceful:

> Regrettably, however, the novel stumbles to a close when the author falls back on one of García Márquez's hoariest literary devices: the discovery of an old manuscript that predicts the family's whole history. Though Allende's debut is full of promise, she still needs to break away from the domination of her unwitting mentor before she can fully display her distinctive voice.[2]

Blake's interpretation has several flaws. First of all, the revelation that the book is being written by a person related to the story, using Clara's manuscripts, can hardly be described as a device that springs up as the novel "stumbles to a close, since Alba gives this information very early on (page 73). Moreover, the narrator reveals her existence several times through the use of personal pronouns, surely noted by a careful reader (pages 73, 78, 263, for example). Second, it is hard to believe that Blake really thinks that such a literary device as the discovery of a manuscript was invented by García Márquez, or that Alba's realistic work of reading journals and writing her story has anything to do with Melquiades's magical manuscript.

Criticism specifically directed at the book's political content was also widespread in the English-speaking press. For example, Christopher Lehmann-Haupt wrote in the *New York Times:*

> I still have my quarrels with *The House of the Spirits*. One never stops feeling impatient with the symmetry of good and evil . . . there are simply no good right-wingers and no bad revolutionaries. More

> seriously, the real evil of repressive police states seems trivialized by the cheap psychology rung in to explain the story's inquisitor, Col. Esteban García, the policeman-torturer who is Senador Trueba's bastard son. The message implied is that we should be kinder to the children we thoughtlessly spawn. Somehow, that won't really do.[3]

Richard Eder, of the *Los Angeles Times*, also thought the book's politics superficial, and gave the following explanation:

> Allende, niece of Chile's socialist president who was overthrown and possibly killed by the military rebels, tells a story of political growth and social change. She tells it from the point of view of the Latin American Left, with a mix of romantic idealism and revolutionary zeal.[4]

Claudia Rosetti in the *Wall Street Journal* is even more blunt:

> As history, the account of the coup is a cursory whitewash of Allende.[5]

D. A. N. Jones of the *London Review of Books* was frankly hostile about the book's political content:

> Pinochet? But he's *real*. What is he doing in this farrago of feminist "magical realism"? A plain man's irritation must be expressed. Before 1973 Chile was unaccustomed to dictatorships and military coups. It was not like Bolivia or Paraguay. DeGaulle said that Chile was "the pilot country of Latin America." John Gunther wrote in 1967 that Chile was "one of the most civilised countries in the world," and that the general line of government was, "roughly that of the New Deal of Franklin D. Roosevelt or even the British Labour Party." There is not a hint of such humdrum worthiness in the ninety years of *The House of the Spirits*. Isabel Allende presents her novel as "a portrait of Latin America, not only Chile," and that means the same old Hollywood film set. . . . The trouble with this book's political stance is that it gives the impression that nothing can be done about Chile's notorious government—you know what South Americans are like, ha ha!—and that Pinochet's regime is no worse than its predecessors. This is surely untrue.[6]

Ironically, in Europe Allende has sometimes been criticized for not being leftist enough, and for appealing too much to popular tastes. Such criticisms are typified in interview questions like this one put to Allende by *Der Spiegel*:

> Haben Sie politisches Pamphlet und Schulze vermischt, um einem sicheren Bestseller zu produzieren?[7]

> (Have you mixed a political pamphlet with a kiosk love story to produce a surefire Bestseller?)

Víctor Claudín, in *Liberación,* (Spain) is much more sympathetic but still describes Allende as a more intuitive than logical soul:

> Sus palabras sonaban con una suavidad y un encanto que convertían las historias que contaban, sus verdades: "yo creo que los buenos van a ganar." . . .[8]

In fact, Allende has herself insisted repeatedly that the book is a personal vision, not an intellectual treatise. Quoted in the *Roanoke Times and World-News:*

> "I am not an intellectual," she says with a laugh. "That book is based on emotions. When people ask me literary questions, I try to look intelligent and don't say anything."[9]

This chapter has attempted to analyze clairvoyance in *La casa de los espíritus* within its proper context, i.e., as a novel and not a work of political science or history. In summary, what such an analysis has revealed is that as a literary device, clairvoyance functions very well in *La casa de los espíritus* to reflect the tormented and conflicting political postures of the novel's characters. Besides this, while some see in this clairvoyance a similarity to García Márquez's *Cien años de soledad,* the use of it in *La casa de los espíritus* has been seen to be specifically appropriate both to the book, and to a historical event that occurred in 1973. Indeed the metaphor of clairvoyance permeates the book and underscores its political argument. Whether or not this point is true and historical is not for me to say, but rather for readers to decide, based on what they can find out through observation and study. In fact, I suspect that that is exactly what Isabel Allende would want them to do.

4
"MAGIC BOOKS" AND THE MAGIC OF BOOKS

> Quede claro, pues, que a mí me gustan estos narradores [Tolkien, Verne, H.G. Wells, Kipling, Stevenson, Salgari, Poe, Zane Grey, Conan Doyle, etc.] por las mismas razones que a los niños, es decir: porque cuentan bien hermosas historias, que no conozco razón más alta que ésta para leer un libro. . . .
> —Fernando Savater, *La infancia recuperada*

> Soy un lector simple que busca entretenerse con lo que lee. Me parece una falta de respeto aburrir al lector. . . .
> —Isabel Allende, in *Informaciones*

No discussion of *La casa de los espíritus* would be complete without mention of the so-called "libros mágicos" from the "baúles encantados" of Uncle Marcos. Allende's capacity for forging phrases with the sonorous memorability of epic epithets "la bella Rosa," "la gran casa de la esquina," "el túnel de libros," etc.), which in their simple straightforwardness suggest all sorts of impossible enchantments, is evident. In the early life of Clara del Valle (described in that portion of the book in which magic is presented most literally), the "libros mágicos" are presented as if they were quite literally magic, capable of transporting a young reader to a distant place or time, or of preserving him from other worldly evils. But as the story progresses, the "magical" title acquires a more metaphorical acceptance, related to the power these tales hold over the childish imagination of their readers. By Blanca's generation some of the specific books are actually identified, and it turns out that they are not unpronounceable incantations in forgotten mystical tongues, but rather universal classics that have delighted children and adults for generations:

> . . . Sandokán, Robin Hood . . . el Pirata Negro, las historias verídicas y edificantes del Tesoro de la Juventud . . . el diccionario de la Real Academia de la Lengua Española . . . historias imposibles, los duendes, las hadas, los náufragos que se comen unos a otros después de echarlo a la suerte, los tigres que se dejan amaestrar por amor, los

> inventos fascinantes, las curiosidades geográficas y zoológicas, los países orientales donde hay genios en las botellas, dragones en las cuevas y princesas prisioneras en las torres. (126–27)

In fact, the wide variety of this reading matter testifies to the astonishing capacity of children who read almost anything. There is magic in the reader, but the most literally magic aspect of the books is their capacity to "poblar los sueños" of those who open them (23).

The transmission of these "magic books" is depicted as an act of love in the novel, either from mother to daughter (as in the cases of Clara to Blanca, and Blanca to Alba), or from one lover to another, as when Blanca commemorates her first stirrings of adolescent love for Pedro Tercero, offering the books to him as proof of affection (126).

Later, the retelling of these very tales is also an act of love. Blanca and Pedro Tercero, for example, shout them good-naturedly into the age-deafened ears of old Pedro García, something that he, we are told, "agradecía mucho" (127). In exchange, he responds lovingly with some of his own oral folklore. Blanca also expresses her love for her daughter Alba by trying to reconstruct remembered tales from the trunk. Although her poor memory magically transforms them and they miraculously metamorphose into something completely different, the act of love is still the same, and the final effect is much appreciated by Alba:

> [Blanca] le contaba [a Alba] los cuentos de los libros mágicos de los baúles encantados del bisabuelo Marcos, pero que su mala memoria transformaba en cuentos nuevos. Así se enteró Alba de un príncipe que durmió cien años, de doncellas que peleaban cuerpo a cuerpo con los dragones, de un lobo perdido en el bosque a quien una niña destripó sin razón alguna. (269)

Moreover, reading these "libros mágicos" has another magic effect: it stimulates the young reader to write or create on his or her own, and a mention of reading the books is frequently linked to an urge to write, within the text. For example, in one paragraph we are told of young Clara's voracious reading habits:

> . . . Leía mucho . . . y le daban lo mismo los libros mágicos de los baúles encantados de su tío Marcos, que los documentos del Partido Liberal. (73)

In the very next sentence the author calls attention to Clara's nascent practice of writing things down in journals:

> Llenaba incontables cuadernos con sus anotaciones privadas, donde fueron quedando registrados los acontecimientos de ese tiempo que gracias a eso no se perdieron borrados por la neblina del olvido. (73)

Already, some of the deeper magic of these "libros mágicos" begins to emerge. They stimulate the readers in their turn to learn how to tell a good story, and the telling of tales results in two effects of paramount importance within the cosmos of *La casa de los espíritus*. First of all, tale-telling entertains honestly, and such entertainment brings teller and listener closer together. Second, it can preserve history, whether that of a family, country, or continent.

The magically stimulating effect of the "libros mágicos" can be seen again when the reading of them, along with syndicalist literature, helps Pedro Tercero García to develop spiritually and intellectually and to pass from childhood to adolescence. In this period, the boy "leyó y releyó mil veces los libros mágicos de los baúles encantados del tío Marcos" (139). At the same time, this period of intense reading is the birth of Pedro Tercero's creative productivity, and prompted by the magic of the books and the magic of his love for Blanca, the youth begins composing his first songs.

The "libros mágicos" also have an important catalytic function in Alba's beginnings as a writer. Blanca attempts to recount the tales from memory to her young daughter, with the confusing results that have already been mentioned. In spite of the oddity of these tales, they enchant the tiny Alba, who wants to hear them repeated:

> Cuando Alba quería volver a oír esas truculencias, Blanca no podía repetirlas, porque las había olvidado, en vista de lo cual, la pequeña tomó el hábito de escribirlas. Después anotaba también las cosas que le parecían importantes, tal como lo hacía su abuela Clara. (269)

Again we see the magic function of books, how they stimulate the imagination toward artistic creation—a phenomenon quite literally inexplicable according to natural law and therefore eminently magic. In this sense, the books from the "baúles encantados" come to stand for all childhood reading in general. The very looseness of the designation, "baúles encantados" in the plural lets the imagination fill in exactly how many trunks it takes to hold the treasures of childhood reading, and exactly how many and what are the books contained. Some of the books are identified, but no index of them is ever given, and in this way Allende contrives to make these magic trunks miraculously expand or contract to hold the childhood favorites of each individual reader.

The connection between the "libros mágicos" and the stimulation of artistic creation can now be seen more clearly on page 73, where the magic books, Clara's notebooks, and the rarely intrusive "yo" (belonging to the older, retrospective Alba) all join together. After mentioning the "libros mágicos" and the notebooks of Clara, the narrator adds, "y ahora yo puedo usarlos para rescatar su memoria" (73). It is as if these two sources, beloved childhood readings and family oral history, are presented here as the raw ingredients of the novel we hold in our hands. These two sources do not contain the actual motivation for Alba's "writing" this book, but they certainly do contain her raw materials.

Reading the "libros mágicos" stimulates the imagination of a child; moreover, within the world of this novel it is a fairly significant factor in determining who will later turn out well and who will not. For example, Jaime and Nicolás are saved in part from the unimaginative rigors of their strict "colegio inglés" by such stimulating reading. By contrast, Esteban Trueba's bastard grandson, Esteban García, in being excluded from his physical birthright within the family is also excluded from the spiritual birthright represented by the magic tales. His frustrations cannot find the creative, constructive outlets that Pedro Tercero forges through song and political activism; rather, his distorted soul resorts to torture and force. The seeds of the adult Esteban García will become are already present in the child, and at our first view of him we can already perceive a dangerous inability to imagine the suffering of others. He is described as "ocupado en ensartar los ojos a un pollo con un clavo" (170). The child, unsupervised and uninstructed by maternal tales lovingly told, so completely lacks the imagination to suppose the pain of the creature he tortures that when he discovers his grandfather dead, he tries to do the same to the old man until Blanca stops him.

Rather than finding compassion, morality, and idealistic adventure in the stories told to him as a child, Esteban García finds embitterment. Instead of the loving accounts of the del Valle history that Nívea tells Clara during the latter's period of muteness, instead of the fascinating adventures that Uncle Marcos relates, instead of the confused but well-intentioned stories that Blanca tells Alba, by contrast, Esteban García's childhood has been poisoned by the bitter tales that his grandmother, Pancha García (the first woman raped by Estaban Trueba) whispered into his ear from the time he was old enough to understand:

> Su abuela, Pancha García, antes de morir alcanzó a envenenarle la infancia con el cuento de que si su padre hubiera nacido en el lugar de Blanca, Jaime o Nicolás, habría heredado Las Tres Marías y podría haber llegado a Presidente de la República, de haberlo querido. (170)

A childhood imagination is such a delicate thing, according to this novel, that malicious stories, told in a susceptible period of childhood, can serve to permanently deform a young character.

Such serious consequences are seen in the "pious" lie Blanca tells Alba about her "father," Jean de Satigny. Because Blanca invents a very believable tale in which the count dies of a fever in the northern desert, Alba actually has nightmares:

> Soñaba con un hombre joven . . . caminando por el desierto a pleno sol. En su sueño el caminante acortaba el paso, vacilaba, iba más y más lento, tropezaba y caía, se arrastraba de rodillas un trecho sobre las ardientes arenas, pero finalmente quedaba tendido en la inmensidad de aquellas dunas lívidas, con las aves de rapiña revoloteando en círculos sobre su cuerpo inerte. (236)

This is clearly a frightening, even damaging effect from adult abuse of the power of storytelling, and Alba reproaches her mother for this when she discovers at last that her father was really Pedro Tercero García:

> Alba . . . sacó un hilo de voz temblorosa para preguntar por qué no le habían dicho antes que Pedro Tercero era su padre, así se habría ahorrado tantas pesadillas de un conde vestido de blanco muerto de fiebre en el desierto. (317)

But fortunately, this abuse of storytelling is counterbalanced by a loving and careful use of the power of books and tales for the most part in the rest of Alba's childhood:

> [La historia del conde] fue uno de los pocos infundios que tuvo que soportar en su infancia, porque . . . su tío Jaime se encargó de destruir el mito de los niños que surgen de los repollos o son transportados desde París por las cigüeñas y su tío Nicolás el de los Reyes Magos, las hadas y los cocos. (318)

By truthfully answering Alba's serious questions about sex, Christmas, and what is under the bed at night, her uncles have not spoiled a childish fantasy world for her, but rather they have permitted her to enjoy the books of enchanted stories, while at the same time knowing that not everything in them is literally true. Thus Alba, the most modern and moderate of the Trueba/del Valle women, enjoys a synthesis between the fantastic and spiritual ways of her grandmother and the practical intelligence of her grandfather. In a way, a wise use of storytelling has been an important factor in seeing to it that Alba falls heir to much of the best of each grandparent.

Other characters are not always so fortunate in the effects that reading and hearing tales have on them. For example, Blanca is determined to convert her passion for her childhood love, Pedro Tercero García, into "un amor de novela" (276). This romanticism causes her to fear the prosaic realities of daily life with someone and ultimately nearly costs her that great love forever.

La Nana as well is adversely affected by a series of "folletos terroríficos" that she cannot even read but whose pictures nevertheless serve as the inspiration for the horrifying costumes with which the good woman does herself up in an attempt to frighten the child Clara out of her muteness. Even pictures can tell a story, and in this case they have a disastrous effect (76).

The "libros mágicos" themselves can have a negative effect if taken too seriously. It has already been mentioned that Alba's reading of the magic books was tempered by her uncles, who always kept her "en un estrecho contacto con las prosaicas verdades de la existencia" (236). Young Clara, by contrast, did not have such a balancing force against the extravagances of her Uncle Marcos, and thus her reading actually leads her to interpret the worst from the most traumatic incident in her childhood—the moment when she accidentally witnesses kindly old Dr. Cuevas performing an autopsy on her sister Rosa.

> El doctor Cuevas, ese hombronazo bonachón y dulce, de amplia barba y vientre opulento, que la ayudó a nacer y que la atendió en todas sus pequeñas enfermedades de la niñez y sus ataques de asma se había transformado en un vampiro gordo y oscuro como los de las ilustraciones de los libros de su tío Marcos. (40)

Once again, pictures have inflamed a suggestible imagination, just as they did in the case of La Nana, and without the counterbalancing effect of an adult to carefully help separate some of the fantasy from reality (without crushing the enjoyment of the fantasy), the imagination is overstimulated to unhealthy ends.

But the telling of tales is not only an important part of childhood in *La casa de los espíritus*. It is also a privileged part of the adult world. Those adults who can tell a good story are given a special position in the narrative, whereas those who use storytelling for malicious ends are veritable personifications of archetypal evil.

Nívea, Clara, and Blanca all tell the best stories they know to their children, stories handed down both from family history and from the magic books of Uncle Marcos. But some other mothers in the book, though often well-intentioned, simply have no good stories to tell. The illiterate Pancha García, for example, can only recount her own poisonous family history over and over. Thus she becomes, as has already been mentioned, one of the first sources for Esteban García's monumental resentment and hatred. On a lesser scale, Ester Trueba tries to be a good mother to Esteban, and on her death, the young man's fondest memory is of her reading with him, "se había inclinado con él sobre las páginas de un libro" (81). But unfortunately, Ester lacks imagination in her choice of reading matter, and as she gets older and more ill, she sits day after day, "sin más compañía que las lecturas piadosas de sus libritos píos de vidas y milagros de los santos" (43). Although her intentions are very good and although the "milagros" alluded to seem to promise magic sparks, the dismal reality of these books is a sadistic distortion of morality that is at least one factor in pushing daughter Férula toward her masochistic relish of self-humiliation.

In fact, books are so important in *La casa de los espíritus* that figures are frequently characterized by what they read. The mention of Ester's bedside reading matter helps to flesh her out immediately in our imagination as someone of limited and somewhat morbid intellectual horizons. By contrast, Alba's beloved Uncle Jaime lives in a "túnel de libros," a monument to a love of reading. What is more, the ultimate statement of intimacy between uncle and niece is seen in the phrase, "compartían los mismos libros" (295). It does not matter that they totally disagree about all they read; this mutual passion for books so unites them that it transcends differences of opinion:

> . . . Ambos se perdían en una oratoria confusa que los dejaba agotados, acusándose mutuamente de ser más testarudos que una

mula, pero al final se daban las buenas noches con un beso y quedaban ambos con la sensación de que el otro era un ser maravilloso. (296)

Jaime's veneration for books has been apparent since his childhood days in English schools, where one of the "extrañas manías" that sometimes separated him from other boys was that, "no le gustaba que . . . le pidieran libros prestados . . ." (167). In a novelistic universe where books play such an important role, it is no wonder that a reluctance to part with valued books foreshadows a great man to be.

By contrast, the unlikable Jean de Satigny is a determined dilettante when he reads, and is damned with the physical description of his hands, "manos . . . de un hombre que no tiene nada interesante que contar" (236).

As the book comes closer to contemporary times, another important function of storytelling begins to emerge: tale-telling as a motivation for action, specifically as a force for political and social change. Through his political awakening, Pedro Tercero becomes convinced of the need for social change among the residents of Las Tres Marías. Initially he passes out syndicalist pamphlets that leave the workers confused and indifferent. But then a "magic" story intervenes, recounted by old Pedro García from the stories of his oral tradition:

> Un día el viejo . . . les contó . . . el cuento de las gallinas que se pusieron de acuerdo para enfrentar a un zorro que se metía todas las noches en el gallinero para robar los huevos y devorarse los pollitos. . . . Pedro Tercero . . . se quedó toda la tarde pensativo, rumiando el cuento del zorro y las gallinas, y tal vez ese fue el instante en que el niño comenzó a hacerse hombre. (128)

Eventually, Pedro Tercero writes a song that recounts the story, and from that point on, the tale comes to represent his songwriting as a whole. By taking an oral tradition, transforming it to the best of his abilities, and adapting it to his own special talent—song—Pedro Tercero has begun to grow into a man. And within the world of this novel, developing artistically is clearly seen as one of the highest goods. Besides, Pedro Tercero discovers to his surprise that by telling his parable in song, he achieves much more than through the prosaic distribution of pamphlets. His father notes this development proudly:

> Cuando escuchaba canturrear algunas de las canciones de gallinas y zorros, sonreía pensando que su hijo había conseguido más adeptos

> con sus baladas subversivas que con los panfletos del Partido Socialista que repartía incansablemente. (157)

In fact, teaching through storytelling is an ancient, time-honored custom in Christianity, and was a favorite pedagogical method of Christ himself according to the Bible. *La casa de los espíritus* takes the ratio of good parables to Christ-like behavior very literally, and the use of parables becomes for example, a good test to determine the virtue or hypocrisy of a priest within the book. The most favorably presented priest in the story is, of course, Padre José Dulce María, the renegade Jesuit whose specialty is transforming biblical parables into calls to socialism. Even after he is banished by the Compañía de Jesús to a forgotten corner of the world, his conviction remains strong and his methods unwavering: "ni por eso renunció a transformase las parábolas bíblicas en panfletos socialistas" (125).

Later, these parables and other books join with the "libros mágicos" to aid in Pedro Tercero's spiritual formation and in the development of his imagination and character. The priest also fulfills the important function of guiding Pedro Tercero into an outlet for his creativity: "también le enseñó a cultivar su habilidad natural para versificar y a traducir en canciones sus ideas" (139). Later, it is once more Padre José Dulce María who convinces Pedro Tercero that he can overcome the loss of three fingers from his right hand and continue making music.

By contrast, the most dislikable priest in the book, Padre Restrepo, is condemned by his distance from simple Christian parables and virtues. Instead of telling straightforward tales to inspire his parishoners to do good, Padre Restrepo uses the power of the pulpit to abuse the patience of his hearers with stories that reflect a diseased imagination and a total lack of reality contact:

> —¡Tú, desvergonzada que te prostituyes en los muelles!—y acusaba a doña Ester Trueba, inválida debido a la artritis y beata de la Virgen del Carmen, que abría los ojos sorprendida, sin saber el significado de aquella palabra ni adónde quedaban los muelles. (10)

Instead of using his eloquence to uplift his hearers, inspire them, or even at least to entertain them, Padre Restrepo chooses to describe such delicacies as the suffering of Hell in such vivid detail that it inflames Ester and Férula Trueba to unhealthy fantasies, while the more sensible Nívea del Valle simply feels sick and worries about fainting.

Another character who uses storytelling to provoke action is Nicolás Trueba. For the imaginative Nicolás, storytelling is first and foremost an art of seduction. After practicing it with success on the country lasses at Las Tres Marías, Nicolás plies his storytelling to great advantage back in the capital. There he woos urban damsels with a fabrication about having learned to dance flamenco in the caves of Sacramonte. As the following passage shows, he was a very convincing teller of tales:

> Nicolás andaba esos días con la novedad del baile flamenco, que decía haberlo aprendido de los gitanos en las cuevas de Granada, aunque en realidad nunca había salido del país, pero era tal su poder de convicción, que hasta en el seno de su propia familia comenzaron a dudar. (195)

Such powers of deception are hardly surprising in a fellow who spent his adolescence arguing both sides of every issue with his brother Jaime (168). Still, Nicolás's powers of storytelling are limited to the same degree that his own spirit is limited, deformed by his later life, and lacking in the ability to imagine the sufferings of others, especially Amanda. This is so much the case that when he eventually sits down to write a book, it sounds without a doubt to be one of the most boring ever printed:

> Después de corregidas e impresas, las mil y tantas cuartillas manuscritas se redujeron a seiscientas páginas de un voluminoso tratado sobre los noventa y nueve nombres de Dios y la forma de llegar al Nirvana mediante ejercicios respiratorios. (242)

Here is an example of a book that is quite literally about a magical subject but that nevertheless could certainly never qualify as a "libro mágico." Nicolás writes, but he does not *tell;* by not availing himself of the storytelling arts, he creates a book that exists literally only as a physical object, not as a transcendental means of arriving at a different reality that is to be found, for example, in an adventure tale, it is no wonder that this highly unimaginative tome soon ceases to be considered as a book at all, and is reduced to its purely physical dimensions:

> Los cajones de la edición terminaron sus días en el sótano donde [la pequeña] Alba los usaba como ladrillos para construir trincheras. (242)

The "libros mágicos" of Uncle Marcos miraculously capable of holding an entire world within themselves, but by contrast, Nicolás's book is nothing more than the pages and binding, a physical mass. It is not enough that a book be about magic for it to be a magic book. Part of what constitutes a "libro mágico" is that it must stimulate the imagination.

But according to the morality of this novel, even works that stimulate the imagination must do so wisely in order to be considered "magic." When the stimulation is random, manipulative, or malicious, then the books in question are not magic at all. Consider with what scorn the text speaks of the books that Jean de Satigny brings to Las Tres Marías. Every piece of literature that this man introduces produces a negative effect, from the "revistas de moda," which promote styles totally impractical for the active country man or woman; to the "folletines de guerra que se habían popularizado para crear el mito del soldado heroico"; and the "novelas románticas para Blanca" (236), which as was discussed earlier, are a factor in her nearly losing the love of her life, Pedro Tercero. All of these types of reading matter are abuses of storytelling, distortions of reality and emotional manipulation. Within this novel, storytelling is viewed almost as a sacred responsibility, associated with acts of love and the very perpetuation of life itself. Therefore it is no surprise that corrupt stories and books should emanate from a character who is presented as morally degenerate.

If the characters within *La casa de los espíritus* can be judged by the stories they tell and the books they read, then Esteban Trueba poses a special problem. The narrator and *lazarillo* throughout much of this novel, he tells a tale of his own life that is first and foremost compelling reading. His, we are certain, are the hands of a man who *does* have something interesting to relate, and his story proves it. Does this mean that the association of good storytelling with a strong moral base falls down in the character of Esteban Trueba? This question can be answered by remembering *when* it is that Trueba begins to tell his story. Although his tale begins chronologically when he was a young man, this is not the point in time from which he is "writing." Rather, as the novel explicitly states, Trueba begins writing all of these remembrances only *after* Alba has returned home, mutilated by her captors, and therefore after Trueba has been forced to change some very deeply held prejudices and beliefs. His written narration, then, is part of his spiritual regeneration, and he can be allowed within the morality of the book to tell a good tale because that is literally part of his expiation for past sins.

Even before his spiritual epiphany, the brusque Trueba associated the telling of personal tales with intimacy. He defines his friends thus:

> Con ellos discutía mis negocios, hablaba de política y a veces de la familia. (278)

But before his spiritual regeneration, brought about through recognition of his errors, Trueba is guilty of some gross abuses of storytelling. Probably the most glaring of these are his terrifying stories of what would happen if the socialists were to win the election. Fittingly, it is his bookish son Jaime, who lives in a "túnel de libros," who is most offended by his father's tactics:

> La única vez que Jaime perdió la paciencia fue cuando una mañana encontró la ciudad tapizada de afiches truculentos donde aparecía una madre barrigona y desolada, que intentaba inútilmente arrebatar a su hijo a un soldado comunista que se lo llevaba a Moscú. Era la campaña de terror organizado por el Senador Trueba y sus correligionarios. . . . Aquello fue demasiado para Jaime. . . . Cerró su túnel . . . y se fue a dormir al hospital. (297)

This distortion of storytelling into which Trueba falls is nothing new in terms of his political methods. Earlier in the novel, he kept his workers in line at election time with a mixture of alcohol, rare friendliness, and lies. But this distortion of truth and the abuse of the power of a story cleverly told to move the masses is especially condemned within this book as it pertains to the Right in general and the leaders of the coup in specific.

As the Junta takes power after the coup, a succesive degeneration of storytelling occurs until even words, the most basic unit of storytelling, fall into degeneration.

The first action of the military leaders after the coup is to attempt to find "witnesses" to swear to a story that is completely false within the novel, i.e., that el Presidente has committed suicide in a drunken stupor. It is fitting that it should be Jaime, with his love for books and veneration for tales that convey beautiful truths, whose last act of courage is to refuse to appear on nationwide television and propagate the story:

> —Haga esa declaración usted mismo, conmigo no cuenten, cabrones—respondió Jaime. Le sujetaron de los brazos. El primer golpe le cayó en el estómago. (327)

Through fear of retribution, moreover, Alba's first act when the military seizes control is to begin destroying Jaime's "túnel," along with all of the other written records that she foresees may be dangerous. Alba, with her grandmother's clairvoyance, senses that the military will launch an attack on these very documents and will destroy directly and indirectly much personal and national history, in the process of contraverting one of the sacred duties of storytelling. As the Junta continues in power, censorship begins to attack the language itself:

> La censura que al principio sólo abarcó los medios de comunicación, pronto se extendió a los textos escolares, las letras de las canciones, los argumentos de las películas y las conversaciones privadas. Había palabras prohibidas por bando militar, como la palabra compañero, y otras que no se decían por precaución, a pesar de que ningún bando las había eliminado del diccionario, como libertad, justicia y sindicato. (337)

The destruction of the language is symbolized by the death of el Poeta. The cause and effect, according to the novel, is clear: "Estaba enfermo y los acontecimientos de los últimos tiempos agotaron su deseo de seguir viviendo" (341). In addition to their crimes against humanity, the leaders of the coup are guilty of literal "lèse culture," and the body of world literature was truncated as a result.

Eventually, the destruction of truth becomes so great that all important events begin to be told by means of a blackly magical conundrum:

> [La] casa azul [del Poeta] estaba medio en ruinas. . . . No se sabía si era obra de los militares, como decían los vecinos, o de los vecinos, como decían los militares. (341)

After so many lies, the truth of any important historical event becomes all but impossible for an outsider to determine. Did Allende kill himself, as the army claims, or did the army kill him, as the Allendes claim? Did the economy of Chile fail because the wealthy withdrew their money, or did the wealthy withdraw their money because the economy was failing? Did the upper-class women march in the streets because no food was being delivered, or were both a ploy to harass the Allende government? Again, it is not the role of this study to answer such historical questions. But what is appropriate is to point out how neatly the conundrums Isabel Allende comes up with in her book match the frustrating situation she depicts in her novel. In

La casa de los espíritus the situation is at last reduced to the ultimate conundrum, which Esteban Trueba himself articulates:

> El país está en guerra, guerra contra el comunismo internacional, o contra el pueblo, ya no se sabe. (366).

As the moral pretext for the coup and the resultant Junta disintegrates, the storytelling becomes more and more distorted, and less convincing, until finally it deteriorates into obvious lies that can only be believed by those making a conscious effort to avoid the unpleasant truths:

> Los periódicos dijeron que los mendigos en las calles, que no se veían desde hacía tantos años, eran enviados por el comunismo internacional para desprestigiar a la Junta Militar. (336)

With answers like this one, the Junta begins to feel free to say anything with impunity, even to change world history and national boundaries in the schoolbooks the children study.

No moral storytelling can come from this entity so opposed to clear speech and the direct transmission of a tale. The closest thing to literature that the Junta is capable of producing is a document of terror, "una lista negra que manejaba la policía política" (338)

Eventually, the Junta steals from the people their most precious words and stories. For Isabel Allende, this is the ultimate crime. This is seen most clearly after Alba has been tortured. The final effect of such destruction of the truth is the loss of words themselves, and the loss of words, for Alba, is the spiritual equivalent of death:

> Nadie resistía mucho tiempo [en la perrera] . . . antes de perder . . . el significado de las palabras . . . o, simplemente, empezar a morir. (362)

But it is at precisely this point in the narration that the real importance of storytelling become most clear. On the surface, destruction has proved stronger than creation, and the agents of evil have burned in a demonic pyre all the "libros mágicos" that filled so many of the del Valle and Trueba children with dreams. Without their stories, their language, their words, the moral storytellers of *La casa de los espíritus* must surely die, mustn't they? But no, such a grim outcome is far from being Isabel

Allende's message. Pedro Tercero García, that teller of parables through song, escapes into exile. Of course this escape requires a degree of moral compromise, but nevertheless, he lives. The Junta may declare him a nonperson, smash his records the way soldiers deliberately smashed Esteban Trueba's record collection for sheer pleasure, and even prevent his name from being mentioned, but they cannot prevent his songs from living on in the hearts of his listeners. The same is true of the words of el Poeta, and for those of el Presidente. Alba, who survives solitary confinement and torture by "writing" in her head the history of her country along with that of her family, proves stronger than the forces that seek to blot out her tale.

The "libros mágicos" that began this chapter can be physically destroyed by the "pira infame" that burns "por error," along with the supposedly politically damaging works when Alba is arrested (23, 353). But the imaginative, creative forces that the books have inspired are not so easily blotted out. The triumph of Alba's survival is at least in part her continued ability to tell her own story and that of the women and men who shared her fate in prison. It is by preserving memory and continuing to tell this tale that the hopeful predictions found in el Presidente's last words can be fulfilled.

By writing, Alba manages to overcome her strict desire for vengeance and to forgive, just as Esteban Trueba manages through his writing to arrive at a much-needed absolution that enables him to die in peace. Thus, writing according to *La casa de los espíritus*, can be a spiritual experience.

The stimulations for a writer can be many, but the foundations for writing, as seen in this novel, come from two basic sources, both rooted in childhood. The first source is based on the stories of family history, which in this book the mothers are especially responsible for transmitting. The second one is drawn from the "libros mágicos," the childhood books that filled the childish imagination the way no other books read later are ever quite able to do. In order to transform these basic sources (the first of which influences content, and the second, style), something magic is needed. Perhaps the influence of the "libros mágicos" is one of the most literally magic in all of the so-called "magical realism" of this book, because it may be from their stimulus that the desire to write arises. Most people who read voraciously as children experience at one time or another the desire to write something as good as their childhood favorites. In the case of Alba, this stimulus combines with a good education (something her mother and grandmother lacked), a rich family history, and living through a historical moment whose telling is important to many people. This mystical configuration, according to the fiction of the book produces Alba's narrative, and it is a magic one indeed, somehow much greater than the sum of the parts that make it up.

I have shown the "libros mágicos" in *La casa de los espíritus* have a number of important implications: they stand for the magical adventure of childhood reading, for the well-told, compelling tale, and even as models for the writing of fiction. Moreover, I have shown how the "magic" aspects of these books—their ability to inspire the readers and even to stimulate them to write—is constant from the beginning to the end, with even more importance at the end. Once again, this goes to disprove the idea that a bit of magic is dropped into the book to get things going at the beginning, but that it is abandoned later on for a more realistic mode of narration. If anything, the "libros mágicos," though physically destroyed by the end, have a more literally magic power at the end of the book than they did at the beginning.

What are the "magic" books in Isabel Allende's personal "baúles encantados"? Surely they are some of the same ones that Alba read. Yet as the "baúles" magically expanded with her later reading, one can guess at others they stretched to encompass—Gabriel García Márquez, William Faulkner, Henri Troyat. . . . But in the end, part of the magic of this secret store is that it is hers alone, and of dimensions that only she really knows. "Alba no soy yo," she has said on various occasions (*Der Spiegel*, Vera Jarach, Michael Moody, for example). Therefore, we cannot ascribe to her all of the literary make-up of her character, Alba. What is more, an important part of Allende's writing background—her experience in journalism—is not shared by Alba, but rather is more similar to the background of the protagonist of *De amor y de sombra*, Irene Beltrán. But in spite of this, one assumption seems very safe to make in conclusion to this look at books, storytelling, and writing within *La casa de los espíritus*. That is that for Allende, telling a good story is an act of love, and that in addition to all of the other things that this book is, it is also Isabel Allende's gift of love to us.

5
CALLING SHAPES AND BECKONING SHADOWS: INVOKING THE SPIRITS

> *Glendower:* I can call spirits from the vasty deep!
> *Hotspur:* Why, so can I, or so can any man;
> But will they come when you do call for them?
> —William Shakespeare, *I Henry IV,* 3.1

As Harry Hotspur so insolently pointed out to Glendower, anyone can summon the spirits. It takes a special kind of magic, however, to make the spirits actually appear. Isabel Allende has this power, for when she summons the spirits, they hear her and report in droves. The pages of *La casa de los espíritus* are crowded with spirits of all descriptions. But what exactly are these insubstantial creatures who give the title to this book? And what are they good for once they have been summoned? What is their role within the context of this novel?

The first spirits that come to mind are of course the ones represented most literally. These, naturally, are the actual spirits that the narrator tells us Clara del Valle and her friends are literally able to summon from the Great Beyond. Yet even as the author manages to convince us of their authenticity, she undercuts their importance, often with a gentle humor. For example, when Clara is forced to take on adult responsibilities for the first time in her life a cataclysmic earthquake injures her husband and leaves Las Tres Marías in ruins, she struggles to maintain a "delicado equilibrio entre los espíritus del Más Allá y las almas necesitadas del Más Acá" (148). But these elusive creatures, the literal ghosts who appear in the corridors of the *gran casa de la esquina* are by no means the only spirits in Allende's novels. Other types of spirits appear from the very first page on, making themselves felt thematically so that they are ultimately much more important than the literal ghosts.

To begin with, young Clara is sort of a spirit herself, as she sleepwalks with her similarly somnambulistic dog through the house at night:

> . . . era común verlos paseando por los corredores, como dos fantasmas flotando en la pálida luz. (75)

Related to the child Clara is the evil spirit, the demon that Padre Restrepo accuses Clara of being possessed by in the first chapter. Interestingly, this accusation comes when Clara chooses to doubt the magical reality of the myths of heaven and hell, especially the latter, which the priest has been spinning from the pulpit with legendary eloquence:

> —¡Pst! ¡Padre Restrepo! Si el cuento del infierno fuera pura mentira, nos chingamos todos . . . (14)

the priest's response is immediate and damning:

> —¡Endemoniada! ¡Soberbia endemoniada! (14)

The reader tends to agree with Clara's parents that "la posesión demoníaca y la soberbia eran dos pecados demasiado grandes para una niña tan pequeña" (14). Therefore, the literal idea of an evil spirit as suggested by Padre Restrepo is devalued. In its place is the possibility of a larger, amorphous evil spirit that seems, in fact, to be controlling Padre Restrepo, and perhaps even a part of the organization he represents. It should be pointed out that the book is not strictly anticlerical, for it includes heroic priests as well as men obsessed with evil. But for Allende, the men of the cloth seem to be divided into two clear categories: those who are a part of the problems of Latin America, and those who are part of the solution. She does not denounce priests as a group, but she expects them to literally fight the good fight and to be actively involved in trying to improve the plight of the poor. One of her "good" priests, Jesuit Padre José Dulce María, sums it up this way to Pedro Tercero:

> Hijo mío, la Santa Madre Iglesia está a la derecha, pero Jesucristo siempre estuvo a la izquierda. (139)

With these references Allende encourages the reader to think about the spirit of a priest who dares to defy earthly authority in his order to obey what he believes to be a higher law. Thus the spirit of priests like Padre José Dulce María, who risked or gave their lives to further what they believed to be a struggle to bring divine justice to earth, is celebrated. The spirits who rustle and murmur in the upstairs halls of *la gran casa de la esquina* suddenly seem vague and unimportant by comparison. What is more, for the reader knowledgeable in Chilean history, the legendary spirits of real-life Chilean priests may also be evoked.

The next group of spirits inhabits this book from the very first page, and also has a whispered message to bring us. Who are these pale creatures? Why, they are the other children of Severo and Nívea del Valle. As we stop to think of it, although Nívea is the mother of fifteen children, we really only come to know two of them, La bella Rosa and the youngest daughter Clara. The rest are mere spirits on these pages, vague presences whom we scarcely see. Oh, they take up a certain space; at Mass for example, "Nívea y Severo ocupaban, con sus hijos, toda la tercera hilera de bancos" (11). But we never meet any of them individually for more than a second, or get the slightest description, in frank contrast to the pages of description of Rosa and Clara. In fact, only three of them even have names. Son Luis appears briefly twice. First he is thrown by his horse and crippled for life. But the incident is told not to introduce us to Luis and his "cadera desviada," but rather simply to confirm Clara's prophetic powers. Later, he marries Clara's pregnant French nanny in an anecdote of a few sentences. Again, the incident is included not to tell us about Luis, but rather to shed light on the subject of Clara's early education.

The other two children whose names are given are daughters mentioned in passing to Esteban Trueba when he comes to ask if there are any marriageable daughers left at home:

> Sacaron sus cuentas y le informaron que Ana se había metido a monja, Teresa estaba muy enferma y todas las demás estaban casadas, menos Clara. . . . (83)

How is it possible to make ghosts of thirteen of what must have been a lively brood of fifteen children? And why does Allende choose to populate the early part of the tale with these spirits? The answer goes to the heart of the novel's narrative structure and reveals a sharp contrast with *Cien años de soledad*.

One might first argue that since Clara is the main character of the book, of course the emphasis is on her. Within the novel, however, such emphasis is explained casually by simple parental favoritism:

> Nívea, a pesar de haber tenido quince hijos, la trataba [a Clara] como si fuera la única. . . . (78)

Rosa is the only other del Valle child to receive close attention in the book. Because she is important to Esteban Trueba's story (through her engagement to him) and because of her hyperbolic beauty and her dramatically foreshadowed death, she is a logical novelistic inclusion. But is it natural that the rest serve as nameless, faceless extras—walk-ons in the story of Clara, holding down a levitated salt shaker or two? The answer is yes, it is natural, when we consider that although the novelist pretends to evoke the house of Severo and Nívea as if the events were actually unfolding during the telling, this is clearly an illusion. For within the confines of the text, there is actually a "present" from which the story is being told, and this corresponds to the young womanhood of Alba Trueba. Alba, of course, is three generations removed from Severo and Nívea, who were killed before her mother, Blanca, was born. It is natural, then, that she should have little interest in great-aunts and uncles whom she likely never met and who left no anecdotes behind (unlike Juan del Pedo, for example). One of the essential concerns of the story is the writing of history, the attempt to "burlar la mala memoria," and this history cannot, ultimately, be written magically. It must be compiled by the work of the last person in the chain and must be told through his or her perspective.

One remembers here that earlier a number of criticisms were examined that insisted on a kinship between *La casa de los espíritus* and García Márquez's *Cien años de soledad*. In particular, several pointed to the detail of the manuscript's being written by Alba as a flaw in structure, at best a clumsy homage to García Márquez, or at worst, a hackneyed device. In particular, the words of *Time*'s Patricia Blake come to mind:

> Regrettably, however, the novel stumbles to a close when the author falls back on one of García Márquez's hoariest literary devices: the discovery of an old manuscript that predicts the family's whole history.[1]

In fact, nowhere are we told in the novel that Clara's notebooks predicted the future of her family, rather than recording it. To the contrary, Alba emphasizes the research that went into her task as she collected an assortment of documents in an attempt to work the magic of evoking past events through writing history. First, she assembled all the old family photo albums and examined the pictures they contained. Then she collected the other documents, of which Clara's notebooks were only a part:

> Los cuadernos de Clara, las cartas de mi madre, los libros de administración de Las Tres Marías, y tantos otros documentos que ahora están sobre la mesa al alcance de la mano. . . . (379)

What is more, an important percentage of the text is not due to Clara's notebooks at all, but rather to the first-person narration of Esteban Trueba. According to Alba, he was the force, the spirit, behind beginning the history at all, not Clara:

> Mi abuelo tuvo la idea de que escribiéramos esta historia. . . . Empecé a escribir con la ayuda de [él], cuya memoria permaneció intacta hasta el último instante de sus noventa años. De su puño y letra escribió varias páginas (378)

There is, in fact, nothing impossible at all about the way Alba says these documents were collected. On the contrary, she says that the two writers prepared their materials in the ordinary, human manner. The idea of the text predicting the future is an interesting one (one supposes that if Clara were really prescient, then she could have done this), but the text never even suggests such a thing. This seems to be a magical invention of Ms. Blake, in fact. Of course, there is the detail that we are told that Clara's spirit helped in the writing of the text, but again, as in the best moments of magical realism, the "magical" suggestion serves as a correlative for a deeper truth from everyday reality. Yes, Clara's spirit literally appeared to grandfather and granddaughter:

> tal como era en sus mejores tiempos, riéndose con todos sus dientes y alborotando a los espíritus con su vuelo fugaz (378).

But the phrase "también nos ayudó a escribir" also has a metaphorical acceptance that, as with the best magical realism, resonates. The spirit of Clara, understood as her essential or activating principle—her will—is what metaphorically motivates the granddaughter to write her account. The word "spirit" is derived from the Latin *spirare,* meaning "to breathe," or *spiritus,* meaning breath,"[2] and the legacy of Clara's spirit is really the breath of life for Alba when she is in the *perrera.* This legacy of spirit is the real inheritance Clara's descendents have from her, not the jewels carelessly stuffed in socks. It is this spirit that Alba succeeds in calling forth when she combines memory with writing. In the role of the literary medium, Alba serves as a stand-in for Allende herself, calling forth the spirits of her characters and invoking them to appear on the pages as shadows of people from real life. For what such corroboration is worth, this interpretation is strengthened by statements from Allende like the one she made to Vera Jarach:

> El personaje de Esteban Trueba es mi abuelo, y Clara del Valle es mi abuela.[3]

Thus one begins to see that there is actually a clear contrast between the text that Alba and Esteban Trueba have written and the magical text produced by Melquíades in *Cien años de soledad.* Melquíades's text is a mystical, impossible creation, at once being written and occurring at once occupying past, present, and future, circling endlessling in a magic Möbius strip of time. By sharp contrast, the text that Alba presents at the end of *La casa de los espíritus,* although it contains magical elements, is actually produced in the old-fashioned way—by meticulous collection of sources, reflection, and the ordering of the past into words. The vague spirits of the del Valle children in the beginning of the book emphasize the fact that this story is actually being told from Alba's viewpoint and that she, not Clara, is the narrator of the apparently third-person passages. To Clara, presumably her own brothers and sisters would have held some passing interest at least, and if she were to tell the story of her own childhood, then one would expect her siblings to figure more prominently. But for Alba, it is hardly of great interest to write about anonymous great-aunts and great-uncles who, being much older than Clara, most likely died before Alba was even born. By treating these characters as mere spirits, Allende underscores the traditional nature of her text. Quite the opposite of being a hoary device from the canon of García Márquez, the revelation of Alba as "author" actually performs a function seen so frequently in the novel up to now: it goes beyond magical realism once more to say that perhaps for Latin America the most important texts are the ones written by real people from their own experience, not imagined by wandering gypsies in a vacuum of time. Perhaps one could read here the suggestion that magical realism, as a literary device, has limitations for telling an important human history.

An enumeration of the spirits in this novel by no means ends here. There are still a number of other apparitions to be called forth. The next group of spirits are the ones that Blanca, pregnant and distraught, is sure she hears passing her door at night in the gaudy manse she shares with her husband, Jean de Satigny. Jean, as Blanca discovers, is involved in the disreputable business of stealing native art treasures and selling them to foreign collectors. Oddly, the most popular items for sale are Indian mummies. Blanca sees them thus:

> Estaba acostumbrada a ver . . . siluetas transparentes paseando por los corredores de la casa de sus padres. . . . Pero las momias eran diferentes. Eso seres encogidos, envueltos en trapos que se deshacían en hilachas polvorientas, con sus cabezas descarnadas y amarillosas, sus manitas arrugadas, sus párpados cosidos, sus pelos ralos en la nuca, sus eternas y terribles sonrisas sin labios, su olor a rancio y ese aire triste y pobretón de los cadáveres antiguos, la revolvían el alma. (227–28)

Blanca cannot imagine what kind of person could actually want to collect dead bodies, but Jean de Satigny tells her that when mounted in a glass case, they make a fine addition to many a European millionaire's art collection.

She begins gradually to imagine that she sees them moving through the hallways at night. Still the text specifies that these visions are hallucinatory:

> Blanca soñaba con ellas, tenía alucinaciones, creía verlas andar por los corredores en la punta de los pies, pequeños como gnomos solapados y furtivos. (228)

When she writes of her fears to her mother, interestingly, Clara answers minimizes the magical in favor of the pragmatic, suggesting that her daughter should fear the living more than the dead, "porque a pesar de su mala fama, nunca se supo que las momias atacaran a nadie" (228).

At last, however, Blanca discovers that the mummies are not the cause of the nocturnal stir at all. In fact, the nightly traffic through the halls is actually caused by the Indian servants, whom Jean de Satigny exploits in life just as he exploits the Indian artifacts in death. The "count" has coerced the staff into participating with him in "acongojantes escenas eróticas que revelaban su oculta naturaleza" (231). Once again Allende caps a dramatic scene by proving in yet another instance that the real can have more force than the fanciful. Once more she undercuts magical realism with plain realism:

> Esas escenas desordenadas y tormentosas eran una verdad mil veces más desconcertante que la momias escandalosas que había esperado encontrar. (231)

Again the idea of the phantasm is presented as a real possibility, and then devalued. As has been systematically observed throughout the course of the study, the magical aspect is ultimately subordinated to the real. The "spirits" in the hallways are really nothing more than the servants whom Jean de Satigny controls not through witchcraft and not even, we suspect, through the magic of his personal charm, but rather through the hard realities of economic slavery. The reader recalls now that Blanca said of them earlier:

> Circulaban como espíritus, deslizándose sin ruido por las habitaciones. . . . No respondían cuando ella les hablaba como si no comprendieran el castellano, y entre sí hablaban en susurros o en dialectos del altiplano. (222)

The word "spirit" has now shifted meaning with regard to these dispirited servants, forced to the margin of Hispanic society, living in physical and spiritual poverty while their history is stolen away in bits and pieces with every artifact that leaves the country. This is the spirit that Jean de Satigny degrades and forces into submission with irresistible bribery in the face of abject poverty. Even the Indians' literal spirits—their ancestors—are defiled by the Frenchman. In fact, the evil spirits here are not the *momias,* but rather the *momios,* and the *momio* in question is Jean de Satigny himself. The word *momio,* a Chilean coinage of wide circulation in Alba's time, was a slang term used by leftist (or leftish) people to describe anyone whom they felt to be unacceptably right-wing. Joan Jara, widow of singer/director, Víctor, defines it this way:

> *Momio* was . . . the popular term for anyone with a reactionary position. In my mind I have always associated the term with a character in a play by Raúl Ruiz which Víctor had directed some time before . . . an ancient landowner who appeared to be disintegrating in his wheelchair, attended by a servant as decrepit as himself. He would call out querulously for his binoculars and peer out . . . as though over the vast expense of his estates, a symbol of the decaying yet petrified oligarchy, jealously protecting their lands and privileges.[4]

A hostile witness to the term is a member of the Chilean Fuerza Armada who wrote a history of the Allende government under the pseudonym of Vicente Chávez Lira. He defines "momio" simply as: "conocido insulto marxista . . . que carece de seriedad política."[5] By either definition, the affected Jean de Satigny seems to merit the epithat. He would have been a *momio* by Alba's definition, certainly. Satigny examplifies the author's belief that the *momios*, with their decadence and lack of respect for the human spirit, are more to be feared than the *momias* of some sad Indians, long dead. Once more, Allende has begun with magical possibilities and then shifted focus to a more-frightening demon of the flesh-and-blood variety.

After Clara dies, the literal spirits of *la gran casa de la esquina* become dimmer and dimmer, until, by Alba's generation, they are scarcely seen at all. Other spirits have arisen to replace them, however, and they too make rustling noises in the labyrinth of the upstairs rooms. The first of these are heard when Alba leads her young lover, Miguel, upstairs in order to avoid the expense and embarrassment of going to a hotel:

> —Si las empleadas oyen ruidos, creerán que han vuelto los fantasmas. (292)

Later, another rustling "spirit" turns out to be Pedro Tercero García, whom Blanca has hidden from the police. Pedro Tercero is the first in a long series of flesh-and-blood spirits who pass through the maze of the house during the times of terror. Pedro Tercero accepts Blanca's offer of help in the face of great danger, but his active spirit cannot long endure the forced inactivity of hiding. Eventually Blanca musters all her spirit to ask her father for help, and the two lovers finally escape into exile. More will be said about the spirit of Pedro Tercero García and what it might represent in the next chapter. After Esteban Trueba, finding some humanity, helps his old enemy to escape, the rustling noises continue. Again Esteban Trueba attributes the noises to ghosts. In his self-created isolation, he imagines that Clara's spirits have returned to the upstairs rooms. He tells the reader that he hears the sounds literally enough, but with his long practice in accepting the unreal as possible, he does not even bother to investigate.

As the reader has already come to suspect, the spirits Esteban Trueba hears rustling about are actually political refugees being sheltered by Alba, following her mother's spirited example, until she can get them safely out of the country. Often, these "spirits" do not even have names, as it would be dangerous for Alba to know any details about them. This anonymity adds a spiritlike transparency to the characters, and they drift through these pages much the way Clara's spirits drifted through earlier ones. Once again Allende multiplies almost magically the number of interpretations that the word "spirit" might have.

First, there is the spirit of the refugees who have survived against great odds. Their spirit contrasts with the "evil spirits" of those who may have secretly denounced or persecuted them. These faceless, nameless informers are allowed, according to the soulless proceedings of martial law, to bring about the deaths of men, women, and children without ever openly facing the accused and giving him or her the chance to respond to the accusations. According to Allende, the scores of characters who fulfill the role of "evil spirit" point to a deep spiritual malaise in the country portrayed and correlate to a national schizophrenia. A country so divided in spirit can hardly produce healthy offspring, and this spiritual disease of the fatherland is in part responsible for the unhealthy spirits of characters such as Esteban Trueba and his grandson, Esteban García.

The word "spirit" up to this point has gone through a series of changes in meaning. It has been used literally and ironically to designate supernatural beings; it has evoked the concept of "the Holy Spirit" in connection with Padre Restrepo; it has referred to the essential and activating principle of a person, as in Pedro Tercero's revolutionary spirit; it has meant a mood or emotional state, as in the high spirits of the supporters of the newly elected president; it has stood as a synonym for loyalty or dedication, as in Jaime's spirit as he goes to work in the hospital every day. In its plural English form, "spirits" are even synonymous with alcohol—as in the spirits that accidentally killed La bella Rosa. Now we have come a full circle and return once again to the more literal meaning of "spirits" as suggested by the title—supernatural beings.

By the last quarter of the novel, the ghosts in question are no longer "ángeles distraídos," benign mummies, or unseen, rustling ghosts. At this point we are faced not with airy spirits, but demons—beings with human form but lacking in human passions or pity. These demons illustrate Allende's idea that the most horrifying ghost story pales by comparison to the actual cruelty that real human beings are capable of inflicting on each other. Alba's time in the hands of Esteban García, her torture, rape, amputations, and final enclosure in the *perrera* represent for her a literal descent into a hell populated by horrifying devils.

On her capture, Alba cries out to her grandmother's spirits, begging them to protect her, "pero ellos parecían haberla abandonando, porque la camioneta siguió por el mismo camino" (354). Later there is a brief respite from the torture, "que aprovechó para invocar a los espíritus comprensivos de su abuela, para que la ayudaran a morir, pero nadie vino en su auxilio" (358). Is Allende's point that good spirits have no force against evil ones? Or is it more what has been observed up to now that the pleasant magic of orchid storms and insomnia plagues is entertaining, but in the last analysis not the kind of art that Latin America needs to solve its problems—if indeed, that is what art ought to do? In fact, this very obsession with the magically real may well be a distraction useful for keeping the poor more content in servitude. Marx said that religion was the opiate of the people, but perhaps in Allende's novelistic world "religion" might be constructed to include superstitions of all kinds, including the belief in magic. When Esteban Trueba's conservative friends insist throughout the book that "el marxismo no contempla el lado mágico de las cosas," they are condemning both Marxism and also the backwardness that they perceive in their own country. In proof of this is Esteban Trueba's sickened reaction to the excess of pomp and show in the rule of the Junta following the coup:

> El país se llenó de uniformados, de máquinas bélicas, de banderas, himnos y desfiles, porque los militares conocían la necesidad del pueblo de tener sus propios símbolos y ritos. El senador . . . comprendió lo que habían querido decir sus amigos del Club, cuando aseguraban que el marxismo no tenía la menor oportunidad en América Latina porque no contempla el lado mágico de las cosas.
>
> "Pan, circo y algo que venerar es todo lo que necesitan," concluyó el senador, lamentando en su fuero interno que faltara el pan. (337)

To say that Marxism lacks an understanding of the magical side of things is at once a criticism of the ideology's stuffiness and at the same time an odd tribute to its innocence. It criticizes the practical, utilitarian doctrine that at best seems to lack an understanding of the motives for human behavior. At the same time, it recognizes that the masses sometimes opt for immediate satisfaction of their need for "símbolos y ritos" over what might in the long run be good for them. By the very structure of her novel, whereby magic is consistently undercut by reality, Isabel Allende may be, consciously or unconsciously, questioning the very morality of continuing to use magical realism as a dominant literary mode in Latin America, while at the same time acknowledging her inability to to totally abandon an intuitive, sometimes frankly supernatural view of life.

The spirits evoked in *La casa de los espíritus*, then, belong to a long list of beings from ghosts to mummies, from hallucinations to wishes, from figments of youthful imagination to delirious visions of illness and age. There are fictional and remembered characters, real people trying to pass unobserved, and unreal apparitions trying to make themselves felt. There are some live demons, and some who are idealized by others as angels. But rising above all of these spirits is the spirit of the book's unnamed country, which is so like Chile. Simón Bolívar wrote of the Chilean spirit:

> Si alguna república permanecerá largo tiempo en América, me inclino a pensar que será la chilena. Jamás se ha extinguido allí el espíritu de la libertad.[6]

Perhaps, like the spirits of Clara's ghosts, the spirit of liberty in Allende's fictional country has not been defeated but is merely waiting for an appointed moment to resurge. In the meantime, there are several legendary figures in the true-life fall of the Allende government, figures whose spirits find echoes in this novel. These legendary spirits are the topic of the next chapter.

6
THE LEGEND OF "EL CANTANTE"

> Porque . . . es el hombre que canta,
> el que muere muriendo sin muerte.
> —Pablo Neruda, "La barcarola"

La casa de los espíritus is a novel bursting with hyperbole, as a glance reveals. There is la bella Rosa's attempt to embroider the largest tablecloth in the world; Esteban Trueba's broken bones, which are too numerous to mention; Clara's "incontables cuadernos" (73), the colds caught by the children at Las Tres Marías "en una cadena sin fin" (100); Férula's "amor desmesurado" (102) and Esteban Trueba's "amor desmedido" (119) for Clara; Blanca, who is a "prodigio de equilibrio y serenidad" (130); the earthquake that wounds Esteban Trueba, "la más fuerte [sacudida] que se había registrado . . . en este país de catástrofes" (144); Clara's superhuman silences: and the "vertiginosa popularidad" of Pedro Tercero García (284), to name just a few of numerous examples. In the midst of all of this hyperbole are three figures who rise above even the intensified vitality of the novel and stand apart. These three figures are the legendary giants of Chilean history of the time period echoed in the novel, and they are names everyone on the continent knows: Pablo Neruda, Salvador Allende, and Víctor Jara.

Isabel Allende represents the first two of these in true legendary form—with titles rather than names. Allende appears as "el Candidato," and later as "el Presidente," while Pablo Neruda appears simply as "el Poeta." If anyone doubts the real-life inspiration for either of these two characters, she has made it abundantly clear in interviews, in comments like the following to Vera Jarach:

> En mis libros he querido contar la tragedia de este torturado continente y la esperanza de los hombres y mujeres que, como Salvador Allende y muchos otros, desean un mundo mejor.[1]

She has even commented that her novelistic description of the funeral of "el Poeta" was taken from her own journals, in which she wrote down a personal account of her own attendance at the funeral of Pablo Neruda:

> . . .Por ejemplo, en *La casa de los espíritus,* el entierro del Poeta es exactamente lo que yo viví en septiembre de 1973 cuando caminé detrás del féretro de Pablo Neruda, llevando un ramo de claveles rojos en la mano. Esa noche le escribí una carta a mi madre, contándole mi emoción. Ella guardó esa carta, y años después la utilicé en mi novela. Este tipo de documentos tiene para mí mucha importancia.[2]

In fact, the funeral of "el Poeta" brings a curious question to mind. In *La casa de los espíritus,* Isabel Allende describes the scene thus:

> De pronto alguien gritó roncamente el nombre del Poeta y una sola voz de todas las gargantas respondió, ¡Presente! ¡Ahora y siempre! . . . Otro gritó, ¡Compañero Presidente! y contestaron todos en un solo lamento, llanto de hombre: ¡Presente! Poco a poco el funeral del Poeta se convirtió en el acto simbólico de enterrar la libertad. (341)

But the reader familiar with recent Chilean history must note almost immediately that one legendary giant is missing from a triumvirate of martyrs who rose above the thousands of dead and disappeared at the time of the Chilean coup. In *La casa de los espíritus,* many historical accounts of Neruda's funeral that correspond otherwise to Isabel Allende's novelistic one, the roll call at the funeral stops strangely short of asking for "¡Compañero Cantante!" Why is he not "¡Presente! ¡Ahora y siempre!"? In fact, compañero Cantante is strangely, totally absent. Where is the figure of Víctor Jara, the respected theatrical director and protest singer who, though not known outside of Chile to the same extent that Allende and Nobel laureate Neruda were, was certainly a giant within the country, one who was executed by the military in the days following the coup? Why does a novelist so interested in summoning up spirits and so devoted to evoking actual history choose *not* to complete her trinity of legendary martyrs by adding the most dramatic one of all, el Cantante? In searching to suggest some possible answers to this question (and certainly one can do no more), one comes face to face with one of the most interesting mixtures of legend and reality in all this novel that deals so skillfully with the blend of magic, myth, and history in Latin American literature and life.

For the historians of the Chilean coup, Jara is a prominent figure. In *Storm Over Chile*, for example, Samuel Chavkin treats the death of the poet and the martyrdom of the songwriter together in a chapter titled, "The Agony of Pablo Neruda and the Murder of Víctor Jara." In it he equates the political importance of the two men as follows:

> In many ways Jara and Neruda were more of a threat to the anti-Allende forces than the oratory of its political opponents or even armed resisters. A speech can rouse hundreds and thousands . . . but with time it becomes an echo. . . . A machine gun is as good as its supply of bullets . . . but a song that catches fire or a poem that takes wing can stir people indefinitely. Music and verse can become a part of a continuing present. They can be hummed or recited in the privacy of one's home or among friends. And the images they bring to life each time can reinforce personal dedication. In effect, even posthumously Jara and Neruda were able to reach over the heads of the Junta generals. . . .[3]

If Jara's influence was so great, then, why does Allende neglect to include him as a spirit or a character in her book? In order to postulate a response, it is necessary to step briefly outside the confines of the text, but before we do, let us look at what is within. In fact, Allende has created a character who has some superficial resemblance to Víctor Jara. This character is, of course, Pedro Tercero García, lover of Blanca and former peon on the land of Esteban Trueba. Both Jara and Pedro Tercero García rise from poverty to become the number one protest singer in the country—and a big similarity that is! If you mention to virtually anyone in Latin America the number one protest singer of Chile, steeped in folk traditions, a man who reached his greatest popularity just before the coup, the listener will immediately respond with the name of Víctor Jara. Pedro Tercero García's meteoric rise to fame, his use of song as a political tool, his ability to make a simple metaphor (like the fox and the chickens) respond, and his dedication all combine to remind the reader greatly of Víctor Jara. Yet despite this great similarity, almost all of the minor details differ. Jara was a product of a *población* of Santiago; Pedro Tercero García has a *campesino* background. And although each one fathered one daughter, Jara was married and had a stable home life with Englishwoman Joan Turner, their daughter Amanda, and Jara's stepdaughter, Manuela. Pedro Tercero García, by contrast, alternates between affairs with young groupies and his passion for the bourgeoise Blanca Trueba. Their daughter, Alba, never even knows that Pedro Tercero is her father until she is an adult. Víctor Jara considered himself to be primarily a theatrical director (noted for numerous productions, including the Chilean premiere of Egon Wolff's *Los invasores*) who really only began singing professionally after the saw the power his songs had to move his beloved working class. By contrast, Pedro Tercero is more exclusively a singer, and his songs are all basically merged and represented by just one song that we hear of over and over—the ballad of the chickens who band together to rid themselves of a marauding fox. But probably the most startling difference of all between these two is that while Jara went to well-known martyrdom on around 16 September 1973, by sharp contrast, the folksinging Pedro Tercero escapes to Canada with Blanca, his bourgeoise bride-at-last, where they live happily ever after, with Pedro Tercero becoming rich:

> Escribía para los trabajadores, los estudiantes, y, sobre todo, la alta burguesía, que las había adoptado como moda, traducidas al inglés y al francés con gran éxito, a pesar de que las gallinas y los zorros son criaturas subdesarrolladas que no poseen el esplandor zoológico de las águilas y los lobos de ese helado país del Norte. (351)

What is the purpose of this startling disparity between the folk singer of legend, and the novelistic one, if indeed it has a purpose?

The most obvious answer to this (and the obvious should never be ignored) is that here Isabel Allende is writing fiction, and the very word implies that one is allowed, even expected to make things up. She has, after all, no obligation to anyone to take character X or Y from life, and in fact is at perfect liberty to do just the opposite, to blend the real with the imagined, to combine several people into a composite, or to invent a whole being out of thin air. It could very well be that the similarity between Pedro Tercero García and Víctor Jara is simply accidental, or incidental, and is of no major thematic importance to the novel. Of course in a sense of critical honesty this possibility should be noted.

But what if it is not an accident? What, then, is the point of giving such a mundane, undramatic exit to the novelistic singer of protest songs? Surely not to diminish the stature of Jara—such an explanation verges on sacrilege! Perhaps, on the other hand, Allende's goal was just the opposite—to enhance the legend of Víctor Jara as it is told and retold in the real world outside the novel, and to not even attempt to freeze it in one specific telling or another. For the death of Víctor Jara, perhaps even more than those of Allende and Neruda, has become an authentic oral legend in the Spanish-speaking world.

The events surrounding Jara's death are, of necessity, known sketchily at best. After all, they occurred at a time of martial lawlessness when the army was not required to render account to anybody.[4] All of the scanty evidence about it today is taken from oral accounts—the testimony of anonymous fellow prisoners who were with Jara in the Estadio Chile (ironically, the scene of some of his most successful concerts) and the report of his widow, Joan, who recovered and buried his body.

The bare facts, as Joan Jara recounts them in her biography of her late husband, *An Unfinished Song: The Life of Víctor Jara,* are as follows: Jara was captured on the morning of 12 September 1973 (one day after the coup began) when tanks took over the Technical University where he was gathered with fellow partisans and students. From there he was marched some six blocks with the others to the Estadio Chile, where he was beaten, and denied food, water, or sanitary facilities for days along with some five thousand prisoners. Friends last saw him when a group of guards took him away on the 16th, and that night some frightened *población*-dwellers reported seeing his dead body dumped with six others in a vacant lot. On the 18th his body was recognized by a morgue worker who, though he described himself as a *momio,* notified the singer's wife. She gives the following description:

> It was Víctor, although he looked thin and gaunt. . . . What have they done to you to make you waste away like that in one week? His eyes were open and they seemed to still look ahead with intensity and defiance, in spite of a wound on his head and terrible bruises on his cheek. His clothes were torn, trousers round his ankles, sweater rucked up under his armpits, his blue underpants hanging in tatters round his hips as though cut by a knife or a bayonet . . . his chest riddled with holes and a gaping wound in his abdomen. His hands seemed to be hanging from his arms at a strange angle as though his wrists were broken, but it was Víctor, my husband, my lover.[5]

From the morgue, Joan Jara took the body herself to the cemetery and buried it without funeral, friends, or ceremony. From prisoners who survived the incarceration in the National Stadium Jara reports that she heard two more bits of information about her husband's last days:

I have two more glimpses of Víctor in the Stadium, two more testimonies. . . . A message of love for his daughters and me . . . and then once more being publicly abused and beaten, the officer . . . losing control of himself, "Sing now, if you can, you bastard!" and Víctor's voice raised in the stadium after those four days of suffering to sing a verse of "Venceremos." Then he was beaten down and dragged away for the last phase of his agony.[6]

This account, built partly on the oral versions of the prisoners, is the closest thing to a full story of the death of Víctor Jara, as seems possible to obtain, unless the unlikely occurred and his executioners were to come forward and tell their side. One must rely on the word of Joan Jara, who reports that she saw the body with her own eyes, and then somewhat less on the second-hand accounts of Jara's fellow prisoners in the stadium. Just as Joan Jara tells the story, it is replete with drama, enough, one would think, for the death of any hero. And yet with the passing of time, the story has evolved, changed, gained epic proportions, and become a legend.

It is not surprising that this should have happened. News of the way Jara died, after all, had to circulate orally, since the truth could be not published. Says Joan Jara:

The newspaper *La Segunda* published a tiny paragraph which announced Víctor's death as though he had passed away peacefully in bed: "The funeral was private, only relatives were present." Then the order came through not to mention Víctor again. But on the television, someone risked his life to insert a few bars of "La plegaria" over the sound-track of an American film.[7]

When something of importance to a great number of people is censored in the traditional communications media, the result is that the information is propagated the old-fashioned way, by word of mouth, with unlimited possibilities for distortion. Just a few days after Víctor Jara's death, the Argentine magazine *Crisis* carried the following account:

Víctor Jara, una de las principales voces de la canción popular chilena, fue asesinado en los camarinos del estadio Chile. Los militares le habían destrozado las manos a golpes de culata, porque Víctor Jara encendía el ánimo de los presos cantando y batiendo palmas. Lo tirotearon en las piernas y lo dejaron desangrarse:

—¡Canta ahora! . . .—le decían—a ver si ahora cantas huevón. . . .[8]

Already, though the oral story has only traveled a few days and across one border to appear in this published account, changes have appeared. The hands, which were possibly hanging at odd angles (and we noted that Joan Jara was careful not to insist on this point) have gone from possibly injured to definitely, "destrozadas a golpes de culata." And the gunshot wounds, fatal enough as Jara described them in the abdomen, have sunk to the legs and a further degree of cruelty.

Galvarino Plaza also insists on the injury to the hands[4] as does Samuel Chavkin in his 1982 book, *The Murder of Chile*. Chavkin even includes reflections he attributes to Joan Jara about the almost magical specialness of Víctor Jara's hands[10] and adds an explicit quote that he cites as from her: "his beautiful hands were broken and swollen."[11] In his 1974 account, Camilo Taufic also insists strongly on injury to Jara's hands.[12]

The next step in the evolution of the myth of Víctor's Jara's hands is even more dramatic, as we see in the supposed eyewitness account by Chilean writer, Miguel Cabazas, included in *O canto-arma de Víctor Jara*, by José Jorge Letría, published in Lisbon. This is what Cabazas claims happened when one of Víctor's captors discovered his identity:

> Chamou quatro soldados para imobilizarem Victor e ordenou que se colocasse uma mesa no centro da 'cena' para que todos assistissen ao espectáculo que se iria desenrola a sua frente. Levaram Victor e mandarm-no por as mãos em cima da mesa. Nas mãos de um oficial, um machado surgiu. . . . De uma pancada seca, cortou os dedos da mão direita. Ouviram-se os dedos a caírem sobre o tampo de madeira; vibravam ainda. O corpo de Victor tombou inesperadamente. Ouviu-se o urro colectivo de 6000 detidos. Esses 12000 oljos viram o mesmo oficial lançar-se sobre o corpo do artista gritando: 'Canta agora, para a puta da tua mãe!' e continuava a agredi-lo com pancadas. . . . De repente, Victor tentou penosamente levantase . . . [gritando] 'Vamos a fazer a voluntade ao comandante!' Momentos depois conseguiu endireitar-se e, levantando a suas mãos encharcadas de sangre, numa voz de angústia començou a cantar o hino de Unidade Popular, que toda a gente tomou em coro.
>
> Enquanto, pouco a pouco, 6000 vozes se levantavem, Victor, com as suas mãos mutiladas, marcava o compasso. . . .
>
> Era demais para os militares, disparram una rajada. . . .[13]

Before I discuss discrepancies between this account and previous ones, of course it should be pointed out that as a reader in North America in 1987 I claim no right at all to judge the truth or falsity of what this writer says he saw. If is completely possible that this is the most true account available of Jara's death, and that others are incorrect for whatever reason. Or, it is also possible that Cabazas actually witnessed this scene, but the person whose hands were amputated was someone other than Víctor Jara. Such a suggestion is not terribly farfetched, when one takes into account the numerous stories of mutilated corpses in the morgue at this time (Joyce Horman, for example).[14] But if, on the other hand, there is a touch of embellishment in this version, the student of literature does have the right to look at the effects such embellishment creates.

The differences between this story and Joan Jara's account are significant. First and foremost, the torture and murder have been moved from the dark, secret bowels of the stadium dressing rooms and brought out into the light in front of the prisoners—for Cabazas, six thousand bodies and twelve thousand eyes. The result of this change of venue is not necessarily simple sensationalism. By removing the murder of Jara from the dark and bringing it out before the eyes of all, the teller is developing the legend. In the legend, it is important to the tellers that the hidden (and very real) murder of Jara become public, that the crime be known, reported, and acknowledged. Every prisoner in the stadium must now be an eyewitness, for together they stand for the entire population of Chile. Jara's courage (as evidenced by the fact that, unlike Pedro García, he stayed in the country) must now have a literal representation. Just as Pedro Tercero García understood that to spread the idea of union to his workers he must tell the story in a parable that they could understand, with everyday creatures like foxes and chickens, in the same fashion the tellers of the Jara story want to convey the death of their hero such that his heroism is literally represented.

T. S. Eliot writes of finding an "objective correlative" that should serve as a "formula" for a particular emotion ("Hamlet and his Problems").[15] Here, the many nameless forgers of the Jara myth have seized on his hands as an objective correlative for what they deeply believe his martyrdom to be about. Hands, in fact, are the inspired choice. To Jara, hands were the symbol of both the force and the humility of the working class. One need only look at the album cover of *Pongo en tus manos abiertas* (dedicated to the founder of the Chilean labor movement, Emilio Recabarren) to understand this. Joan Jara reports that her husband personally selected the cover photo of a worker's rough palms, spread open as if to receive a gift.

Hands, indeed, become the objective correlative for Jara's artistic gift and political dedication. Both of these were literally cut off by his early death. It is fitting, then, that in the legend form, simplified for telling so that the monstrosity can be grasped by even the slowest of hearers, the artist's hands should literally be cut off.

Supreme eloquence against tyrants from a man whose hands have been cut off is, in fact, also a deeply rooted motif in Chilean literature. In Alonso de Ercilla's epic poem, *La Araucana,* which narrates the Spanish struggle for dominion over the Araucanian Indians, the cruel Spaniard Hurtado de Mendoza orders that both hands be cut off the captive Galvarino, who nevertheless manages to return to his comrades-in-arms and, holding up his bloody stumps, to harangue them to greater bravery. Even in Pedro de Oña's subsequent, anti-Indian retelling of the story, *El Arauco domado,* Galvarino's loss of hands and resultant eloquence still appears. Thus, the image may have special resonance for Chilean readers.

In any case, to return to the specific instance of Víctor Jara, it is impossible to document all of the endless permutations of his story, for they are first and foremost oral tradition, with no one final, finished form. I have personally heard many versions of this story, from Bolivian and Chilean students in the United States, from Chilean artists exiled in Spain, and even from Joyce Horman, on whose experiences the movie *Missing* was based.[16] The common elements of the story, repeated over and over with infinite variety by tellers of many nationalities, educational levels, and social classes, are Jara in the stadium; the defiant order, "Canta ahora, huevón, si puedes . . ."; the cutting off of fingers, hands, and sometimes whole arms and legs; and, last but not least, Jara's spirit rising superhumanly above all adversity to continue doing what he did so beautifully in life—stirring and uplifting people through song. Those who tell the story of Víctor Jara's death thus, "they cut off his fingers, but he kept on singing, they cut off his hands, but he kept on singing . . ." are not really sensationalizing history; they are using a myth to convey the deepest truth of their feelings about Jara in terms that can be grasped. Perhaps most men could not sing or even retain consciousness after such amputations, let along beat the bloody stumps together to the rhythm of "Venceremos." But the figure of Víctor Jara in this story is not an ordinary man. Like Prometheus chained to a rock, where his liver is endlessly devoured by an eagle, Víctor Jara is a symbol of the human spirit. Galvarino Plaza writes:

> De la canción popular, Víctor Jara es hoy una figura mítica . . . seguirá viviendo.[17]

The myth has come to stand for those who are downtrodden everywhere. Perhaps the first person who embroidered the tale (if such a thing ever happened) was somehow afraid that his hearer would not fully understand the horror and the implications of cultural homicide for Chile unless the atrocities were more literally represented. Then gradually the legend of the Víctor Jara who kept singing and singing even after overwhelming physical mutilation, comes to represent for the teller of the tale the spirit of Chilean resistance, or resistance to injustice in general, indomitable, in spite of repression and terror. Deep down, that may be what the myth really means to convey—that Víctor Jara's songs are still sung, and that his spirit lives on.

I return, now, to the hypothetical question posed earlier of why Allende chooses not to represent Jara as "el Cantante," telling his tragedy thinly disgused by fiction, as she did with Neruda and Salvador Allende. After tracing the development of the Jara myth, I think we can see some of the special problems that would have been involved. The most outrageous version of the myth could have been recounted with ease by García Márquez, for the Nobel prizewinner specializes in taking popular hyperbole and legend, pushing them to the limit, and making us either believe his stories or at least believe that if they happened, people would react the way he says they do. But Allende's touch is definitely lighter. Moreover, the death of "el Cantante" would have corresponded in the narrative to the phase in which, as I have shown, "magical" occurrences have been driven underground and replaced by factual horrors. It would have been difficult to decide *how* to tell the story. Should she go for realism or opt for myth? If she had chosen realism, there would have been little pleasure for readers in hearing one of their most cherished myths debunked. On the other hand, a mythical, hyperbolic telling would have opened her to the charge of historical inaccuracy by someone who knew Joan Jara's account.

Wimsatt and Beardsley have already eloquently pointed out the folly of pretending to guess at what a writer intended on composing a work of fiction. Even if one were to ask Allende, the witness she might bear would still be subordinate to the evidence of the text. It is probably more profitable, then, to ask not what Allende intended, but what she *achieved* in her handling of Pedro Tercero, basing conclusions on the text of the novel.

What is the result of reading about Pedro Tercero García's defection? Readers who know some version of the story of Víctor Jara are likely to stop and say "Wait a minute; that's not right!" The easy placidity of Pedro Tercero's happily-ever-after contrasts starkly with what the reader knows (or believes) of Jara's martyrdom. Automatically, the legend of Jara begins to vibrate in contrast to the text. Of course these reverberations can only be perceived by a reader with a certain political IQ level, just as allusions to Shakespeare in T. S. Eliot can only be perceived by a reader with a certain literary IQ. But when that level is present, the reader fills in the space left by Pedro Tercero's defection to Canada with the spiritual presence of what he imagines Víctor Jara to have been. How much better literarily, such an effect is than having told a mythical story that many cold-hearted skeptics would have found spoiled by improbability, or a realistic one that would have disappointed others by the omission of their beloved objective correlative.

Quite a good case can be made for the notion that the text deliberately sets these reverberations in motion. For example, there is the existence of a character (Jaime) who is obsessed by the memory of a woman named Amanda. The name is just a whisper of a song lyric, but it happens to be from one of Jara's most famous songs:

> Te recuerdo Amanda . . .
> la sonrisa ancha
> la lluvia en el pelo. . . .

The name Amanda, as Joan Jara points out, was the name of both Jara's daughter and his mother and, as such, had a special, magical significance for him.[18]

Another, much more convincing piece of evidence in support of the deliberate evocation of Jara within the text is the detail that as a young man, Pedro Tercero has three fingers from his right hand cut off by an enraged Esteban Trueba wielding an ax. The resonance of such an occurrence is hard to miss. In spite of his mutilation, Pedro Tercero has the greatness of spirit to go on making music. He learns how to strum his guitar with the thumb and forefinger of his right hand and despite his handicap arrives at a "vertiginosa popularidad que ni él mismo esperaba" (293). Here, in the missing fingers are part of the objective correlative that functions so perfectly in the Jara myth. Like Jara, Pedro Tercero García continues to sing in spite of mutliation, and his song rises above his adversity to carry the spirit of his message. What is more, the force that severs Pedro Tercero García's three fingers from his right hand is in political terms equivalent to the one that truncated Víctor Jara's life and art, though on a smaller scale. Esteban Trueba represents not the military but the *momios* who gave the military its power, never suspecting that the power would not be returned. Esteban Trueba is motivated by a violent class hatred toward Pedro Tercero and by blind belief in rule by the strong.

Fingers are very important to the Jara myth. Recall Cabazas's insistence that he actually saw them vibrating on the table. Here the loss of fingers and the graphic description of the scene is very likely to trigger a memory of Jara for the reader who has heard the story. The fingers in *La casa de los espíritus* evoke the myth, yet they do not attempt to match it, digit for digit. Pedro Tercero García loses only three fingers, and then it is in a conflict that, while it has deeply symbolic political overtones, also has an important selfish side as well (his love for Blanca). The contrast comes unbidden to the reader's mind—Víctor Jara gave everything, his life and his art (or both hands, in the literal terms of the myth). By evoking the Jara legend in this way, Allende allows the reader to mull it over alone, deciding without being told what the legend means. Moreover, she is surely a canny enough storyteller to know how hard it is for people to give up their favorite legend. A novelist has nothing to gain by debunking a popular myth that people want to believe. Yet a novelist who is also a journalist and historian may have ethical objections to retelling a myth she knows (or suspects) to be distorted. So, by choosing the liberty of fiction to create a new character, she masterfully overcomes these difficulties.

But the references to severed fingers do not end with Pedro Tercero. They become an obsession with his cousin, Esteban García, as well. Esteban García is the illegitimate grandson of Trueba who was cheated out of a reward he felt he had earned by revealing Pedro Tercero's hiding place to Trueba. After García rises through the military to the rank of colonel during the events leading up to and including the coup, he takes advantage of his power to torture Alba, cutting off three of her fingers in symbolic vengeance for his truncated childhood dreams, his stolen patrimony, and his illegitimacy. Thus the novelistic use of the objective correlative is spread out between two characters, father and daughter, and over two generations. This division of the symbol suggests a number of interesting readings. One might be a cautionary note to those who love to tell the Jara story over and over—see how ugly is the vengeance of a hand for a hand! Remember him, but do not demand a literal payment for his suffering, for the chain of retaliations can be endless.

Another possible reading of this dividing of the objective correlative of amputation is as a reminder that the tragedy of figures like Víctor Jara did not end with the political murder of the father. The children of such a man are left with a permanent loss, as if a part of the body had been amputated. The effects of torture and repression do not end with a single generation, but rather make themselves felt for generations to follow, often in ugly ways. Again, at the end this brings us to the notion that the chain of inherited grievances and vengeances must at some point be arbitrarily stopped.

This chain of hatred cannot be broken until a character like Alba, who bears the scars of conflict in her own flesh, has the magnitude of spirit to consciously put her past behind her and not exact an eye for an eye, a finger for a finger. Is this the warning for subscribers to the Jara myth? Is she saying that it is important to remember the hero in him more than the martyr? The people's brilliantly forged objective correlative of hands is good insofar as it leads them to remember Jara's art, but it could become evil if it were allowed to grow into a cry for vengeance.

Alba tells us she writes "para burlar la mala memoria" and that her "misión no es prolongar el odio" (379). Surely this is at the heart of the book's message. People need to remember and write down their legends, and to preserve the stories about their heroes. But if these stories lead them to violence or disaster, then they need to be reexamined, reevaluated, and perhaps even cut down (the way Nívea cuts down the traditional climbing tree in the yard). Maybe some of the stories should even be replaced by fictional versions!

All of these possible readings—each individual, and dependent on a reader's personal tastes—are suggested by Allende's skillful contrasting of myth and reality with regard to el Cantante. Whatever the author's intentions may have been, she has succeeded in creating a richly ambiguous facet to the text with the character of Pedro Tercero García. His characterization is just one more bit of the novel's overall magic.

7
THE GIRL WITH GREEN HAIR

> Sé que me quieres azul,
> sé que me quieres verde,
> sé que me quieres rosa,
> pero al caer la tarde,
> sólo me quisiste roja. . . .
>
> —Cecilia, "Fui"

> Eres como la rosa de Alejandría . . .
> colorada de noche, y blanca de día. . . .
>
> —"Eres alta y delgada," canción popular castellana

One phenomenon that is clearly magic, if by that we mean contrary to natural law, is the fact that two of the main female characters are endowed with naturally green hair. In this chapter, some of the effects and the possibility of these verdant tresses will be explored.

The first character so endowed is, of course, la bella Rosa, who has it from birth:

> Con el cabello verde y los ojos amarillos, la criatura más hermosa que había nacido en la tierra desde los tiempos del pecado original, como dijo la comadrona, santiguándose. (12)

Immediately this unusual beauty is associated with maritime images, and we are told that adolescence accentuated "su gracia marítima" (12). The undersea flavor lingers after her death, and Esteban Trueba laments that he will never again find, "en todo el universo, otra mujer con su pelo verde y su hermosura marina" (37). Later, as he passes the night of Rosa's funeral next to her tomb, he is overcome with the desire to "soltar el verde manantial de su cabello y hundirse en sus aguas más profundas" (39).

This undersea aura to the descriptions of Rosa has a superficial explanation that Isabel Allende has offered to the public on many occasions. For example, she told Vera Jarach:

> El personaje de mi tía Rosa era, en la realidad, una mujer muy bella a la que se recuerda por fotografías desteñidas, color sepia. Decían que era hermosa como una sirena, y yo me imagino a las sirenas con el pelo color verde. Por eso en la novela tía Rosa sale con el pelo verde.[1]

Here is one simple explanation for the green hair of la bella Rosa in *La casa de los espíritus*—a child's poetic associations with the word "sirena" combined with the faded, deceptive tones of an old photograph that could not convey any true coloration. Moreover, as with the best uses of magical realism, the seemingly impossible event underscores a deeper truth—that memory fades and distorts the color of events and individuals, much as it does that of concrete details. A lock of baby's hair, for example, preserved in an old album, naturally dulls with time and takes on a greenish cast. So it is no surprise that Alba's baby book should contain "también unos mechones verdosos" (233). In this context the color stresses the passage of time along with the unreliability of memory.

If it were true, as many have suggested, that the outright magic in this novel is limited to the early pages, then we should not be surprised to find the initial appearance of green hair in the character of Rosa. However, the motif does not end with Rosa but, on the contrary, reappears in the last and supposedly realistic portion of the novel in the person of Alba. Given the pragmatism of Alba and her contemporary existence, is it logical to attribute her green hair once more to Allende's fanciful connections between mermaids and undersea plants? It should be remembered that Alba resembles her aunt Rosa only in the color of her hair, not in "mermaidlike" beauty, for while Rosa was tall and generously endowed, Alba is small, thin, and considered normal to paltry-looking by the family (including her grandfather, who considers middling looks a reason for sending the girl to school, since he fears she may not marry) (266). When Alba falls in love with Miguel, she laments her looks:

> Por primera vez en su vida, Alba sintió la necesidad de ser hermosa y lamentó que ninguna de las espléndidas mujeres de su familia le hubiera legado sus atributos, y la única que lo hizo, la bella Rosa, sólo le dio el tono de algas marinas a su pelo, lo cual, si no iba acompañado por todo lo demás, parecía más bien un error de peluquería. (294)

Alba, from this humorous description, sounds nothing at all like Allende's distantly remembered "mermaid" aunt. But if faded memory or childish confusion is not the explanation for Alba's green hair, is it merely accidental, like the "error de peluquería" Alba suggests? Or does it have a close thematic relation to the rest of the novel? This chapter will attempt to show other possible explanations for and effects created by the succession of tinted tresses.

Besides its verdant color, the hair of la bella Rosa is endowed with a plantlike quality. To young Clara, for example, it appears to hang "como un helecho," or to fall "como una cascada vegetal" (31). This vegetable quality is very appropriate in Rosa, for she is something of a vegetable herself, a magical extreme of passivity who is described as "inmune a la vanidad . . . ausente," who has become engaged to a man in whom "rara vez pensaba," and whose only goal in life is to embroider "el mantel más grande del mundo" (12–13). The passivity of both Clara and Blanca has already been discussed at length in chapter 2, but compared to Rosa, they both seem veritable models of enterprise. The relation between docility of spirit and limpness of coiffure is even passed on to Clara, who enjoys such slavish attentions from la Nana that even her hair shows it:

> [La Nana] le cepillaba el pelo hasta dejárselo brillante y dócil como una planta de mar. (91)

A problem arises, however, in associating the del Valle hair with docility when green hair is introduced in the character of Alba. It is hard to imagine a young woman less passive than the valiant Alba, who joins student protests, stockpiles illegal arms, steals food from the family larder to give to the poor, and repeatedly risks her life to help political fugitives. Is Alba's green hair a fluke, a facile touch of peroxide magic right out of the bottle, put there to literally add color to the tale? Or is it part of a coherently developed theme that is integral to the novel, not just painted on?

One starting point in the search for an answer to this question is Clara's fixation with the notion that each person has an "aura" in which his animic state can be read by those who have eyes to see it. For example, in later life, Clara always wears the color white, "porque decía que era el único color que no alteraba su aura" (118). Moreover, "seeing" the color of a person's aura is a major factor in the success of Clara's clairvoyance. She knows that Getulio Armando will cheat her father "porque se lo leyó en el color del aura" (74). She also predicts her husband's plots and misdeeds "por el color de sus irradiaciones" (118). Later, when

Blanca's love for Pedro Tercero García deepens and becomes sexual, Clara suspects "porque podía ver un nuevo color en el aura de su hija y creía adivinar la causa" (142).

To understand the incorporation of auric color schemes into *La casa de los espíritus*, it is useful to examine briefly some prevailing notions on the subject.

According to David V. Tansley in *The Raiment of Light: A Study of the Human Aura*, the idea that individuals radiate light according to the state of their spirits is nothing new:

> Since time immemorial man has illustrated the aura to express the spiritual nature of man. For example, in Christian art, the halo or nimbus around the head is a common feature filled with meaning. . . . If you look carefully you will see that the nimbus around the head of Jesus differs from those placed around the heads of the disciples.[2]

Simply put, those who believe today that each person has an aura of colored light radiating from his head and visible to people with psychic ability think that this aura is related to the spirituality and virtue of the wearer, and that the aura tells much about a person at a glance. Writes Tansley:

> Various colors appearing in the aura express information with respect to the individual's past, present, and future life.[3]

It is interesting to note here the connection between auric colors and the prediction of the future, a concept often avowed by believers in this phenomenon. Tansley quotes the experiences of one Edgar Cayce to describe how viewing the aura works, and it is striking to observe how similar this personal account is to the fictional powers of Clara del Valle. Says Cayce:

> Ever since I can remember I have seen colors in connection with people. I do not remember a time when the human beings I encountered did not register on my retina with blues and greens and reds gently pouring from their heads and shoulders. It was a long time before I realized that other people did not see these colors; it was a long time before I heard the word aura, and learned to apply it to this phenomenon which to me was commonplace. I do not even think of people except in connection with their auras; I see them change in my friends and loved ones as time goes by.[4]

Although one hesitates to rely too heavily on the authority of a man who believes (as Tansley does) that the problem of world air pollution could best be controlled by having each individual on the earth use the power of positive thinking to clean his own aura, still he presents the theory of auric color lucidly and with a flair for metaphorical interpretation. Most convincing are his arguments for a persistent belief in some sort of colored aura in many cultures at different times. For example, consider these reflections on biblical tales:

> Wherever we look in spiritual literature we will find references to light and colors with respect to the inner nature of man. The biblical story of Joseph with his coat of many colors is a metaphor for his aura, and the colors are his radiant energies. So outstanding was his "coat" that it lead to jealousy and he was sold into bondage.[5]

This example seems strangely pertinent when we recall that the biblical Joseph, like Clara del Valle, is subject to dreams by which he tells the future through extracting a symbolic meaning from an oneiric event that on the surface is nonsensical.

It would be dangerous indeed to venture a guess as to whether or not author Isabel Allende believes in the literal existence of the aura. What seems more to the point to assert, however, is that she has created for her character Clara a strong belief in the "science" of auric coloring much like that outlined in Tansley. When we consider that many of the effects of color within the novel may be calculated to create special effects that illuminate the personality of certain characters, a number of visions suddenly appear to our previously untrained eyes.

Each of the colors of the auric spectrum is traditionally associated with certain characteristics, and it is interesting to note that these color associations are frequently very revealing within the novel.

Of course the character with the most sensitivity to these color associations is Clara. Her "cuadernos de anotar la vida," for example, are not ordered chronologically but, rather, are "separados por acontecimientos," and the divisions are "atados con cintas de colores" (380). Color, then, is her instinctive tool for separating events by type and flavor. Color is also a tool used by author Allende to divide and present the events of her narration to her readers.

For example, the Mora sisters are always associated with a "perfume de violetas silvestres," which the women insist is a natural emanation. The name "Mora," what is more, suggests "morado," or purple, along with the berry, "mora," which is also a deep purple in color. Thus the association between the color purple and the Mora sisters is evoked every time their name is mentioned. Moreover, their house, a converted windmill, is uniformly referred to as "su extraordinaria morada," a choice of words that again evokes the color. Given this, it is interesting to note the traditional associations with purple as an auric color, according to Tansley:

> Violet is the high spiritual color of the adept and the initiate. It indicates love, wisdom, soul power and true greatness. Some psychics claim that the color is seldom seen in the aura of the average person.[6]

How well the Mora sisters fit this category! As Clara's spiritual mentors, the Mora sisters introduce her to the gamut of abstruse parapyschological phenomena, which the author presents to us with tongue firmly in cheek:

> Las tres hermanas Mora eran estudiosas del espiritismo y de los fenómenos sobrenaturales, eran las únicas que tenían la prueba irrefutable de que las ánimas pueden materializarse, gracias a una fotografía que las mostraba alrededor de una mesa y volando por encima de sus cabezas a un ectoplasma difuso y alado que algunos descreídos atribuían a una mancha en el revelado. . . . [Se] presentaron con sus propias barajas impregnadas de fluidos benéficos, unos juegos de figuras geométricas y números cabalísticos de su invención, para desenmascarar a los falsos parapsicólogos, y una bandeja de pastelitos comunes y corrientes de regalo para Clara. (115)

Later, on a much more serious note, it is Luisa Mora who announces the disasters of the impending coup d'état and Alba's suffering at the hands of her captors. In a more somber way, this again points to the Mora sisters as possessing spiritual powers far beyond those of any ordinary person, just as the auric color scheme set out by Tansley claims.

But the association of the Mora sisters with the color purple is not the only such correspondence to be found within the novel. Esteban Trueba is also defined by his predominant color, and the color that most frequently accompanies him in the text is red. It does not take a spiritualist to see the red in Esteban Trueba's aura; his angry force is visible in the blood that so frequently accompanies his actions.

Trueba's first move on arriving at Las Tres Marías is to shoot an impertinent dog. Later, after a bad dream, in which he sees la bella Rosa and perceives her peaceful aura, he responds by angrily kicking a chicken to death, "dejándola agónica en un charco . . ." (68).

Blood in great quantities also accompanies Esteban Trueba's engagement to Clara del Valle, when someone chooses that moment to stick a butcher knife in Clara's outsized dog, Barrabás, who appears at the elegant engagement party:

> En ese momento . . . entró Barrabás . . . desangrándose como un buey . . . el hocico babeando en un hilo de sangre. . . . El perrazo se acercó a [Clara], y se quedó mirándola . . . mientras el blanco encaje de Chantilly, la seda francesa del sofá, la alfombra persa y el parquet se ensopaban de sangre. (86)

Blood is also implicit in the string of rapes that Esteban Trueba carries out, both the actual blood spilled in the rapes of young virgins like Pancha García and also the transmission of Trueba's troubled blood through his practice of "sembrando la región de bastardos" (62).

Eventually the red of murder victims' blood is also reputedly on his hands:

> Dos veces aparecieron cadáveres de campesinos de otras haciendas acribillados a tiros de escopeta y a nadie le cupo duda que había que buscar al culpable en Las Tres Marías. (62)

Before long Trueba even draws blood from his own wife and daughter. When Jean de Satigny informs on the midnight rendezvous of Blanca and Pedro Tercero García, Esteban Trueba catches his daughter, "la golpeó sin piedad, propinándole un azote tras otro," and then he brings her home to her mother, "cubierta de barro y de sangre" (179).

When Clara protests, Trueba turns his fury on her, an act he regrets for the rest of his life:

> Inmediatamente una ola de sangre le subió a la cabeza. Perdió el control y descargó un puñetazo en la cara de su mujer. . . (179). Clara abrió los ojos. Botaba sangre por la nariz. Cuando abrió la boca, escupió varios dientes, que cayeron al suelo y un hilo de saliva sanguinolenta le corrió por la barbilla y el cuello. (179–80)

Blood, then, becomes a recurrent motif very closely associated with Esteban Trueba. The most shocking of all these blood-soaked incidents, of course, is the scene in which he chops three fingers from the hand of Pedro Tercero with an ax. The immediate result is that Esteban Trueba's aura is contaminated literally with red as blood spurts at his head: "Un chorro de sangre me saltó a la cara" (184). The scene itself is bathed in blood, as Pedro Tercero escapes, leaving behind "un reguero de sangre," and the child Esteban García picks up the severed fingers "como un ramo de espárragos sangrientos," then drops them in the sawdust, "tiñiéndolo de rojo" (184).

Red, then, is the dominant color associated with Esteban Trueba, a violent red that tinges everything he does. When he decides to pay his peons with scrip instead of money, for example, he uses "papelitos rosados" (63). Ironically, he does this to avoid "cosas que, según él, olían al comunismo" (63). Even in his hatreds, Esteban Trueba is dominated by the color red, and he becomes completely obsessed by communists, whom he despectively refers to as "los rojos." Ultimately, Trueba's rabid collaboration with the military and with foreign advisers helps bring about the novel's bloodiest period—the coup d'état and the events that follow it. Unwittingly, Trueba helps into power the very people who later brutally murder his son and then torture and maim his granddaughter.

After presenting all of the evidence of the frequency with which red is associated with Esteban Trueba, I find it significant to note the auric associations of the color according to Tansley:

> Red is a predominantly physical color, the symbol of life. It denotes strength, force, vigour, passion and capability. . . . Dark red can denote a fiery temper or personality. Red almost always means nervous trouble and overconcern about self. Pride, avarice and selfish affections show up as red. . . . Individuals with a lot of red in their aura are often physically strong and willful, with a rather materialistic outlook in general.[7]

How closely this description fits Trueba! Physically, he is a very strong man, able to live through the accident that he asserts would have left a weaker man "inválido para siempre . . ." (159). His force lifts Las Tres Marías from disrepair into precise function, and his passion drives him to the compulsive pursuit of neighborhood girls. His fiery temper has already been demonstrated, and his obsession with the idea that he is shrinking clearly indicates an overconcern about himself. He is proud, strong, and willful, and his life goals, from the moment he enters the mines to win la bella Rosa (something she never required of him), show his generally materialistic outlook.

However, not all of the auric associations with the color red are negative, and these tendencies can sometimes be turned into something positive by the force of will. Tránsito Soto, for example, emerges from the pointedly named Farolito Rojo with many of the good qualities that the color red can portend, according to Tansley. He gives the following list of positive characteristics associated with the color:

> Red, first ray of will and purpose:
>
> Purposefulness
> Natural leadership
> Positivity and drive
> Strength of will
> Directness
> Ability to lead, initiate and govern
> Fearlessness[8]

Some of these strengths could be attributed to Esteban Trueba as well. But in this case, they seem outweighed by the negative attributes, which Tansley lists as:

> Ambition
> A love of power
> Impatience and irritability
> A domineering attitude
> A conviction of being right
> Tyranny
> Pride
> Contempt
> Rigidity[9]

It is only with age that Trueba manages to dim the red from his aura and approach a purity in his case attainable only through suffering. This final change is physically represented by his "blanca melena leonina," which is the color of purity (372). The change for the better in his aura is at first nothing more than an "halo misterioso," which becomes clearer "a medida que mi abuelo fue perdiendo para siempre la rabia que lo atormentó durante toda su existencia" (378). The color white is very important to the text. The chain of del Valle and Trueba women in the novel pass on names denoting whiteness and clarity from mother to daughter—Nívea, Clara, Blanca, Alba. In addition, later in life

Clara insists on wearing only white, "porque decidió que era el único color que no alteraba su aura" (118).

But white cannot be said to be the auric "color" of these women because white, strictly speaking, is of course not really an individual color at all, but rather the blending of all the rays of the visible spectrum together.

The first definition of "white" offered in the *Funk and Wagnalls Standard Dictionary,* for example, is:

> Having the color produced by the reflection of all the rays of the solar spectrum.[10]

The *Diccionario Universal Salvat* expresses it thus:

> El color compuesto resultante de la combinación de todas las radiaciones correspondientes al espectro visible de la luz solar.[11]

If we view "white" scientifically as the combination of all colors in the visible spectrum, then the association of white with the women in this novel is rich with possibilities. While characters like Esteban Trueba are driven to extremes by an excess of auric color (red, in Trueba's case), these women, according to their names, may have no one dominant ray to color their auras, but rather could be seen as representing balance, blend, and unity. Each of the women, from Nívea to Alba, has a name that could suggest the color white, and each represents a kind of ideal of familial unity—especially Clara. Her unifying force in the family is so great that after her death, "todos en la familia sintieron que sin Clara se perdía la razón de estar juntos" (262).

But the color white has other, less obvious implications as well. The theoretical concept of white may be belied by a more practical observation, and any child who tries mixing all the colors of his paint box in an attempt to get white realizes the difference between theory and the muddy gray before him. In the physical world of hues, then, white has another accepted definition, which Funk and Wagnalls gives in this way:

> An achromatic color of maximum lightness, the complement or antagonist of black, the other extreme of the neutral gray series.[12]

Gray as an auric color may, according to Tansley, be related to "depression, gloom and sadness."[13] White, of course, would be the palest of pale grays, but still, one would be hard-pressed to deny a hint of melancholy in Clara's decision to engage in a loveless marriage, Blanca's hypochondria, and Alba's obsession with the family basement.

More obviously within the gray sequence is Férula, whose very name suggests an iron-gray will. Gray is the color of her stern bun (remember that the aura is associated with the head), and the ever-present bunch of keys at her waist. Here is a woman clearly prone to depression, gloom, and sadness. What is more, readers of Carlos Fuentes's 1962 novel, *Aura*, will recall that there the term was used to describe the vision that the aged Consuelo managed to conjure up before the willing eyes of Felipe Montero. Fuentes's character Aura is literally nothing more than an astral projection. Similarly, what else is Férula when she appears to the family at the time of her death? Clara, "con su larga familiaridad con los asuntos sobrenaturales," recognizes this gray aura immediately (134). This vision of Férula's astrally projected aura stresses again the gray in her appearance.

But in addition to being the lightest, hueless shade of the gray sequence, "white" has another, quite different acceptation. Ironically, "white," when applied to the temperature of metal, is a synonym for *incandescent*, which is quite the opposite of the grim associations of gray. Certainly there is an incandescence implicit in Clara's character, with her light, airy clothing, her otherworldliness, and her general lack of mundane cares.

But the associations of the word *blanco* do not end in Spanish with scientific (or even pseudoscientific) explanations. *Blanco* is also the Spanish word for *target*, or as the *Salvat* expresses it:

> Fin u objeto a que se dirigen nuestros deseos.[14]

How appropriate this term is when applied to Clara del Valle! She is the "blanco" of at least three characters' most ardent desires: Esteban Trueba, Férula, and Pedro Segundo García. Blanca, too, is the object of Pedro Tercero García's fantasies from childhood through middle age. As in the case of Clara, part of what makes her that obscure object of desire to him is her inability to decide in his favor, her incapacity to choose a mundane life situation.

One could continue practically ad infinitum playing with the notion of "whiteness," but then since Melville the task is perhaps less challenging. Instead, therefore, let us consider for a moment that perhaps not all that glitters is white. Although reviewer D. A. N. Jones claims with contempt that the names Clara, Blanca, and Alba are rather obvious and easy symbols for purity,[15] in fact author Allende does not claim exactly this. When Alba is born, her mother wants to name her Clara, but grandmother Clara opposes the confusion of names and suggests instead looking up the word in a dictionary of synonyms. According to the narrator, then, Alba is "el último de una cadena de palabras luminosas que quieren decir lo mismo" (234). On the one hand, this is again a gentle spoof of the uncountable Aurelianos and José Arcadios in *Cien años de soledad,* for Clara frequently refuses to repeat names, insisting, "eso siembra confusión en los cuadernos de anotar la vida" (233). Even when author Allende does repeat names, as in the case of the García family, with the purpose in mind of showing how each succeeding generation inherits the same burden of misery and is not seen as individual by the *patrón,* she helpfully assigns them numbers, both as proof of the landholder's lack of consideration and also in deference to her readers, so that they do not get mixed up.

However, in spite of all this, the colors involved in the names, "Nívea, Clara, Blanca, and Alba," are not totally free from ambiguity. The adjective *claro,* for example, may be applied to any color to mean a light shade, but it does not forcibly suggest pure white. And the noun *clara,* meaning egg white, is not really white at all in its virgin state, but clear and colorless. Nívea and Blanca, by contrast, are the least equivocal, with the color white strongly evoked by both. However, with the name *Alba,* "el último de una cadena de palabras luminosas," there is a particularly interesting ambiguity (234).

On the surface, of course, the adjective *albo* is a synonym for *white,* coming from the Latin word *albus.*[16] But by making it feminine, *alba,* the author adds some new elements, for *alba* in the feminine is the Spanish word for *dawn.* The *Salvat* defines "alba" as "la primera luz del día antes de salir el sol," and when one honestly begins to think of it, the first light of day is not, chromatically, strictly white in most cases.[17] In fact, dawn is frequently associated with a pink hue. This connection is so persistent and long-standing in the tradition of western literature that C. Hugh Holman uses the phrase, "rosy-fingered dawn" to illustrate the Homeric epithet in his *Handbook to Literature.*[18] In this way, Allende subtly introduces Alba's onomastic affinity with her aunt Rosa, with whom she also shares the aura of green hair.

Rose and pale green are complementary tones, and the suggestion of both colors is present in Rosa and Alba. It is interesting to read the value that Tansley assigns to rose pink in the auric field:

> Rose pink is the color of refinement. . . . It is the color of the emotional body and thus . . . friendship and physical love. Rose pink acts upon the nervous system to help vitalize the body. . . . It increases the will to live.[19]

When one considers these qualities as they relate to Rosa and Alba, it seems clear that some of these qualities lay dormant in Rosa but were given a chance to flourish in Alba. Rosa's capacity for physical love and her will to live were cut short by her untimely death—due to a real act too strong and swift to be overcome (her accidental drinking of the poisoned brandy). Alba, though she lacks some of her great-aunt's splendid beauty, surpasses her ancestor in vitality and energy. Moreover, her will to live (possibly hinted at in her rosy-fingered name) enables her to survive an ordeal that would have defeated many strong men.

All of these suggestions of auric color within *La casa de los espíritus* have been hypothetical readings invited by the novel's playful introduction of the theme. One may take them just as seriously as one takes Clara's spirits, mummies, and UFOs. It is hard to say how seriously Allende herself means for the reader to take any of this, or how deeply she probed into the study of auric colors before writing her book. Some of the parallels drawn here may, of course, be accidental. But one case in which auric color definitely does seem to be stressed is in the case of Alba's green hair, and with this I return to my initial question: *why* the green hair? Alba, the narrator of the book and one of its most important characters, is charged with giving a message of hope at the end of the novel, a message on which Allende elaborated in an interview:

> Soy una incorregible optimista. No creo que la humanidad se autodestruirá en un holocausto nuclear o algo parecido. Al contrario, creo que avanzamos en una espiral ascendente, a veces parece que andáramos [sic] en círculos sin movernos del mismo nivel, pero no es así. Progresamos, crecemos, aprendemos.[20]

Alba, with her very human maternity and her near-divine capacity for forgiveness, must be the human representative of this progress within the novel. And to this end, her aura of green hair is a banner of hope, for according to Tansley, green is one of the most positive of all the colors in the auric field, the color of the continuation of life itself:

> Green is the color of nature and healing. . . . It is beneficial to have a good clear green in the aura. . . . People with green in their auras are

> usually lively, thoughtful, versatile, and adaptable. Green governs the mental levels of consciousness and indicates a plethora of ideas. It is the color of regeneration, of new life springing up . . .[21]

With Alba, life continues in spite of obstacles, and the persistence of her spirit is echoed in the healthy green of her hair. Once again, a bit of magic that was merely fanciful in the early part of the novel, with the mermaid tresses of la bella Rosa, has taken on a deeper significance in the later part of the book, where it is interwoven with the work's most basic theme: the continuation of life. Although Alba laments her hair in adolescence, by the end of the novel it has become a fitting halo for a determined heroine.

In Joseph Losey's 1948 B-film, *The Boy with Green Hair*, a young boy's hair turns green when he learns that his parents were killed in an air raid. Other war orphans encourage him to parade himself publicly as an image of the horror and futility of war. The film makes its muddled and pretentious point in the typical Hollywood fashion of the times, and eventually the boy's hair returns to normal color after being shaved off by his grandfather, a garrulous Pat O'Brien. But with Isabel Allende, the green tresses are more subtle—sometimes washed with bay rum or chamomile tea by loving nannies, "lo cual tuvo la virtud de mitigar el color, dándole una tonalidad de bronce viejo" (12). Once, at the instigation of her eccentric Uncle Nicolás, little Alba even decides to shave it off for religious reasons, and her grandfather finds her "con la cabeza rapada como una bola de billar repitiendo incansablemente la palabra sagrada OM" (265). In contrast to the Hollywood tale, not even shaving causes Alba's hair to grow out a different color. With Alba, the green hair is not a confused antiwar slogan, but rather a tenacious, plantlike symbol for life itself that reappears undaunted even after being cut off at the root. In fact, the stubborn growth reminds us of another plant that Allende frequently alludes to when describing this novel:

> Cuando hice la maleta para irme de Chile, eché unos puñados de tierra del jardín en una bolsa. En Caracas la puse en un macetero y planté en la tierra chilena un nomeolvides. Durante esos años no ha hecho mas que crecer y crecer. Como mi nostalgia. (Back cover, *La casa de los espíritus*)

In the end, in fact, Alba's green hair and Allende's *nomeolvides* are the same plant, flowing out, haloing the tale, and providing the assurance of the continuation of life in spite of all man's mean efforts to the contrary.

8
THE INCREDIBLE SHRINKING MAN

> Hombre pequeñito, hombre pequeñito
> suelta a tu canario que quiere volar. . .
> yo soy el canario, hombre pequeñito,
> déjame saltar.
>
> —Alfonsina Storni, "Hombre pequeñito"

> An aged man is but a paltry thing,
> A tattered coat upon a stick unless
> Soul clap its hands and sing and louder sing
> For every tatter in its mortal dress. . . .
>
> —William Butler Yeats, "Sailing to Byzantium"

Another major piece of magic that is realized to the fullest degree in the latter part of *La casa de los espíritus* is the shrinking of Esteban Trueba, in accordance with the curse put on him by his sister, Férula, when he exiles her from the house:

> —¡Te maldigo, Esteban!—le gritó Férula—. ¡Siempre estarás solo, se te encogerá el alma y el cuerpo y te morirás como un perro! (121)

The shrinking of Esteban Trueba operates on many levels and is one of the best examples of how Allende blends magic, reality, and an occasional homage to García Márquez in order to create a magically real effect that is very much her own, and that also grows logically from beginning to conclusion in the novel.

Esteban Trueba's anxiety over his perception that he is shrinking is probably the strongest emotion we see in his part of the narrative after his love and mourning for Clara and his later preoccupation with the safety of Alba. He mentions the shrinking from the very first physical description he gives of himself:

> . . . alto y flaco como yo era entonces, antes de que se cumpliera la maldición de Férula y empezara a achicarme. (37)

The inevitable, inexorable process of shrinking hangs like a curse over Esteban Trueba's head even before he alienates Férula and provokes her words. The introduction of the ominous foreshadowing so early in the text gives Esteban Trueba's shrinking the weight of grim inevitability.

Soon after Férula's expulsion, Esteban Trueba's anxiety over his supposed shrinking begins to manifest itself. He adduces physical evidence such as ill-fitting clothing in an insistent attempt to convince the reader of the truth of the phenomenon:

> El fue el único que se dio cuenta de que se estaba achicando. Lo notó por la ropa. No era simplemente que le sobraba en las costuras, sino que le quedaban largas las mangas y las piernas de los pantalones. Pidió a Blanca que se la acomodara en la máquina de coser, con el pretexto de que estaba adelgazando. . . . (163)

At the same time, he desperately searches for a scientific or even pseudoscientific explanation for the phenomenon—anything but that it is the result of an earned malediction from his sister:

> . . . [S]e preguntaba inquieto si Pedro García el viejo no le había puesto al revés los hueso y por eso se estaba encogiendo. (163–64)

Trueba's anxiety increases in direct proportion to his loneliness as he moves further and further away emotionally from his family. As this happens, Trueba's need to find a scientific explanation for his troublesome decrease in size grows stronger, and at last he determines to set out on a pilgrimage to what he perceives as the mecca of scientific knowledge and hard facts—the United States:

> Cansado del dolor de huesos y de aquella secreta enfermedad que sólo él percibía, tomó la decisión de hacerse examinar por médicos extranjeros, porque había llegado a la conclusión que los doctores latinos eran todos unos charlatanes más cercanos al brujo aborigen que al científico. (216)

Thus, his personal anxiety reveals a fair dose of self-disparagement, evident in his deprecating opinion of things autochthonous—his country, and by extension, himself. Nevertheless, the third-person text continues to stress that no one but Trueba perceives the decrease in size—leaving more than a little room for the reader to question whether the shrinkage is real or merely a product of Trueba's guilty imagination:

> Su empequeñecimiento era tan sutil, tan lento y solapado, que nadie más se había dado cuenta. (216)

Again and again the text insists on the lack of evidence visible to anyone but Trueba himself, and in doing this, leaves the reader free to consider the phenomenon a product of Trueba's imagination. An ironic note comes in when Trueba decides that his head is shrinking as well:

> Un día se puso el calañé que no había usado en todo el verano y vio que le cubría completamente las orejas, de donde dedujo horrorizado que si estaba encogiendo el tamaño de su cerebro, probablemente también se achicarían sus ideas. (217)

The irony of this is that of course the reader has already observed the increasing narrowness in Trueba's ideas ever since he began to run Las Tres Marías, and that such progressive shrinking of horizons is unfortunately all too common in many people who do not have the convenient excuse of a physically shrinking head. This obvious fact again inclines the reader to conclude, along with the gringo doctors:

> . . . que eran puras ideas suyas, que no pensaba estarse encogiendo, que siempre había tenido el mismo tamaño y que seguramente había soñado que alguna vez midió un metro ochenta y calzó cuarenta y dos. (217)

Trueba's reaction to the problem casts further doubt on the landowner's reliability:

> Esteban Trueba acabó de perder la paciencia y regresó a su patria dispuesto a no prestar atención al problema de la estatura, puesto que todos los grandes políticos de la historia habían sido pequeños desde Napoleón hasta Hitler. (217)

Napoleon, of course, is the classic identification of a man with delusions of grandeur, and Trueba's reference to him practically forces the question of the man's sanity. Moreover, his naming of Hitler as one of "los grandes políticos de la historia" is a clear evidence of Trueba's shrunken ideas, regardless of his past or present hat size. Thus we see that throughout the supposedly "magical" period (up to Clara's death), actually a scientific explanation for Trueba's supposed shrinking is strongly hinted at in place of the literally magic one Trueba perceives.

In his grief over Clara's death, significantly, Trueba feels another surge of anxiety over the loss of his stature: As he lies down on the bed with his wife's corpse, his sense of loss at her beauty is joined to his belief in his loss of size:

> [Clara] había adelgazado y creí que había crecido, que estaba más alta, pero luego comprendí que era un efecto ilusorio, producto de mi propio achicamiento. (260)

According to Sigmund Freud in *The Problem of Anxiety*, this coupling of anxiety and grief is not surprising.[1] Both are emotional reactions to a sense of loss, one actual and one perceived as imminent. In fact, the two are so closely related that sometimes it is difficult to tell them apart. Writes Freud, "the question is, when do we have one, and when do we have the other?"[2]

Of course, in Trueba's case, the tangle of anxiety and grief is especially hard to unravel since Trueba had already begun to lose the object of his affections (Clara) while she was still alive. From the moment he destroys his matrimonial relationship with Clara by striking her, Trueba plunges himself into an anxiety-ridden state brought on by an incomplete loss—one he can neither regain nor properly mourn. As Freud defines the two states, "grief is the reaction specific to object loss, anxiety to the danger this object loss entails. . . ."[3] Therefore, it is suggestive that when Esteban is faced head-on with the final, irrefutable proof of the loss of his object of affection (Clara)—her corpse—he should react with a compulsive inventory of his shrinkage. He adds this, oddly, to the end of his account of preparing Clara's body for interment:

> Yo me había achicado diez centímetros. Me nadaban los zapatos y tenía el pelo definitivamente blanco, pero ya no lloraba. (260)

It is as if the affirmation of his physical loss of stature, measured with scientific precision ("diez centímetros") somehow comforts and reassures Trueba at the loss of his wife. Once more, the reader feels more than a hint of suspicion that the real loss is that of Clara, and that Trueba's anxiety over the diminution of his physical size may be just that—mental distress over something that has not yet occurred.

After the climactic moment of Clara's death, references to Trueba's shrinking become less frequent; he seems to resign himself to the permanent impression of being smaller. At the same time, other shrinking effects begin to make themselves felt—notably in his fortune: "esta parecía irse mermando desde la muerte de Clara" (273). But, as with the decrease in size, once the loss of his most prized object is final, Trueba soon arrives at a posture of near indifference:

> No se alarmó porque supuso que en el orden natural de las cosas estaba el hecho irrefutable de que en su vida [Clara] había sido un soplo de buena suerte. (273)

The shrinking becomes less and less important, in fact, to Trueba, but sometimes when he is reminded of his guilt, it recurs. For example, after he buries Clara with her sister Rosa in his mausoleum, "junto a otros seres queridos, como . . . la misma Férula, quién espero que me haya perdonado," he begins to be plagued by insomnia (277). As he wanders the house at night he feels disproportionately small, "arrastrando las zapatillas que me quedaban grandes" (277). But with the return of the work day, the sense of smallness diminishes, replaced by the sense of impatience to be at work:

> Con la luz del sol, sin embargo, recuperaba el deseo de vivir . . . ponía al día sus asuntos de negocios. . . . (277)

Up to this point, throughout the so-called magical portion of the book, realistic explanations for Trueba's shrinking have been insistently offered (the settling of age, combined with anxiety-ridden imaginings). Ironically, it is in the so-called realistic conclusion to the book that the narrator Alba finally offers concrete evidence of a magical explanation—a photograph of her grandfather:

> cuandro era joven y medía un metro ochenta, prueba irrefutable de que se cumplió la maldición de Férula y se le fue achicando el cuerpo en la misma medida en que se le encogió el alma. . . . (378)

In yet another example, then, we see a most magical act, one that defies natural explanation, insisted upon in the final section of the novel. Again this tends to disprove the notion that *magical realism* is a term only applicable to the early chapters of this novel, and that the ending is starkly realistic.

In order to demonstrate that the magic element not only exists at the end of the novel, but also that its importance grows logically, organically from the beginning, it is necessary to examine not just the fact of shrinking but also its metaphorical implications. It is important to remember that although Esteban Trueba becomes obsessed with his physical decrease in size, this is only one part of Férula's curse, and indeed, to many it would not be the most frightening.

"Siempre estarás solo," Férula's curse begins, and in fact, this lonely solitude is at the root of Esteban Trueba's pathetic old age, not any real or imagined shrinkage. "Se te encogerá el alma y el cuerpo," she continues (121). First and foremost in the curse is the spiritual diminishment, taking precedence over the physical one. The curse ends with the ominous prediction, "ye te morirás como un perro" (121). It is revealing that of all the curse, Trueba seems only to have heard the physical threats—the shrinking of his body, the dying like a dog. By contrast, he seems never to spare a moment's worry over whether his soul may be undergoing a reduction in size parallel to that of his body.

By coupling the dissimilar elements of size and soul in the curse, of course, Allende invites the reader to associate them. On the most superficial level, Trueba's shrinking body is nothing more than a physical manifestation of his dwindling humanity. Trueba's physical reduction of size is measured in centimeters, in shoe and hat size, in sleeves taken up. At the same time, his spiritual limitation is measured in the distance he keeps from his family, in his smear campaign against el Candidato, and most tragically, in his short-sighted participation in the coup d'état.

The shrinking is also a natural metaphor for the withering effect of age on a flower, a human body, or in some cases, an intellect. In *Cien años de soledad*, Gabriel García Márquez carries the notion of shriveling up with age to its extreme with the aged Ursula. As always in the best magical realism, there is a seemingly fantastic, exaggerated occurrence (an adult shrinking to the size of a baby) juxtaposed with a hard reality (that children and grandchildren of an elderly person sometimes treat them as little more than objects):

> Amaranta Ursula y Aureliano la llevaban y la traían por el dormitorio, la acostaban en el altar para ver que era apenas más grande que el Niño Dios, y una tarde la escondieron en un armario del granero donde hubieran podido comérsela las ratas. Un domingo de ramos entraron al dormitorio mientras Fernanda estaba en misa, y cargaron a Ursula por la nuca y los tobillos.
>
> —Pobre la tartarabuelita—dijo Amaranta Ursula—, se nos murió de vieja.
>
> Ursula se sobresaltó.
>
> —¡Estoy viva!—dijo.
>
> —Ya ves—dijo Amaranta Ursula, reprimiendo la risa—, ni siquiera respira.
>
> —¡Estoy hablando!—gritó Ursula.
>
> —Ni siquiera habla—dijo Aureliano—. Se murió como un grillito.
>
> Entonces Ursula se rindió a la evidencia. —Diós mío—exclamó en voz baja—. De modo que esto es la muerte.[4]

The heartless play of Amaranta Ursula and Aureliano with their shrunken great-grandmother, whom they drag around the room like a doll, is at the same time fantastic and yet based on an unpleasant reality, and the exaggeration does no more than give a literal representation to a figurative truth (i.e., "they treat her like a piece of furniture," or "they drag her around from relative to relative," and the like).

By contrast, the shrinking of Esteban Trueba in *La casa de los espíritus* is not so dramatic or complete but lends itself to other possibilities. Like Ursula, Esteban Trueba is a person whom age eventually robs of position and authority. His shrinking, like hers, has the inevitability of encroaching old age. But the main difference between the two is that while physical shrinking comes upon the outrageously elderly Ursula ("la última vez que la habían ayudado a sacar la cuenta de su edad . . . la habían calculado entre los ciento quince y los ciento veintidós años)"[5] without particularly surprising or troubling her, by contrast, the shrinking of Esteban Trueba sets in at an early age and is a source of grave anxiety to the man. Whether he will admit it or not, on some level he must sense that the decrease of size is linked to a decrease of the soul. Moreover, this condition is not the inescapable effect of age on all the characters of the book, for as Trueba himself points out, his wife actually appears to have grown taller at her death:

> Creí que había crecido, que estaba más alta, pero luego comprendí que era un efecto ilusorio, producto de mi propio achicamiento. (260)

It may be that this passage reflects a piece of popular mythology about death—the notion that after death, bodies actually "grow" a little. The phrase, "el último estirón" refers to the supposed phenomenon, and many educated people continue to believe in it despite all scientific evidence to the contrary. But what does scientific evidence matter in the face of popular tradition? Though doctors tell us that neither hair nor fingernails nor any other tissue can grow after death, these popular myths still abound.[6] And although those in the know assure that on death muscles contract, and that after *rigor mortis* passes off the body begins to decompose, but does not grow taller, still in Hispanic society, many people continue to be fond of the idea of an "último estirón," as if in recompense for dying, the body had a growth spurt as proof of immortality.[7] Isabel Allende would be the last to debunk popular myths about death; rather she would be much more likely to weave them into the rich tapestry of her fictional world.

In a strictly practical sense, however, the idea of a dead body growing runs counter to what today's scientists tell us they believe to be true of natural laws.

Thus, when Trueba measures himself against Clara del Valle's corpse and finds her to be taller, it is evident that this event belongs to the "magic" portion of the narrative. Whether or not Allende may believe in the idea of an "último estirón," it seems clear that here she has used the comparison to reveal Esteban Trueba to the reader psychologically. A live person comparing himself in size to a dead one is not, in fact, without literary antecedents. Shakespeare has Brutus do just this in *Julius Caesar*, for example. On the battlefield of Philippi, realizing that the battle is lost and that his military career is finished and his life effectively over, Brutus sees Caesar's ghost in a vision. To the desperate Brutus, Caesar's ghost seems larger than ever. "O Julius Caesar," he tells the apparition, "thou art mighty yet!"[8] For Brutus, it is apparent that the mighty Caesar has grown in popularity even after death, while he, Brutus, has shrunk miserably in the public esteem. Similarly, Esteban Trueba's comparison of his size to his wife's reveals much about his inner state: deprived of his wife he feels shrunken and alone.

Another special component of Trueba's anxiety over shrinking is that besides being closely allied to his sense of loss of his wife's love, it is also akin to his anxiety over a perceived loss of masculinity with age. According to Freud, the castration complex is one of the most basic of all anxieties, and what better objective correlative for the fear of losing one's potency than actual, physical shrinking! After being cursed by Férula, Trueba increasingly believes his masculinity to be in doubt. This particular sense of loss begins with his alienation from Clara. No longer the young man who raped country girls in the blink of an eye, Trueba has become obsessed with his need of Clara, who has all but lost interest in him and complies with his wishes only when absolutely necessary to maintain her socioeconomic status:

> Un día Clara hizo poner un pestillo a la puerta de su habitación y no volvió a aceptarme en su cama, excepto en aquellas ocasiones en que yo forzaba tanto la situación que negarse habría significado una ruptura definitiva. (162)

As with their physical sizes, Clara's power over her husband appears to grow while his on her shrinks to practically nothing, and his obsessive attraction to her, the unattainable object, leaves him all but impotent in other situations:

> Mi sensualidad se había hecho más selectiva con la edad. . . . Ella sabía donde estaban mis puntos más sensibles, podía decirme lo que necesitaba oír. A una edad en que la mayoría de los hombres está hastiado de su mujer y necesita el estímulo de otras para encontrar la chispa del deseo, yo estaba convencido de que sólo con Clara podía hacer el amor como en los tiempos de la luna de miel, incansablemente. (162)

In Trueba's pathetic attempts to seduce his wife he goes so far as to drill a hole in the bathroom wall in order to see her undressed but when this proves too frustrating, he makes a show of going to el Farolito Rojo to visit the prostitutes. Clara's only comment is that "eso era mejor que forzar a las campesinas" (163).

Reduced by his wife's indifference and provoked by her comments, Esteban Trueba actually goes so far as to attempt raping country girls once again, but the results are anything but reassuring to his masculinity:

> Pude comprobar que el tiempo y el terremoto hicieron estragos en mi virilidad y que ya no tenía fuerzas para rodear la cintura de una robusta muchacha y alzarla sobre la grupa de mi caballo, y mucho menos, quitarle la ropa a zarpazos y penetrarla contra su voluntad. Estaba en la edad en que se necesita ayuda y ternura para hacer el amor. Me había puesto viejo, carajo. (163)

The connection between Trueba's anxiety over loss of masculinity and his anxiety over shrinking is apparent in the words immediately following these confessions: "él fue el único que se dio cuenta que se estaba achicando" (163). This juxtaposition neatly transfers attention from Trueba's fear of loss of masculinity to his preoccupation with shrinkage. Like Trueba himself, the reader is distracted by the inexplicably "magical" event from the all too explicable real one.

By the end of the novel, Trueba's loss of power and potency is all too clear, and the connection between the two is delineated in a scene in which a broken Trueba visits Tránsito Soto in her "cooperativa de putas y maricones" to enlist her help in finding and freeing his granddaughter. "En vista de que no ha venido a hacer el amor," Soto tells him, "vamos a hablar en mi oficina, para dejar este cuarto a la clientela" (365).

Ultimately it is Tránsito Soto, using a power acquired through falsifying the potency of love, who is able to get the best of the new regime and negotiate Alba's release. Esteban Trueba's power, by contrast, has shrunken to uselessness, along with his sexual potency, his size, and his very soul, until none is of any use to him or his family.

In Jack Arnold's 1957 sci-fi thriller, *The Incredible Shrinking Man*, an ordinary citizen who is caught in a radioactive mist shrinks to micro size. The horror of the plot lies in the inevitability with which a once strong, healthy man is reduced to terror of the family pet and finally even of garden insects. Actor Grant Williams in the title role conveys the horror of a man who finds himself becoming ever smaller through no fault of his own, and who at last achieves heroic (though diminutive) stature when he determines to face the unknown bravely.

There is a similarly inevitable quality to Trueba's shrinking—after all, no one is immune from aging. But age does not impose a diminished spirit on all people, as is graphically evident in the case of Clara, who appears literally and figuratively to have continued to grow throughout her life. Unlike his shrinking cinematic counterpart, however, Trueba deserves his fate. It is only when he recognizes this and begins to atone in some measure for his lifetime of prejudice and domineering ways (for example, by forgiving Pedro Tercero and helping him to escape, and later through his suffering over the death of Jaime, or in his preoccupation over Alba's capture and torture) that he can arrest the terrible shrinking of his body and spirit before it reduces him to nothing. In doing so, he escapes the final most awful prophecy of all in Férula's curse:

> No murió como un perro, como él temía, sino apaciblemente en mis brazos. . . . Ahora está tendido en el velero de agua mansa, sonriete y tranquilo. . . . He abierto las cortinas de seda azul para que entre la mañana y esté alegre el cuarto. (371)

Once more, a magical culminating occurs in the final pages of the novel. Trueba's peaceful death belies the tragic end for which he earlier seemed destined. For a character with the background, upbringing, and life experiences of Trueba, to change and to see the tragic consequences of some of his attitudes is nothing short of a miracle. And if an old reprobate like Trueba can be regenerated, then perhaps there is hope as well for the entire class—the unseeing bourgeoisie—he represents. It is in just such miracles, not in flying saucers or crystal balls, that Isabel Allende puts her hope. In reading her book, we too have trust that such a blend of magic reconciliation with the reality of history may yet occur in fictional countries like that Allende describes, and perhaps in real ones as well.

9
DE AMOR Y DE SOMBRA: MAGIC ABJURED?

> . . . This rough magic I here abjure.
> . . . I'll break my staff,
> Bury it certain fathoms in the earth
> and deeper ever than did plummet sound
> I'll drown my book. . . .
> Now my charms are all o'erthrown
> And what strength I have's mine own.
>
> —(Spoken by Prospero) William Shakespeare, *The Tempest*, 5.1

> Vivo en un continente donde no hace falta inventar mucho, porque la realidad siempre nos sobrepasa, es una tierra de huracanes, terremotos, maremotos, catástrofes políticas. . . . Nuestra historia es alucinante y nuestra realidad a menudo lo es también.
>
> —Isabel Allende, interviewed by Michael Moody

Powerful incantations and editorial sprites could hardly have brought Isabel Allende more glowing initial responses to her second novel than those she received. When Plaza y Janés published *De amor y de sombra*—the subject of this chapter—in 1985, the reaction was one of gushing praise. For example, Miguel Angel Candelas Colodrón enthused in *La Voz de Galicia:* "Isabel Allende ha vuelto a confirmar con *De amor y de sombra* la represión política."[1] Only the *Diario de Granada* hints at a relationship between the political stance and the magical popularity of the book, pointing out that the author, "ya no oculta ser sobrina de Salvador Allende," and then going on to state the unspeakable—flatly saying to the author's face, "yo [que Ud.] no estaría [tranquila]. Su primera novela me gustó mucho más que la de ahora," in a 1985 interview in Granada.[2]

From the New Critics onward, a desire to avoid invidious comparisons and to let individual works of a given author stand or fall on their own merits has been virtuously pursued. Many, moreover, will sympathize with Allende's response to the *Diario de Granada*'s aggressive reporter:

Yo no sé opinar. Es como preguntarle a una madre qué hijo prefiere.[3]

The purpose of this study is not to rank Allende's novels in numerical order according to someone's abstract notion of "goodness." But in an in-depth examination into the workings of magic in both novels, it does not seem out of place to talk about the very magic that keeps the narrative together and holds or fails to hold the reader under the spell of the book. Thus this kind of narrative magic will be the first examined in this chapter.

As the title of *De amor y de sombra* would suggest, love and shadow are the two main themes of the novel. Outside the welcoming acceptance of Spain, some other European reviewers have seen this juxtaposition as forced and unhappy. In Germany, for example, despite the runaway-bestseller status of *La casa de los espíritus* (translated as *Das Geisterhaus*), Allende's second novel (in Germany, *Von Liebe und Schatten*) has sold well but been less kindly reviewed. Swantje Strieder of *Der Spiegel* put the problem to Allende with the magazine's characteristic bluntness:

> Sie beschreiben in Ihrem jüngsten Roman glühende Küsse vor verstümmelten Leichen. Glauben Sie, dass man so der Militärdiktatur Pinochets beikommen kann? . . . Wird die Brutalität nicht verharmlost, wenn man sie mit romantischen Liebesszenen ausschmückt?[4]

> (You describe in your latest novel burning kisses in front of mutilated corpses. Do you believe that one can bring down in this way a dictatorship like Pinochet's? Isn't the brutality rendered harmless when you adorn it with romantic love scenes?)

Allende's response is that extreme situations bring out extreme feelings ("extreme Situationen bringen extreme Gefühle hervor").[5] But the author's general response does not answer the question of whether or not the love story and the political intrigue find a peaceful coexistence within this novel. *De amor y de sombra* is the story of Irene Beltrán, a young woman raised amid the privileges of the unnamed *barrio alto* of a large South American city that again sounds very much like Santiago de Chile, and of her gradual realization of the undercurrents of repression and torture beneath the surface of her placid existence. Aiding her political awakening is Francisco Leal, son of Spanish Civil War exiles, who eventually wins her love and woos her away from her army officer fiancé, as he and Irene discover evidence on a small scale of massive political corruption.

Allende explained the juxtaposition of the love story with the political intrigue to Michael Moody thus:

> Tengo dos obsesiones, dos fantasmas recurrentes: el amor y la violencia, la luz y la sombra. Por eso el título de la novela. Siempre están presentes en mi vida, como dos fuerzas antagónicas. La violencia es una posibilidad, otra dimensión de nuestra realidad. Hay una frontera invisible que separa el mundo aparentemente ordenado, donde vivimos y cuyas leyes creemos conocer, de otro mundo que existe simultáneamente, que nos rodea, que ocupa un terrible ámbito. . . . Eso quería contar en mi libro: un viaje a la violencia y al horror, de dos personas inocentes que nada tienen que ver con eso. . . . Mis protagonistas andan buscando el amor en una primavera radiante. . . . De pronto se ven envueltos en una situación de la que no logran escapar.[6]

The promise of crossing this invisible border to an unseen world of violence hidden beneath the quotidian sounds engrossing, but somehow the trip goes awry shortly after it begins. Allende has frequently described herself as a simple reader who enjoys reading for entertainment, and in *La casa de los espíritus* she proved her ability to narrate a tale that keeps the reader anxious to know what will happen next. But much as one wishes to avoid the odious, the invidious comparison, somehow one feels obliged to point out that this basic narrative suspense is to a large extent missing from *De amor y de sombra*, and love and politics are evenly matched in the book in that from the opening pages, there is very little suspense about anything at all. From the beginning only the dullest of readers can doubt that Irene will leave her close-cropped military boyfriend for the embraces of the long-haired, politically correct Francisco Leal. And there is never any question at all in our minds that once the ominously named Juan de Dios Ramírez takes the young mystic/epileptic Evangelina Ranquileo into custody after she has publicly lifted him off the ground and shaken him, he will find a disgusting way to kill her and then hide the body in a shabby grave that will in all likelihood contain the remains of the five missing members of the Flores clan.

The failure of the book to create any kind of suspense about these two factors is so patent that it merits a closer examination. Let us begin with the love story.

"DE AMOR"

The problems with the love story start with Irene Beltrán herself. In the first place, from the beginning, Irene seems to have more idiosyncrasies than real personality. Like any good pre-hippy, preactivist, Irene enters the book dressed like a third-world gypsy, in cotton ruffles. Allende also resuscitates her much-used epithet for Amanda's costume jewelry from *La casa de los espíritus*, the "abalorios de pitonisa," and uses the phrase quite enough times in this book to wear it out. Later, when Irene's serious political commitment occurs, she opts for a more urban guerrilla look, which Sargento Faustino Rivera describes thus:

> Notó los cambios en la apariencia de la joven y se preguntó dónde quedaron sus pulseras escandalosas, sus faldas de vuelos y el dramático maquillaje de sus ojos que tanto le impactaron cuando la conoció. La mujer que tenía delante, con el cabello recogido en una trenza, pantalón de dril y un enorme bolso colgando al hombro, apenas guardaba alguna semejanza con la imagen anterior.[7]

This change of clothing is of course meant to symbolize Irene's inner evolution as she becomes conscious of the corruption of her country, but the novel's repeated insistence on the correlation between mode of dress and spiritual worth leads eventually to many characterizations that are only skin deep. The work-worn Digna Ranquileo is good, while the well-dressed, coiffed, and manicured Beatriz Alcántara is bad; long-hairs are daring political opponents, but short-hairs are fascists. The dress code *does* reverse itself in the case of male homosexuals; there the elegant Mario is good, while the dirty heterosexuals with broken fingernails from his hometown are bad.

The insistence of Irene's change of dress accompanying her change of heart makes her seem at times like an actress, now playing at gypsy, now at intrepid reporter, and now at committed leftist, each time with appropriate costume changes.

Further characterization of Irene is similarly facile. Her kindness to the elderly residents of "La Voluntad de Dios," the rest home she and her mother operate on the ground floor of their house, extends to paradigmatic extremes, including letting child-like grandfathers feel her up as she delivers imaginary mail she has written to keep them happy. That these public fondlings distress her mother is presented as proof of the mother's petty class prejudices and her all-too-conventional way of viewing the world:

> De pronto el abuelo erótico se acercó a Irene y le colocó ambas manos sobre los senos, oprimiéndolos con más curiosidad que lascivia. Ella se detuvo, inmovilizada por unos instantes interminables para su madre hasta que una de las cuidadoras se dio cuenta de la situación y corrió a intervenir. Pero Irene la detuvo con un gesto.
>
> —Déjelo. No le hace mal a nadie—sonrió. (14)

The book asks us to see Irene, through this introductory scene, as a generous free spirit, unrestrained by narrow-minded bourgeois taboos. Irene's volunteer dabblings as sex surrogate might, however, suggest other interpretations to some readers, such as mild exhibitionism, a desire to annoy her mother, and an unusual sense of the erotic. However, the last possibility, unfortunately, is not borne out by the rest of the book, for in spite of the fact that the author assures us over and over that when Irene finally sleeps with Francisco, "no había amado así" (191), and "no recordaba haber sentido tanto gozo, comunicación profunda, reciprocidad" (191), theirs and all the other love scenes in the novel have a consistently generic, lackluster quality, summed up in the most hackneyed of terms, as when Beatriz refers to her dalliance with Michel as "una noche inolvidable" (91). In fact, the only sex scenes described with any enthusiasm at all are the ones involving the rape and murder of Evangelina Ranquileo. Perhaps a touch of imbalance ignites Allende's pen more than the descriptions of her committed pair of lovers, but whatever the reason, the fact is, the two give off few sparks. Maybe they are too earnest, too euphemistic, too egalitarian, or simply too skinny to be sexy. Or maybe the problem is that we know that Francisco has been "amamantado más allá del plazo normal" (206). In any case, when the magic erotic flame fails to blaze, it is very difficult to say why. But the descriptions of sex that, along with the rest of the narrative, were so unforced and convincing in *La casa de los espíritus* have become here laborious exercises in euphemisms through which the reader glimpses only a confused tangle of unidentified body parts. The word *retozar* for making love seemed fresh and fitting in the historical setting of *La casa de los espíritus;* here its endless repetition seems coy. Even more coquettish are Irene's repeated references to sex as "la fiesta recién vivida" (194) and "la fiesta de los sentidos" (192). In fact, a reader might prefer to have overused phrases like "caricias recién inventadas" (191, etc.) replaced once in a while with some specifics. Moreover, there is room for doubt on reading that "una formidable represa estalló" in Francisco's "vientre, inundando a Irene de aguas felices," as to whether the man orgasmed or wet the bed (192). In the case of a man who in childhood continued to nurse long after he could talk, it might be well to specify.

The sad part is that "el novio de la muerte," Irene's love who returns from a long military outing turgid with testosterone only to discover that he has been supplanted, is much more complex and appealing than Francisco. It is almost as if Allende realizes near the end that she has made him sexier than her hero, for she promptly emasculates him literally and figuratively, involving him in a wild-eyed plot to overthrow the military junta that brings about his speedy torture and death.

"DE SOMBRA"

The love story, for all of this, is just part of the novel, half of the title. If the side represented by *amor* is problematic, what about the part of the narrative that falls under the heading of *sombra?* To answer this question, we must look at what it is that draws Francisco and Irene over the line of normalcy into the nether-world of shadows. The wheels are set in motion by a magical event—the "miracles" attributed to the adolescent Evangelina Ranquileo. Word of these miracles attracts spectators, including journalists Irene and Francisco, along with Teniente Juan de Dios Ramírez. But before this encounter takes place, the reader has been advised that all five adult male members of Evangelina's family (she was switched with another baby in the hospital at birth) have been "disappeared" for belonging to the *sindicato agrícola* during the times of the brief Agrarian Reform (34). With such a setup, it is no surprise at all to find that when Evangelina, in the middle of her seizure, publicly humilitates Ramírez, he returns at night and takes her into custody. The hints have been so strong from the outset that Juan de Dios Ramírez is to blame (not the least of which being the fact that he arrested all concerned), that the reader cannot help wondering why on earth Irene and Francisco are so slow to pick up on it. On page 194, *after* witnesses have told the pair that Evangelina was in the power of Ramírez when last seen (either dead or unconscious), *after* one of Ramírez's underlings has led the reporters to Evangelina's grave, and *after* the girl's mother and brother have filled in what pieces Ramírez's underling did not, the reader is astounded to find Irene and Francisco still *wondering* if Ramírez might be implicated. After all of this evidence has been presented, the author tells us as though we ought to be surprised, "también Irene y Francisco sospechaban del oficial" (194).

The fact is, the reader knows from the very beginning that all the bones will be found mixed together in a hidden grave but keeps going for three hundred pages to find the mysterious revelation that will make it seem like more than a pathetic news clipping. The details of the story were, in reality, inspired by just that. Allende told *Der Spiegel:*

> Diese Toten gab es wirklich. Da tauchten 1978 zum ersten mal die Skelette von Regimeopfern auf.[8]

> (These deaths really happened. In 1978 skeletons of people the regime murdered appeared for the first time.)

In her interview with Michael Moody, Allende went into more detail:

> Mi segundo libro se basa en un hecho acontecido en Chile, en la localidad de Lonquén, a 50 kilómetros de Santiago. En unos hornos abandonados de cal se encontraron 15 cadáveres de campesinos, asesinados durante el golpe militar. Este descubrimiento se hizo a través de la Iglesia Católica, en el año 1978, cuando yo estaba ya en Venezuela.[9]

She also stresses the factual research she put into weaving the story into a novel:

> Me tomó un buen tiempo recopilar todo el material para escribir mi historia. . . . Para realizarlo trabajé mucho, investigué, leí, busqué.[10]

The personal side of the tragedy, according to Allende, convinced her to place it in a novelistic setting:

> En la vida real hubo cinco miembros de una familia Maureira que fueron asesinados en Lonquén. Leyendo eso en la prensa de Venezuela, tuve una terrible impresión. No dejaba de pensar en las mujeres de esta familia, para mí adquirieron las características de la tragedia griega. . . . Pensando en esas mujeres y sintiendo su pena en mi corazón, me despertaba sobresaltada por las noches, se me aparecían en el día. A veces iba distraída manejando el automóvil y me asaltaba su recuerdo con el impacto de una descarga de adrenalina. Comprendí que debía exorcizar este dolor y dejar testimonio,

> por eso escribí el libro, a pesar de que la historia me parecía poco atractiva, muy sórdida, muy patética.[11]

In her interview with the *Diario de Granada,* Allende frequently mentions the word *solidaridad.* Her interviewer remarks, "hace dos años me pareció Ud. menos comprometida," to which the author responds:

> Ahora me cuesta no estar comprometida. Y no hablo del compromiso con un partido político, que no tengo ninguno, sino de un compromiso contra los abusos, contra la opresión, contra cualquier militarismo. . . . Mi compromiso es con la solidaridad.[12]

Perhaps it is a combination of the factors that the author attests to above that accounts for the lack of suspense in the telling of this tale. First, it is based on a real occurrence taken from the newspapers, not woven from her family's oral tradition. Second, what is researched has a way of getting used—and in respect for the real victims, perhaps Allende felt she should not stint on proofs of the factuality of her tale, instead of trying to convince the reader of the reality by more literary means. For example, regarding Lieutenant Ramírez she says:

> En *De amor y de sombra* hay algunas partes tomadas casi textualmente de las declaraciones de los militares y testigos, por ejemplo, la confesión del Teniente Ramírez. En la vida real no se llamaba así, pero sus palabras están en mi libro. Llamé los Riscos a la localidad de Lonquén y cambié algunos detalles, pero todo lo demás es casi exacto.[13]

But in her desire to be faithful to a historical substructure, perhaps Allende is false to the superstructure of fiction. More specifically, by building the discovery of the grave around one, solitary responsible party—Teniente Juan de Dios Ramírez—does she not by implication limit the borders of corruption in the novel into one neat, aberrant, local package? Ramírez alone corrupted by power, is responsible for the deaths of the Flores men and of Evangelina, as well as for the deaths of the other peasants. When he has been publicly fingered as responsible, even though he escapes punishment, does this not weaken rather than strengthen Allende's novelistic argument that the entire country is riddled with corruption? What is more, the fact that Evangelina is really a Flores again seems to make the situation more local. After all, maybe local superstition is right, and the family is just *gafe,* or jinxed. Even Faustino Rivera, who nails the lid on the case against his superior, doubts that the implications are more than local:

> Unos pocos cadáveres hallados en el fondo de una mina no significa que todos los uniformados sean asesinos. (231)

Allende herself saw the implications of the case differently:

> No fue el único caso, ni el primero. Se han descubierto muchas tumbas, pero hasta entonces siempre fue posible echarles más tierra y mantener los asesinatos en la sombra. Esa era la primera vez que se publica abiertamente sobre los crímenes de la dictadura, porque la intervención de la Iglesia impidió que se ocultara, como siempre se había hecho.[14]

Still, Allende's airy gift of hyperbole that aided the narration of major disasters in *La casa de los espíritus* seems constrained here, and novelistically, the main point of all this investigation seems to be how it relates to the personal lives of Francisco Leal and Irene Beltrán. For Irene, as for Manuel Puig's theatrical hero Molina in *El beso de la mujer araña,* there is undeniable personal grandeur attached to being gunned down by faceless baddies in a speeding car, while in the pursuit of noble, if somewhat vague ideals. As Puig's Valentín wonders in a morphine-induced dream:

> ¿Por una causa buena? uhmm . . . yo creo que se dejó matar porque así moría como la heroína de una película. . . .[15]

Unlike Molina, Irene survives her cinematic assault to escape into exile. On this point the plot again wanders into trouble. While Irene is in the hospital, Mario, the make-up artist, assures Francisco that their lives are still in danger and that Irene is under surveillance by men who will stop at nothing to get her—men who have already turned her house upside down, assaulted her jolly housekeeper, and shot her dog. Mario, "con su célebre maletín de las transformaciones," disguises the pair so that they can leave the hospital unrecognized and then offers to hide them in his apartment until Irene is well enough to travel (252). So far so good, but when they arrive at Mario's, Francisco immediately begins to telephone and visit his parents frequently, conveniently forgetting former worries about tapped phones and tails. Fortunately, the shadows are too dumb to connect Mario to his two best friends or to follow Francisco from his parents' home to Mario's apartment. It does seem that if faceless villains had really been intent on killing Irene, they might have thought to keep an eye on Francisco. According to the novel, he has been at her bedside since the accident. Besides, he has on occasion called attention to himself, with behavior like the following reaction to Irene's first spoonful of soup after the assault:

> Enloquecido de alegría, salió brincando por los pasillos de la clínica, se lanzó a la calle, cruzó zigzagueando entre los automóviles y se dejó caer sobre el césped de la plaza. Roto el dique de la emoción . . . reía y lloraba sin disimulo ante la vista asombrada de niñeras y jubilados que a esa hora paseaban al sol. (249)

One can only wonder who finished feeding Irene her soup. The passage goes on to establish that Hilda Leal, Francisco's mother, also came frequently to the hospital, where she could have easily been spotten by anyone observing the place. If the surveillance was really as tight as the book would have us suppose, then why does it conveniently ignore Hilda and Francisco?

> Hasta allí fue a buscar [a Francisco] su madre para compartir su gozo. Hilda pasaba muchas horas tejiendo silenciosa junto a la enferma. . . . (249)

The acute paranoia that surrounds the escape from the hospital conveniently lifts once the fugitives arrive at Mario's, and no one seems to spare a care for what the neighbors think of Francisco's comings and goings, or what they think of noises in Mario's house while he is away. Any pretense of caution drops completely when Mr. and Mrs. Leal actually come to Mario's apartment for a large, noisy farewell dinner that serves no purpose other than an excuse to insert some sentimental dialogue on the heartbreak of exile. The Leals' exile, what is more, seems more than a little illogical by this time, as they argue that they must stay near son Javier's grave rather than return to Spain, their homeland, to be near the still-living Francisco, his bride-to-be Irene, and possible future grandchildren. They seem to prefer a masochistic nostalgia to the attempt to recover some of what they have lost.

The fear of police capture is conveniently resuscitated for the last portion of the book, allowing a dramatic escape scene with more references to the ubiquitous *nomeolvides* plant. The result of all this is that the political implications, which the book labored so painstakingly to present in a personal light, are lost in the aggrandizement of the well-intentioned but bland love story of Francisco and Irene.

Yet another failure of narrative magic must be mentioned: the similarity of the narrative voices that combine to tell the story. In *La casa de los espíritus* there was a clear and masterful difference between the narrative voices of Alba and her grandfather, Esteban Trueba. Here, however, whoever's speech is paraphrased in the exposition, from Digna Ranquileo to Beatriz Alcántara, from Faustino Rivera to Irene, from Josefina Bianchi to Pradelio Ranquileo, they all end up sounding like the same university-educated, journalistically trained, female person.

In interviews, Allende has recognized this problem with the text and claims that the similarity of narrative voices was deliberate, that she did this seeking a "neutral" tone because she did not want to mark the country of the narrative specifically as Chile, but rather wanted it to represent Latin America in general:

> La falta de diálogos es un recurso literario. En la literatura el diálogo es siempre coloquial y sitúa a los personajes en un ámbito determinado, y yo quise huir de ese tipo de identificaciones. ¿Cómo hacer hablar a un campesino chileno sin que hable como tal? Entonces lo evité porque mi propósito era involucrar a toda Latinoamérica.[16]

But somehow this well-meaning excuse does not quite offer a satisfactory explanation for the lack of variation in speech from city to country, and from character to character. It may be that in attempting to create an international text Allende has failed to make the novel function on the basic, literal level she has so often stated she demands of a book that she herself would like to read. Whatever the explanation, it is unimaginable that the taciturn, rustic giant, Pradelio, would spout pages of description of his sexual obsession with his "sister," pages that sound more like warmed-over D. H. Lawrence than rural Chile, full of phrases like "la calentura que abrasaba la sangre," "el ímpetu de su masculinidad" that could "atravesarla como una espada," and the way Pradelio "sentía sus huesos derretidos y algo caliente y viscoso ardiendo en sus venas" (162). All of this leads in grand Lawrencian fashion to dramatic reactions whenever Pradelio is near the cause of his derangement:

> Las fuerzas lo abandonaba, perdía el entendimiento y hasta la vida se le iba a causa de ese olor a humo de su pelo y de lejía de su ropa" (162).

It is quite simply impossible to imagine that Pradelio could have described his obsession to Irene and Francisco, complete strangers, in these words, if at all. Pradelio, noted for his scarce speech, is barely literate, and can only just read the cowboy novels his mother sends him, and one simply does not find it easy to envision him waxing so literary especially after (or in spite of) days in the mountains without proper nourishment. Rather, the mention of the subject seems to trigger an excuse to interject a little illicit sex—usually welcome enough, but here jarring with the characterization of Pradelio, who is always described as of a sepulchrally silent nature and simple almost to the point of retardation. But besides this, the whole basis for the obsession seems somehow to be a bit off. Why does Pradelio torture himself trying to overcome his attraction to a woman who is no blood relation to him? In *The Sound and the Fury* Quentin Compson's obsessive fascination with his sister, Caddy, carries with it the decadent thrill of incest within an aristocratic Southern family.[17] Here, by contrast, Pradelio's obsession with Evangelina reads more like garden-variety adolescent hormones. It is hard not to ask what, in view of this, everyone is so upset about. Why cannot Pradelio simply marry Evangelina?

An even more grating example of the lapses in narrative voice comes with relation to a similar subject when Sargent Faustino Rivera gives his imaginary reconstruction of the death of Evangelina Ranquileo:

> [Ramírez] fue a la parte trasera [del camión], quitó la lona y vio la silueta de la muchacha. Debe haber sonreído con este gesto torcido que sus subalternos conocen y temen. Apartó el pelo del rostro de Evangelina y pudo apreciar su perfil, el cuello, los hombros, los senos de colegiala. Le pareció que a pesar de los hematomas y las costras se veía hermosa, como todas las jóvenes bajo las estrellas. . . . Se abalanzó sobre ella con una violencia inútil, pues no encontró resistencia . . . recuperando así el orgullo de macho que ella le arrebató ese domingo en el patio de su casa. Cuando terminó . . . ella no hacía el menor movimiento, no se quejaba y tenía los ojos abiertos fijos en el cielo, asombrados de su propia muerte. . . . El teniente . . . echó una última mirada a su alrededor para verificar que no había rastros de su acción. Subió al vehícula y enfiló por la carretera. (234–35)

Even if Rivera is one to wax poetic in his notebook, this sounds like much too much for a low-level career military man in a rural outpost with little educational background. What is more,

Rivera's asides to Irene in his normal speaking voice make the passage seem all the more bizarre, and unlikely to be told over a greasy lunch in a fly-stained *parador:*

> —Disculpe mi franqueza, señorita—se interrumpió Faustino Rivera chupando los útimos huesos del almuerzo. (234)

Besides the incongruity of voice, it is awkward having Rivera tell the story at all, since, as he points out, he was not there. And even if he *did* tell it, would he really go on and on inventing details about the way his commander "abrió el cinturón de cuero y el cierre del pantalón" (234) and the like, and would Irene really sit quietly and listen to it all? Well, maybe. We remember her patience with the *abuelo erótico.* As if Allende suddenly realizes the utter atonality of the account, she has Rivera conclude with the lame excuse:

> Admito no tener pruebas de cuanto le he contado, pero podría jurar por la memoria de mi santa madre, que en paz descanse, que las cosas ocurrieron más o menos así. (235)

In summary, in my opinion this novel, though undoubtedly earnest and well-intentioned, fails at times as an entertainment and as fiction because there is no suspense created either in the love story or in the political intrigue, because the different characters have such similar voices, because the "good" and "bad" characters are often superficially and simplistically divided, and because the book struggles with the competing goals of being a novel and being a faithful reportage of the historical occurrences that inspired it. The realistic endowment of both good and bad qualities that made Esteban Trueba such a successful character in *La casa de los espíritus* is forgotten here, and Beatriz Alcántara is shallow right down to the bottom: even while her daughter lies near death in the hospital, she is more concerned with her reputation sullied by her ex-husband, and we see her, "más preocupada por . . . ese enemigo escurridizo, que de la salud de su hija" (252). The recent Argentine film, *La historia oficial,* directed by Luis Puenzo succeeds masterfully in portraying a businessman involved in dirty dealings partly because it also depicts him as a devoted family man and husband. The truth is, villains frequently love their families just as much as anyone else does. By implying that bourgeoise matrons love their wrinkle creams more than their children, the novel loses force. It also loses the healing potential that in *La casa de los espíritus* recognized unifying values between Left and Right and suggested a kind of "feminine" logic that might someday override male militarism. But in this novel Allende's "magical feminism" seems to have derailed. Instead of intuitively wise, infinitely loving mothers, we have Beatriz Alcántara who never bids her daughter farewell, two rural mothers who agree to raise each others' daughters to avoid paperwork, and the exiled Hilda Leal, who chooses to spend her life taking flowers to a dead son's grave rather than share the existence of a living one.

The subtitle of this chapter, "Magic Abjured?" brings up the question of whether, or not Allende has abandoned the sometimes magical mode of expression she used in her earlier novel, and with what result. We saw at the beginning that the Spanish reviewers perceived this novel as a much more realistic effort than its predecessor, "casi una crónica política" (*La Nueva España*),[18] "patéticamente sobria" (*El Europeo*),[19] and a "manifiesto contra la represión" (*Diario de Navarra*).[20]

Curiously, however, the novel is not as completely removed from the "magical" and the inexplicable as might first appear. In fact, "magical" events are the catalysts that cause both the love story and the political one to unfold. The agent behind these events is of course Evangelina Ranquielo, with her supposed "magical epilepsy," or seizures that cause unusual, possibly supernatural events to occur.

MAGICAL EPILEPSY?

Evangelina's is an unusual story worthy of García Márquez, even before her birth; as long as her mother bears children at home, aided by the mystical midwife, Mamita Encarnación, with her "tijeras benditas por el obispo . . . tijeras milagrosas para darle fuerza y salud," all is well (22–23). But the minute it occurs to the peasant woman to take a step away from local superstition, to leave the midwife/witch doctor behind her and have the next baby in the hospital, disaster strikes. Her baby is switched with another, the hospital refuses to admit it made a mistake, and the two mothers are sent home with each other's daughters. All of this is charmingly told, and the negative magic of Progress seems responsible for everything. "A world of made is not a world of born," e.e. cummings might have consoled the women ("Pity This Busy Monster Man Unkind Not").[21] But what happens next defies the logic of the novel. Because of hair color, build, and so on, each mother is absolutely convinced that the other has her child. Nevertheless, both refuse to switch the babies back:

> Los padres sugirieron simplemente cambiar a las niñas y quedarse en paz, pero ellas no deseaban hacer sin legalidad. (34)

In this case it is the men who have common sense and pragmatic vision, while the women concern themselves with trivial technicalities. When fire destroys the records, we are told the mothers decide to keep the exchanged babies and raise them as their own, knowing that each has a sort of hostage of love in the other's home. The story is cute, and it provides a number of narrative branchings for the plot, but ultimately it runs counter to Allende's stated purpose of making the reader feel personally the stories of the people buried in the hidden grave, for it is hard to care much what happens to people who are this dense. Besides, it shows more than a trace of urban prejudice about country dwellers, and Allende should understand that there is a difference between simple, good-hearted country folk and the mentally challenged. If Digna Ranquileo will not claim her own child over silly bureaucratic objections, but instead will placidly accept a substitute the way an animal at times may allow a stray to suckle, then how can we seriously believe that she or her *comadre* is capable of human grief at the loss of another child? Moreover, as has already been mentioned, the event makes all of Pradelio's worries about incest inexplicable, since the whole countryside apparently knows the story of the "Evangelinas cambiadas."

Problematic as the story of the exchanged babies is, it introduces a theme that is central to an examination of magic in the two novels: the clash between old fashioned superstition and newfangled progress. Mamita Encarnación, like old Pedro García in *La casa de los espíritus*, possesses some surprising powers. What is more, in Allende's first novel, a repeated motif was the idea that Marxism failed in Chile partly because it is too coldly logical and European a philosophy, ignoring "el lado mágico de las cosas" (337). This conflict between progress and superstition, "civilización y barbarie," is nothing new to Latin American letters. It has been a constant in works like *Facundo* (1845), *Doña Barbara* (1924), *La vorágine* (1924), *Los pasos perdidos* (1954), and many others. Early positivist beliefs in science as the answer to Latin America's ills were gradually replaced with a cynical view of progress, and eventually the entire vein of Latin American literature that has come to be lumped together as magical realism has actually celebrated superstition and simplicity in areas isolated from urban modernity. Magical realism was the very first tendency in modern fiction to originate in Latin America and to earn legitimacy at last for its authors, including Nobel prizes for Gabriel García Márquez and Miguel Angel Asturias. It occupies, therefore, an almost sacred place in Hispanic letters, and Isabel Allende, like most of the new group of novelists, has been touched by its spell. But is it the most appropriate vehicle for describing modern urban problems of the kind Allende wants to narrate in *De amor y de sombra*? On closer examination, Evangelina Ranquileo and her sufferings could be seen as a (perhaps unconscious) metaphor for magical realism as a narrative means of conveying the problems of a troubled Latin America. The magic produced can cure small ills (like warts), but it produces a convulsive, epileptic effect on the person performing the magic. Like Evangelina, a country or a continent may be convulsed by the conflicts between modern ideas and superstition. Delightful "magic" may be produced by the prolongation of an awe and reverence for old superstitions, but the overall effect of such magic may not be altogether healthy for the "body" inducing the magic. Evangelina Ranquileo is ultimately killed because of her unconscious magic seizures, and there is at least a suggestion that by worshiping at the altar of magical realism exclusively, a body of literature may suffer similarly unhealthy alterations.

In addition to this consideration, magical realism is a narrative technique strongly tied to rural conditions and superstitions, and by contrast very difficult to pull off in a modern, urban setting. Carlos Fuentes succeeds in *Aura* (1962), set in contemporary Mexico City, but he does it in part by reducing the space of the novel to an old-fashioned house after the first couple of sentences, and then building the plot around events that occurred some hundred years earlier. Julio Cortázar managed it with Paris and other cities, but he too either reduces space (as in "Axolotl," or "Casa tomada"), or sends the reader traveling in time (as in "Todos los fuegos el fuego") or employs some other limiting device. But generally, *magical realism* is a term that has not been applied to a novel set in the contemporary big city unless the city can be made to seem from centuries past with a regime older than its buildings (as in the dark underworld of Miguel Angel Asturias's *El Sr. Presidente* [1946] or the endless reign described in *El ontoño del patriarca* [1975], where García

Márquez fills his president's palace with cow droppings and flashbacks to the decrepit ruler's distant youth). Generally, the *magical realism* label has been applied to stories and novels *not* focused on contemporary urban reality. Think of the jungles of Macondo in García Márquez, the backwater Bahia of Jorge Amado, the bucolic quest in Carpentier's *Los pasos perdidos*, or the desolate isolation of Juan Rulfo's *Pedro Páramo* or "Luvina." Juan José Arreola's short story "El guardagujas" happens in the middle of nowhere, and even that urbane master of the urban setting, Borges, sends us back in time and out to the suburbs when his hero takes a magic voyage to "El sur."

In fact, on reflection it would seem logical that magical phenomena—those contrary to natural law—are best believed by readers when set in a time and place far-removed from the readers' own. Allende seems intuitively to recognize this unwritten law of magical realism, for when she uses the technique in her two novels, it is always either in a previous time period or in a rural setting. Since so much of *De amor y de sombra* takes place in a contemporary city much like Santiago de Chile, it is not surprising that the city scenes contain little of anything that could be called magical realism. What magic there is is subtler, without the riotous colors of the jungle or the lonely winds of the altiplano. For example, the magic of great acting transforms the aging Josefina Bianchi[22] as she plays Camille for the residents and staff of "La voluntad de Dios." An innocent belief in the supernatural is behind Hilda Leal's attempts to pray the dictator out of power. But most touching of all the urban bits of magic is the way the child Irene accepts unquestioningly the servant Rosa's magical transformation of her stillborn baby into "el niño que cayó del tragaluz":

> —¿De dónde salió este bebé? . . .
> —Cayó de arriba del tragaluz—replicó Rosa, mostrando una toma de aire en el techo—. Cayó de cabeza y murió, por eso está lleno de sangre. . . .
> —¿Qué haremos, Rosa?
> —¡Ay niña! Nadie debe saberlo. . . . Vamos a tirarlo a la basura.
> —Es una lástima acabar así, Rosa. El pobre no tiene la culpa de haberse caído del tragaluz. . . . (145)

The two bury the baby and plant a forget-me-not on top of the grave. From then on the author manages to create an unsentimental pathos every time the phrase, "el niño que cayó del tragaluz," is repeated, showing she has not lost her ability to coin the kind of compact epithets she made such good use of in *La casa de los espíritus*.

But the touches of bona fide magical realism that again invite comparisons with García Márquez are limited to the rural setting, including a couple of oblique references to the master, such as the hyperbolic size of Pradelio Ranquileo (reminiscent of the corpse in "El ahogado más hermoso del mundo") and the old colonel in "La voluntad de Dios" for whom Irene invents letters which she mails to him saying the letters are "para alguien que no tiene quien le escriba" (54) (echoing García Márquez' *El coronel no tiene quien le escriba*). But the most important of all these magical touches center on the figure of Evangelina Ranquileo. The first phenomenon is the "convención de ranas," which coincides with the beginning of all the Ranquileo family's problems:

> Una mañana las descubrieron muy temprano, dos gordas y soberbias ranas observando el paisaje cerca del cruce del ferrocarril. A poco llegaron muchas más provinientes de todas las direcciones, pequeñas de estanque, medianas de pozo, blancas de acequia, grises de río. Alguien dio la voz de alarma y acudió todo el mundo a mirarlas. Entretanto los batracios formaron filas compactas y emprendieron marcha ordenadamente. Por el camino se sumaron otras y pronto hubo una verde multitud dirigiéndose hacia la carretera. (39)

The hyperbolic nature of this plague has biblical echoes as well as echoes of García Márquez, Horacio Quiroga, and even Allende herself in her first novel. The results here are monumental, as people come to watch "aquel prodigio nunca antes visto":

> El enorme mosaico viviente ocupó el asfalto de la ruta principal a los Riscos, deteniendo a los vehículos. . . . Un camión imprudente intentó avanzar, resbalando sobre los cadáveres destripados y volcándose en medio del entusiasmo de los niños, que se apoderaron con avidez de la mercancía dispersa entre los matorrales. (40)

Modern scientific techniques cannot curtail the invasion but simply enable journalists to observe from helicopters that 270 meters of highway are covered with the creatures, "tan cerca unas de otras que semejaba una brillante alfombra de musgo" (40).

Eventually, of course, what science cannot explain, oriental wisdom clarifies, and a Chinese U.N. delegate at last elucidates the matter:

> Después de observar por algunos minutos aquella gelatinosa multitud, el oriental concluyó que no había motivo de alarma, pues sólo se trataba de una convención de ranas. (40)

Given this simple explanation, the public disperses. One sees here as earlier in *La casa de los espíritus*, Isabel Allende's ability to describe a seemingly impossible or magical event and then to undercut it at the end by minimizing its importance. What are 270 meters of solid frog, after all, if it is merely a Frog Convention? What is the good of playing the piano with the lid down if you cannot move the instrument around the room with the force of your mind? This undercutting the scope of magically real events (things that are maybe possible, maybe exaggerated) carries over from the earlier novel, and once again, the magic seems trivial in the end compared with the stronger force of the reality by its side. For example, just after the Frog Convention, Evangelina has her first "ataque," and those near her begin to report small miracles—warts removed, hemorrhoids eased, and other small problems solved. It is the attention that these miracles attract that eventually brings Evangelina to the notice of the law, combined with her brother's unrequited lust (another kind of magic altogether), and the force of Evangelina's magic seems pathetic indeed when contrasted with the stronger evil power of people like Juan de Dios Ramírez. The seizures that Evangelina suffers provide the novel with a wonderful metaphor for the failures of various institutions to deal with personal problems beyond their ken. Just as the clairvoyance of little Clara del Valle revealed the insensitivity of institutions like that represented by Padre Restrepo toward people who are different, and perhaps artistic, here the "ataques" of Evangelina Ranquileo bring out petty rivalries and all manner of shortcomings in the institutions that try to treat her—from churches, to hospitals, to local witch doctors. Digna takes her daughter first to don Simón, "conocido en todo el ámbito de la región por sus aciertos medicinales," and he emits a swift diagnosis: "le hicieron un mal de ojo" (58–59). His methods for removing the curse are brutal and ineffective:

> La fricción, el susto y el roce de aquellas pesadas palmas, tiñeron la piel de la joven de un tenue color celeste y le produjeron una violenta agitación nerviosa que por poco la conduce a un patatús . . . dejándola desfalleciente y temblorosa. . . . A la semana la muchacha había adelgazado, tenía turbia la mirada y trémulas las manos, andaba con el estómago revuelto y los ataques continuaban. (60–61)

This failure greatly diminishes don Simón's status in Digna's eyes, although she already had doubts:

> Digna había perdido parte de la confianza en don Simón, desde que supo cómo le engañaba su mujer, porque concluyó con razón que no debía ser tanta su sabiduría si era la única persona del pueblo en ignorar sus propios cuernos. (59)

When don Simón's cure leads nowhere, Digna breaks her vow and returns to the hospital where her baby was switched. There the doctor prescribes strong tranquilizers and, when this proves ineffective, electroshock treatments.

When science fails her, Digna attempts to find spiritual guidance, but again, the answers offered are unsatisfying. Her pastor tells her that the cause of the attacks is her husband's sinful refusal to give up alcohol. The Catholic priest, Padre Cirilo, believes the girl to be under the influence of Satan. However, he resists the idea of an exorcism:

> El tenía pruebas irrefutables de la existencia de Satanás, el devorador de almas, y por lo mismo no se sentía inclinado a hacerle frente con ceremonias improvisadas. Por otra parte, si semejantes prácticas llegaban a oídos de su superior, el manto de escándalo oscurecería definitivamente su vejez. (65)

The most he offers to do is say a few *padrenuestros* and splash a little holy water in the hopes that the power of suggestion might cure the girl. For good measure he suggests that Digna reconcile herself with the True Faith, "porque esas desgracias solían ocurrir a quienes desafiaban a Nuestro Señor con sectas impías" (65).

Eventually, as the "miracles" become public property and pilgrimages begin to take place, the issue turns into a mass of confused, contradictory opinions:

> Mientras unos sostenían el origen místico de la crisis, otros la atribuían a un simple maleficio satánico. Es histeria, alegaban en coro el protestante, el cura, la comadrona y el médico del hospital de los Riscos, pero nadie quiso escucharlos, entusiasmados como estaban con aquella feria de prodigios insignificantes. (66)

The consternation caused by Evangelina's daily attacks is startlingly reminiscent of the political confusion that surrounded the election of el Candidato in *La casa de los espíritus*; and one notes that in both cases, an unusual phenomenon provokes fear and confusion in the observers rather than an orderly attempt to seek the truth. A key word in the above passage, moreover, appears to be "insignificantes." The magic produced in both of Allende's novels is of the same delicate breed. Like miniatures, the magical touches produce a sense of pleasure when examined close up but they do not alter the overall picture of a novel any more than a miniature can have much impact on the overall decoration of a room. What is more, the uneducated people caught up in their trivial wonders and led by scientific and spiritual shepherds who treat them like naughty children, seem incapable of advancing and learning more sophisticated solutions to their problems. Thus, the "magical epilepsy" suggested by the figure of Evangelina Ranquileo is more a symptom of the clash of value systems than a description of a solution to the serious social problems this novel depicts. In this novel, then, magical realism may be read as a delightful mode of expression that may not always be appropriate to describe a less-than-delightful world.

But what about the other term coined earlier in this study, "magical feminism"? Is it applicable in any way to this novel? Using the deliberately nonjudgmental definition of "magical feminism" I gave, I think it can be used. After all, Evangelina is the "santa" around whom magic revolves, and in her case it is a defense mechanism developed partly because of the sex-descrimination to which she is subjected. And once again, as such a mechanism, it is less present in a more liberated generation like Irene's, so Irene's intuitions and "pálpitos" are often less reliable.

Reviewer Gloria Bautista found Irene's figure to be clearly a change from male-inspired patterns:

> Irene es el símbolo de la evolución de la conciencia feminina y la realización de la mujer a través de la acción social y la inquietud humana. Lo maravilloso es que esta concientización ocurre dentro de los patrones patriarcales y la autoridad tradicional.[23]

In other words, perhaps the mere existence of a woman who dares to be a feminist in Latin America is a marvelous or magical event, and thus the act of putting such a figure in fiction would be by definition "magical feminism."

All of this is not meant to imply that Irene is any sort of perfect model of feminist strength and intelligence, for she is definitely a human being, deliberately described in the novel with strengths and weaknesses. In fact at times she indulges in downright annoying behavior, such as insisting on taking a huge bag of canned provisions up the steep mountainside to Pradelio, and then making Francisco carry it; fainting right and left; dragging Francisco to a pig slaughtering and then being overcome by fits of vomiting. It is true that Irene, like her literary ancestor Clara from *La casa de los espíritus*, even has touches of clairvoyance:

> En algunos momentos de su vida, Irene se sintió golpeada por la fuerza de la intuición. Creía escuchar las señales del futuro y suponía que el poder de la mente podía determinar ciertos acontecimientos. (129)

Unfortunately, these intuitions do not seem to make Irene a better reporter, as has already been demonstrated earlier in this chapter, and she lags well behind ordinary readers in discovering the culprit.

What is more, unlike in *La casa de los espíritus*, where the feminine magic is presented unquestioningly as good, clear, and healthy for the aura, here there is more than a little suggestion that feminine conditioning to accept superstition more easily is part of what holds women back as a class. For example, the astrologer on the magazine's staff panders to the readers of that publication, with what must be a taste for the supernatural. However, the woman most often is completely wrong when trying to guess the birth dates and signs of people she encounters in the magazine's waiting room. Also, superstitions that in moments of relaxation seem charming can in times of stress drive a practical man to distraction. We see this when Professor Leal rips the habit of the Virgin of Lourdes from his wife, who has put it on in the hope that such sartorial sacrifice will bring about the return of her runaway son. Perhaps again in this novel Allende subtly suggests that a feminine resorting to magic and superstition may be endearing, but that in the end they hold women back, just as magic as a sole means of literary expression may hold her continent back, and just as superstition may hold her people back.

Because of this possible reading, I would say that *De amor y de sombra* does fulfill the requirement for "magical feminism" in certain passages, especially with regard to the magic of the unfortunate Evangelina. In the first place, the novel is femino-centric, as Juan Manuel Marcos points out in his article, "El género popular como meta-estructura textual del post-boom latinoamericano":

> En *De amor y de sombra* se incorporan al primer plano narrativo ciertos sectores que habían sido marginados por el "boom" en bene-

ficio de los personajes de extracción pequeñoburguesa y de sexo masculino.[24]

He clearly sees this as marking a differentiation between Allende and García Márquez:

> La longevidad hiperbólica de García Márquez es reemplazada por una visión realista y profundamente solidaria de los ancianos. . . .[25]

Not only this, but he also sees it as distinguishing her from another "Boom" author, Mario Vargas Llosa:

> La frivolidad machista de Vargas Llosa respecto a las prostitutas es corregida a través del respeto que les profesa Irene, de mujer a mujer, sin ningún naturalismo caritativo: "Permiso, señorita," le pregunta Irene a una, con intención de entrevistarla, "¿usted es puta?"[26]

In fact, the only "Boom" author that Marcos sees Allende as having a connection to is Manuel Puig, partly because of her representation of Mario, the homosexual hairdresser. For all of these reasons, I see the "magically feminist" label as once again being useful in a discussion of Allende's second novel.

Along with her use of magic to call into question the role of women in Latin America in this book Allende also uses it, in my opinion, to call into question the entire concept of magical realism as a vehicle for discussing the problems of Latin America. *De amor y de sombra* could also be seen as a plea for more realistic novels to gain *approval* (though they have certainly always existed) on an international level alongside their magically real cousins on the shelves of bookstores dedicated to contemporary Latin-American fiction. In *De amor y de sombra*, the death of Evangelina Ranquileo and the discovery of her grave do not really suggest any clear answers for the struggles of a country against dictatorship, but rather simply signal a problem, and in the final analysis, the book makes this point coherently. The magical Evangelina is viewed as charming but defenseless, and it is just such people that the state should strive to protect, not persecute and destroy. Though the book gives no answers, the discovery of the grave and the ensuring public testimony do give off a ray of hope for the future. It is not a clear prediction, but rather a feeling, an intuition, that in Isabel Allende's own simple phrase, eventually, "los buenos van a ganar."[27]

10
THE ROLE OF MAGIC IN *LA GORDA DE PORCELANA*

> Amo lo que no tiene sino sueños.
> Tengo un jardín de flores que no existen.
> Soy decididamente triangular.
>
> —Pablo Neruda, "La verdad"

Isabel Allende's 1983 tale, *La gorda de porcelana*, published in the illustrated format of a children's book, is the story of a punctual scribe to a notary, don Cornelio, who one day falls in love with a life-sized porcelain statue of a generously built woman named Fantasía in an antique-shop window. When don Cornelio buys the statue and tries to take it home with him, his life changes completely, and despite the author's insistence that this "es un cuento de verdad-verdadera," unaccountable things soon begin to take place.[1] Allende's favorite forms of magic quickly emerge as Fantasía comes to life, and she and don Cornelio levitate high above the smoggy city and later communicate telepathically with bunnies, bees, flowers, and pine trees, "que odian la Navidad, porque les mutilan sin piedad" (23).

But the real magic Allende is talking about is that which transforms a gray, anonymous city dweller into something more human. In the beginning, don Cornelio is more machine than man, and a dull machine at that:

> Llevaba al cuello una larga bufanda gris y contaba los ochenta y siete pasos que lo separaban del autobús sin mirar hacia los lados porque conocía la calle de memoria. (10)

His job consists of writing all day, "con su hermosa caligrafía, en unos papelotes que luego eran archivados por la eternidad" (6). In his spare time he sets out traps and poison for the mice who invade the *Notaría*. The city in this story is a place that imposes a crushing conformity on its inhabitants, and under its force, don Cornelio does not dare initially to commit even the smallest infraction of social rules, such as feeding the pigeons in the park on his lunch hour or saying hello to the town "loco."

But when Fantasía comes into don Cornelio's existence, she gives him the spine to stand up to the dehumanizing influences of his environment. Significantly, don Cornelio's rebirth begins with a magical trip to the country. When Fantasía holds don Cornelio by the hand, they are able to fly high above the dirt of the city:

> Don Cornelio . . . se echó a reír como cuando era niño. Se sujetó el sombrero con la mano libre y no tuvo miedo cuando sobrepasaron las antenas de la televisión, la torre de los bomberos y la cúpula de la Sociedad Protectora de Animales, dejando atrás los últimos techos de la ciudad. Abajo vieron los bosques como manchas oscuras, las cimas de las montañas cubiertas de suave merengue, el increíble color del cielo en un claro día de otoño. (22)

Just when don Cornelio thinks the excitement could not be more intense, Fantasía brings him back to earth, but this time to an earth nothing like the city he left behind, but one that is rather full of the magic of springtime in the country:

> —¡Bajemos!—rogó el escribiente, que quería verlo de cerca, porque hasta entonces, el único río que conocía era el negro canal lleno de basura que cruzaba la ciudad.
>
> Ella eligió un buen lugar para el aterrizaje . . . y bajó limpiamente como una gaviota. Por sugerencia suya, don Cornelio quitó los zapatos y sus pies sintieron por vez primera la tierra en su estado natural, porque antes sólo la había visto en maceteros. Dio unos saltitos breves, gozando de la nueva sensación, y empezó a bailar, a darse vueltas, loco de felicidad. Pensó que aquella borrachera se debía al reciente vuelo y al exceso de aire puro. (22–23)

The training Fantasía gives to don Cornelio during this day in the country is principally a return to the natural:

> Fantasía le enseñó a ponerse en el lugar de las hormigas, para ver el mundo desde abajo, a revolotear como las abejas, para apreciarlo desde media altura, a ser como los peces, para deslizarse bajo el agua, y a silbar como el viento entre las hojas. Eso fue lo que más entusiasmó al escribiente, porque su más secreto anhelo era silbar en la ducha, pero nunca había podido. (23)

Fantasía also gives the hero a lesson in sensory appreciation:

> También aprendió a palpar el mundo con los ojos cerrados, adivinando por su textura la secreta naturaleza de las cosas, y a diferenciar el olor de la yerbabuena, el tomillo y el laurel. (23)

All of this produces in don Cornelio thrills that seem practically sexual, especially when we note that they are described with Allende's favorite euphemism for erotic pleasures, "pasaron una tarde inolvidable" (23).

When they return to the city, it is not quite as oppressive as before, and moreover, the scribe is fortified against its dehumanizing influences:

> Penetraron en el colchón de humo que flotaba sobre los techos, pero don Cornelio llevaba en los ojos el recuerdo azul del cielo y todo le pareció menos gris y más amable. (24)

Soon a painter covers don Cornelio's dismal gray clothing with bright flowers, and when the scribe is ejected from job and apartment, his transformation is complete and he finds his true vocation as a street vendor, a profession that Allende paints in lyrical terms:

> Al dejar la Notaría encontró su verdadera vocación, que no era copiar documentos en el fondo de una sala polvorienta, sino andar por la calle silbando, conversar con la gente, cultivar la amistad del Loco en la plaza y alimentar con galletas de avena a las palomas, a los ratones y a otras bestias menores. Como siempre hay que ganarse la vida, combinó su necesidad con una ocupación adecuada: se hizo heladero en verano y vendedor de castañas calientes en invierno. (30)

And although La Gorda de Porcelana does not accompany don Cornelio on his daily rounds, "porque excitaría la atención de los transeúntes" (31), they do have other adventures when the work day is done:

> Con la Gorda de Porcelana han vuelto a hacer los viajes increíbles, se meten bajo la tierra, vuelan como aeroplanos, nadan en todos los mares y se introducen en los libros para correr aventuras inolvidables. (31)

On the simplest level, then, the story can be read as the adventures of an ordinary man who finds a magic statue and with it an extraordinary existence. On a slightly deeper level, the tale can easily be seen as an allegory for the importance of fantasy in life, especially in the regimented life of a city dweller. It might not be wise to squeeze this airy tale too much further in search of a deep, philosophical meaning, but several points do remain that are useful in completing our view of narrative magic in the fiction of Isabel Allende.

First is the importance of setting. In the previous chapters it was pointed out that when Allende introduces elements of magical realism into her adult novels, it tends to be either in an earlier time period or in a rural setting. In *La gorda de porcelana*, although some small magic events do occur in the city, for the most part urban mechanization forces "Fantasía" to stay in hiding. Fantasía is at her freest when she is out in the countryside, where the forces of nature are less constrained. As discussed earlier, the countryside is often a setting for magical occurrences in Allende novels. Evangelina Ranquileo's minor "miracles" and Pedro García's faith healing seem possible only in rural settings, aided by the power of local superstition. Moreover, this is not the first time an Allende character undergoes a dramatic transformation on going from the city to the country. We remember that Clara del Valle was transformed, at least temporarily, from a dreamy mystic into a hard-working practical manager because of the harsh realities country life imposed on her.

Next we notice that "magic" for Allende, here as before, has the connotation of that which is ideal, natural, and good. Our definition of realism as mimesis and magic as idealism fits very neatly, and here again Allende's mimetic skills are in a precarious but lovable balance with a search for ideal kindness that loves mice and sees beauty in the homeless "loco" and the old woman in orthopedic shoes, for example.

If realism, as Holman defines it, is the ultimate expression of middle-class values, then here again Allende's introduction of magic into an otherwise realistic situation is the deliberate attempt to upset the bourgeois apple cart, to interject a touch of asymmetry, of bright color, and what she would likely see as healthy chaos. Magic can be that which runs counter to natural law, but in the writing of Isabel Allende, it can also be that offbeat touch that reminds us that the natural laws exist in the first place.

Another technique Allende carries over from previous novels is the playful tendency to introduce a magical event, and then to undercut it by insisting on its trivial or mundane nature. For example, when a mysterious painter appears to decorare don Cornelio's suit with "flores, mariposas y angelotes," the author adds slyly, "dejándolo como una cortina de baño" (25).

Other touches of offbeat "magical" humor come when Fantasía gets hurt feelings and imitates a statue of Santa Rita, "mirando hacia el techo con los ojos húmedos" (27), or from non sequiturs, as in the following confusion over the statue's name:

> —¿Cómo se llama?—preguntó don Cornelio arropando la figura con la bandera.
> —Mi nombre es Baltasar—replicó el vendedor con una inclinación.
> —No, la estatua.
> —¡Ah! Su nombre es Fantasía—replicó . . . con otra inclinación. (15).

But all along the way, a humorously realistic view jostles with a more idealistic one, and magic and reality compete in a kind of magical reality that still falls short of magical realism. Chanady would likely class the story as "fantasía," like its heroine, because of the surprise the statue's antics cause in the originally down-to-earth don Cornelio.

Lastly, the person of Fantasía reminds us of the important role of books and storytelling in Allende's narrative cosmos. The tale informs us that Fantasía and don Cornelio "se introducen en los libros para correr aventuras inolvidables" (31). A child might easily read this sentence literally—believing that by magic don Cornelio and his friend physically enter the fantasy world described in books and actually experience the things described within. But a metaphorical reading—that fantasy is the means that enables a young reader to "enter" a story and "experience" vicariously a world different from his own—reminds us of the reverence with which Allende speaks of a writer's duty through her narrator Alba in *La casa de los espíritus*, or of the magic of the "baúles encantados."

All of the elements mentioned combine to make *La gorda de porcelana* yet another entry in the Allende canon in which natural law is transcended by the supernatural, a force that impels the characters toward a more idealistic life. Fantasía cannot change the city any more than Evangelina Ranquileo's supposed sainthood can prevent her death, or Clara del Valle's spirits can oust a dictator. But what she can do is change one individual so that he is better able to bear his environment. Don Cornelio faces the city at the end, "un hombre vestido de muchos colores" (31). Just as the antique seller promised him, "Fantasía le cambió la vida" (31).

11
EVA LUNA

Luna que se quiebra
sobre las tinieblas
de mi soledad,
¿a dónde vas?
—"Noche de ronda," (canción) Agustín Lara

Like the moon in the popular song, Eva Luna, the protagonist of Isabel Allende's latest novel to date, is a wanderer. A *pícara* in the finest tradition of *pícaros* (and she has much more in common with the male of the species than with, say, La pícara Justina), Eva Luna is a woman who lives by her wits, not her cleavage, experiences both hunger and abundance, works for a series of masters and mistresses, and in the course of her wandering, runs the gamut of Hispanic society from top to bottom.

Eva is conceived much like John Irving's Garp when her mother, a humble housekeeper, decides sex would be useful therapy for a moribund Indian gardener suffering from a bite by a snake with the sonorous name "sucurucú." The treatment is a bang-up success (shall we say); unlike Garp's father, the Indian goes his way with a smile, and nine months later Eva enters the world.

Eva's first years are spent at her mother's side in her place of work, the home of an English mad scientist, Professor Jones, whose main specialty is embalming the dead so artfully that they can be preserved as statuary by their loved ones, but who in his spare time also tries to cure cancer with mosquito bites and mental retardation with sharp blows to the patient's head. In these years, Eva bonds tightly to her mother, as Allende heroines are wont to do, in a love that again is often manifested in the telling of stories. Although Eva's mother, Consuelo, is normally, "una persona silenciosa, capaz de disimularse entre los muebles, de perderse en el dibujo de la alfombra," pushed by love for her young daughter, she offers the gift of stories:

. . . comenzaba a hablar del pasado o a narrar sus cuentos y el cuarto se llenaba de luz, desaparecían los muros para dar paso a increíbles paisajes, palacios albarrotados de objetos nunca vistos, países lejanos inventados por ella o sacados de la biblioteca del patrón . . . . Preservó intactas sus memorias de infancia en la misión de los curas, retenía las anécdotas oídas al pasar y lo aprendido en sus lecturas, elaboraba la sustancia de sus propios sueños y con esos materiales fabricó un mundo para mi.[1]

After her mother's death, Eva remains in the household for another year under the care of her godmother, a large *mulata* who also works in the house, and as an adopted granddaughter of the aging Professor Jones. When the professor dies, however, the household is broken up, so at the age of seven, Eva must go to work for an unmarried brother and sister. Retired workers, each is full of quirks—the woman bosses incessantly, while the man drinks, plays the horses, and seems a little too interested in caressing young Eva behind the potted palm. When Eva rebels at her mistress's bossiness and runs away temporarily, she makes the acquaintance of Huberto Naranjo, a street-wise urchin who instructs her in panhandling, shell games, and petty thievery as ways of survival. Eventually, Eva returns to the old couple's home for a time, where she remains "varios años" (67). There the cook, Elvira, becomes like a grandmother to her. When the *doña* refuses the godmother's demand for a raise, however, Eva is fired and begins a pilgrimage from one service to another. In one house she works for a sculptress who has discovered a marvelous "Materia Universal," and in another she toils for a minister who requires her to empty the contents of a bedpan he has installed in a felt bishop's chair (which she eventually does one last time on his head!).

After this she briefly reencounters Huberto Naranjo, who takes her to live with a kindly madam and her friend, the charming transvestite Melecio. The two do their best to educate the girl and protect her from the environment in which they move, but a police roundup forces Eva back onto the streets, where she is picked up by a harelipped Turkish merchant who takes her to his home in the jungle to care for his wife, and who eventually relieves Eva of her virginity. When the Turk's wife commits suicide, Eva is charged with murder and sees a rural jail from the inside, in finest picaresque style. The resulting scandal forces Eva back to the city, where she again meets the beautiful transvestite, Melecio, now going by the name of Mimí after hormone treatments and plastic surgery. With Mimí's help, Eva studies nights and works days in a factory that makes military uniforms, and in the meantime resumes a friendship and intermittant affair with Huberto Naranjo, now a guerrilla commando.

When the unwanted advances of an army colonel force Eva to leave the factory, she turns her hand to writing and converts her own story into a script for a television soap opera to star Mimí, who has become a well-known actress. Eva must live a dramatic conclusion before she can write it, and the freeing of some of Huberto's companions from a military prison uses all of Eva's skills, both literary and manual. The assault is successful; Eva tells the story of it in her television script and in this way confounds official censorship to let the truth be told publicly. In the end, Eva finds both her literary vocation and a more reliable love in the arms of Rolf Carlé, a German emigrant photojournalist, whose story has been told parallel to Eva's, heightening hers by suspense, serving as contrast, and also making interesting reading in its own right.

After a second novel that was disappointing to some, this third effort again tells an epic story that covers several generations and many social stations and returns to the lush narrative texture of *La casa de los espíritus*. In spite of insightful critical works by people like Juan Manuel Marcos ("Isabel viendo llover en Barataria"), showing profound differences between the Colombian and the Chilean, the first thing many reviewers felt compelled to comment on was again the García Márquez connection. For example, writes Spaniard Luis Alonso Girgado in *El Correo Cultural:*

> [Hay] elementos mágico-maravillosos al modo en que surgen en García Márquez, de cuya prosa es deudora en más de un aspecto la novelista chilena. Porque el desenfrenado vitalismo, el zarandeo del tiempo, la propensión a lo fantástico-legendario y aun milagroso, la capacidad para que lo imaginario se haga normal y lo real extraordinario, la instauración de la realidad como hipérbole y de lo inaceptable racionalmente como cotidiano, la pasión por rodear a cada personaje de su microhistoria particular que lo individualiza—constantes de la narrativa del autor de *Cien años de soledad*—es en *Eva Luna* observable. . . .[2]

In *La Vanguardia* (Spain), Roberto Saladrigas also insisted on the similarity:

> La obra . . . sobre todo evidenciaba las huellas de un modelo inimitable e imitado en exceso. La sombra poderosa de Gabriel García

Márquez oscurecía lo que podía aportar de original Isabel Allende. Confieso que uno de mis serios reparos al texto lo motivaba esa influencia.[3]

He further explains his objections:

En este caso el modelo soñado sigue siendo García Márquez. Un modelo extraordinario, pero me temo que inalcanzable. Por consiguiente, ¿no sería preferible que para bien o para mal Isabel Allende decidiera plantearse ser definitivamente ella misma, asumiendo todas las consecuencias de la propia identidad?[4]

What he doesn't explain, of course, is why magical realism or a magical brand of Latin American feminism cannot be Isabel Allende's true self, or true voice. He seems to feel that Nobel laureate García Márquez has a patent on anything magic, despite the whole long tradition of magically real fictional works that came before the Colombian. Moreover, García Márquez himself has insisted often that the magic nature of his works mirrors Latin American life. If this is true, how absurd for critics to place him on a pedestal as the *only* author now allowed such imitation!

Neither does Saladrigas explain why it is all right for Jorge Amado to have the lively ghost Vadinho, but not all right for Eva Luna to speak to her dead mother; why Flor may speak to African gods through the *candomblé,* but Eva's friends may not practice *santería*; why a Cortázar character may turn into a axolotl, but Eva may not see a mirage in the desert; why Arreola may describe a train that never arrives at its destination, but Allende may not contrive that a cottage be filled with rotting mangos as revenge. In fact, Saladrigas does not explain anything about his dismissal of Allende's right to speak of the marvelous, the strange, and the unusual, favorite literary topics through the ages.

Another review, this time closer to Allende's home, gives further insight into the continual repetition to this facile, one-note put-down of the author's work. Santiago reviewer Ignacio Valente writes in *El Mercurio* that Allende is currently "haciendo profesión expresa de realismo mágico," and that her language is "mas bien proclive a los derroches fantásticos de un García Márquez."[5] He adds:

Desde el comienzo se aprecia el dilema formal de *Eva Luna,* que fluctúa entre los hallazgos y energías de la major narrativa latinoamericana actual, por una parte, y por otra el relato taquillero

> vagamente garcíamarquista, que vende como pan caliente o como licor exótico en los mercados mudiales del libro.[6]

With these assertions, Valente unintentionally sheds new light on the question. Again, the equation seems to be in effect that South America + whimsy or magic = García Márquez, but he adds a new and more envious variation: (Latin American novel) × (big success in Europe) = García Márquez ripoff. In fact, it is quite easy to demonstrate that this is logically false. Since Valente does not specifically mention what any of Allende's supposed vague Garcíamarquian tendencies are, it is hard to refute them specifically, but it is perhaps equally enlightening to point out that if García Márquez is vaguely present, the ghosts of many other influences are haunting with force.

Tributes to great storytellers of all nationalities abound in this novel. For example, it seems to me that one could make a much better case for Allende's similarity to Brazilian Jorge Amado and his novels *Gabriela, cravo e canela* and *Dona Flor e seus dois maridos*. Like Gabriela, Eva enjoys the passionate embraces of her boss, an emigrant of Arab extraction, and like Flor, Eva has friends who practice *santería*, specifically, her *madrina*, who believes in "los santos católicos, en otros de origen africano y en varios más de su invención" (48). Allende adds with a puckish humor that is hers alone:

> En su cuarto había levantado un pequeño altar, donde se alineaban junto al agua bendita, los fetiches del vudú, la fotografía de su difunto padre y un busto que ella creía de San Cristóbal, pero después yo descubrí que era de Beethoven, aunque jamás la he sacado de su error, porque es el más milagroso de su altar. (48)

What is more, the constant references to the aromas of cinnamon and clove that cling to Rolf Carlé's cousins evoke the Amado title, *Gabriela, cravo e canela*. The description of Rolf's aunt preparing her "plato afrodisíaco" cannot fail to remind the initiate of one of the pages of erotic cookery in Amado's *Dona Flor*, to cite another example (86).

Other literary spirits can be glimpsed as well. Eva's prolific output as a scriptwriter of a television soap opera might contain a hint of tribute to Mario Vargas Llosa's *escribidor*, Pedro Camacho, and Allende's parallel narratives and story-within-a-story seem more reminiscent of *La tía Julia* than of *Cien años*.

But Latin American novelists do not have a monopoly on the

fanciful or the odd. On reading in *Eva Luna* of Elvira's escape from the flood in her coffin, it is hard not to remember Melville's *Moby Dick.* North American John Irving's spirit also seems to have been called up here. Besides the similarity between Eva's conception and that of Garp there is also the presence of the big lovable transsexual, best friend to both, and the embalmed puma Eva drags around is no odder than Sorrow—the stuffed dog in Irving's *Hotel New Hampshire.* Come to think of it, there was a stuffed dog in *La casa de los espíritus* as well, wasn't there? And if he was not named Sorrow, Barrabás often prefigured it quickly enough.

And while we are playing the game of looking for that elusive beast, influence, who is to say that Rolf's insistence that his seductive cousins smell like spices and his nephews smell like candles is not Allende's way of translating Benjy's incessant refrain in Faulkner's *The Sound and the Fury* that "Caddy smells like trees"? Except, to be sure, that Rolf is no idiot.

The continuation of the picaresque tradition in this novel, which I have already alluded to, is another element that seems much more important than the shadow of García Márquez. Writes José García Nieto:

> Esta novela picaresca, en el sentido más noble y clásico del género, esta narrada sin énfasis y evitando la caricatura. Es lo real lo que manda y define, lo que limita y sorprende.[7]

José A. Ponte Far goes into more depth:

> La novela nos recuerda las clásicas del género picaresco: relato en primera persona; un personaje (femenino en este caso) que, recorriendo y observando desde dentro los distintos ambientes de la escala social, vive situaciones extremas; que vive sin un programa para desarrollar su vida: siempre a merced de la fortuna, de lo que pueda depararle el siguiente amanecer.[8]

The venerable Spanish tradition of the *esperpento* also lifts its head here, but according to García Nieto, modified by the sense of balance Allende wants to achieve in the novel:

> Cuando alguna vez el esperpento asoma entre la aventura, la autora de la novela puede parecer que quiere equivocarnos, pero en seguida sujeta la rienda de su imaginación y nos queda sólo la noticia de la escena truculenta. . . .[9]

The point of all of this jest is, of course, that it is grossly unfair to Allende to go on reviewing her as if *Cien años de soledad* were the only book either she or her reviewers had ever read. Again, I must insist that it is now not the obligation of Allende and her scholars to go through life proving that she is *not* imitating García Márquez (though I repeat, Juan Manuel Marcos has done an eloquent job of just that), but rather the job of detractors to give hard evidence if they want to keep on making that tired claim.

More than an illegal parentage to García Márquez, I see in this novel evidence of broad readings of the works of the best storytellers both in Latin American and other countries, both in our decade and in many others.

Still, Allende herself is not unaware of the allegation, and with her typical good humor, in her latest novel she has Mimí foster Eva's literary ambitions after being fueled by a literary encounter:

> Desde que vio una cola de gente ante una librería esperando turno para que un bigotudo escritor colombiano en gira triunfal firmara sus libros, me colmaba de cuadernos, lápices y diccionarios. Ese es buen oficio, Eva, no tendrás que levantarte temprano. . . . (207)

But there is another author to whom Allende pays tribute in this novel, one more important than all the others mentioned, even the "bigotudo escritor colombiano," one who has much more effect on the themes and development of this book than anyone else. That author is Allende herself, who, far from repeating here, shows in this novel that she can give her recurring concerns a different fictional development through a completely different story.

There are many elements in *Eva Luna* that will sound familiar to the reader of *La casa de los espíritus*. At the heart of the story is an independent female deeply attached to her mother's spirit, a child who drags around a stuffed animal, and who later evokes her mother's spirit while she is unjustly in jail. There is also a house filled with mummies and occasional spirits, a charming eccentric who believes in tarot cards and astrology, a mention here and there of auras, the occasional attempt at clairvoyance, and a prophetic dream or two. But for all of this, *Eva Luna* is a new and fresh novel, and if some of her characters are similar, they are in new situations and settings. After all, Faulkner's Compsons resurfaced again and again, and no one ever seemed too surprised to see the themes of incest, degeneracy, or suicide recur in Yoknapatawpha County. Besides, as was the case in *De amor y de sombra*, in *Eva Luna* the strictly "magical" occurrences in this new novel are few. The beautiful transsexual Mimí nurses a host of superstitions, and Eva seems to find this endearing, but she does not take them particularly seriously. Eva also "speaks" to her dead mother from time to time, and occasionally "sees" her, but on the literal narrative plane there is nothing more magical about this than the persistence of memory. Once again, there is a deliberate attempt to undercut the superstitions through which some of the characters (and readers?) view the world. For example, the "alma en pena" that Elvira sees at the window turns out to be a friend of Huberto Naranja bearing a message:

> No se trataba de un ectoplasma trashumante, como se supo ese mismo día cuando el negro tocó el timbre y Elvira, espantada al verlo, cayó sentada al suelo. La había enviado el comandante Rogelio y rondaba la calle buscándome sin atreverse a preguntar por mí para no llamar la atención. (243)

Other more nearly "magical" events are downplayed, simply mentioned in passing, like the rain of fish (27) or the "manantial que lava pecados" (252). The "plato afrodisíaco" that Rolf's mother makes can be understood literally or figuratively, and the "Materia Universal" is as much a metaphor for the transformation of matter through art (here sculpture) as a literally "unnatural" phenomenon.

Does all of this add up to "magical feminism?" Once again, remembering the definition I forged for the term, I would have to say that it does. Again, it is a femino-centric novel, and the magic that does appear is within the context of trying to show honestly the trials that Eva Luna encounters, coupled with a sense of optimism with which she goes about trying to solve her problems without falling into prostitution or despair. "Eva Luna . . . es la esencia de la feminidad aceptada," Allende told Rosa María Piñol of *La Vanguardia*.[10] With all its strengths and weaknesses, the book represents a new brand of fiction—books that show women as they see themselves, not as men see them (whether as impossible ideals or perhaps negative stereotypes), and books that try to outline new options, and give women new ways of looking at themselves and their problems.

Once again, the real magic in this Isabel Allende novel comes in the form of human love, storytelling, and tale-telling as a manifestation of love. In this, her thematic concerns seem more in line with, say, Vargas Llosa's exploration of the how and why of the creation of fiction in his novel *La tía Julia y el escribidor* or in plays *Kathie y el Hipopótamo* and *La señorita de Tacna* than with anything from Gabriel García Márquez's canon.

There is a soft magic in Allende's language as well, as Royal Academician José García Nieto has noted:

> La materia verbal es siempre movediza. Cuenta, como sin detenerse, con un castellano muy rico, sin exceso de localismos en los que se podía caer habiendo entrado en el tipismo y las costumbres.[11]

In fact, he calls the novel "un paso definitivo en su carrera de novelista."[12] Still, there is no shortage of dissenting voices.

Juan Carlos Suñen replied acidly to this:

> Si hemos de creer lo que ha dicho hace poco José García Nieto en su crítica de esta mismo novela, que "Isabel Allende ha conseguido un paso definitivo en su carrera de novelista," y que así "se incorpora a la nómina brillante de escritores de *allá*," entonces hemos de creer también que tanto la una como los otros hacen lo mismo que alguien dijo una vez de los cangrejos, avanzan rápidamente hacia atrás.[13]

Allende, apparently unruffled at these or any other comments, replied serenely, "es una novela feliz, una obra que me ha producido placer escribir."[14] She continued, "así vomiten los crítricos, seguiré creando personajes que se amen tiernamente, no tengo miedo que me acusen de cursilería."[15]

This is an attitude that should gladden the hearts of Allende well-wishers, those who would allow the writer all the freedom she needs to continue to weave her magic spells as she sees fit. Now if Eva's *madrina* were to weave a spell on her creator, perhaps she would bless Allende with specifics like the long life of a Jorge Amado, the prolific output of a George Sand, the vigor of a Vargas Llosa, and maybe even high-toned reviews by Thomas Pynchon. On the other hand, in the real world, Isabel Allende's literary career seems to be advancing apace, hyperbolically even, with or without this supernatural help. In fact, if you put it in a novel, maybe no one would believe it.

12

CONCLUSION: THE INFLUENCE OF ISABEL ALLENDE ON GABRIEL GARCÍA MÁRQUEZ

> "It would just lend itself nicely to computerization," Dempsey continued. "All you'd have to do would be to put the texts on tape and you could get the computer to list every word, phrase, and syntactical construction that the two writers had in common. You could precisely quantify the influence of Shakespeare on T. S. Eliot."
>
> "But my thesis isn't about that," said Persse. "It's about the influence of T. S. Eliot on Shakespeare."
>
> "That sounds rather Irish, if I may say so," said Dempsey with a loud guffaw. His little eyes looked anxiously around for support.
>
> —David Lodge, *Small World*

There are those who will look at the title of this chapter and assume it is a joke or a desperate bid for attention, like the one made in the bar scene quoted above by lovesick Persse McGarrigle in an attempt to seduce a beautiful woman with his critical audacity. In fact, it is neither (exclusively, at least), and rather has a serious point to it. Throughout this study I have shown that although there is much that separates Isabel Allende from Gabriel García Márquez, and that although critics (notably Juan Manuel Marcos) have spoken eloquently about their individuality, the label "Garciamarquian" continues to follow Isabel Allende. In this conclusion I would like to suggest that it now makes as much or more sense to speak of Allende's influence on García Márquez.

Although suggestions like Persse McGarrigle's that Eliot influences Shakespeare sound comical at first, Eliot himself, in "Tradition and the Individual Talent," asserted much the same thing.[1] There he held that each new milestone in criticism and art invites or even demands that we reassess what went before, just as Picasso's studies of "Las meninas" force us to look at Velázquez with new eyes. Or, as Persse puts it:

> Well, what I try to show . . . is that we can't avoid reading Shakespeare through the lens of T. S. Eliot's poetry. I mean, who can read *Hamlet* today without thinking of "Prufrock"? Who can hear the speeches of Ferdinand in *The Tempest* without being reminded of "The Fire Sermon" section in *The Waste Land*?[2]

In the same way, one could assert that the publication of *La casa de los espíritus* is such a phenomenon in Latin American literature that no one will ever be able to read *Cien años de soledad* again without remembering Clara del Valle's asides about how repeated names cause confusion in the notebooks that record family life. Throughout this study I have shown examples like this of subtly ironic references to García Márquez in Allende that could indeed be said to influence future readings of Colombian.

But the notion of Allende's influence on García Márquez can be taken even further, if one chooses to speak of influences at all, and can be analyzed in García Márquez's use of magic with regard to love as compared to Allende's. Earlier I cited Juan M. Marcos, who claimed that Allende's "lucidez crítica respecto a la condición social de la mujer latinoamericana" was one of many "virtudes" that distinguished her from García Márquez.[3] In continuation, I would like to assert that García Márquez's latest novel shows an increased sensitivity to the social condition of the Latin American woman, and that in fact he may venture into the terrain of the magically feminist for a time. For those who claim that A's preceding B means that A influences B, this may again prove subversive. By showing how it is possible to claim that García Márquez did this in imitation of Isabel Allende due to simple chronology, I hope eventually to undermine the original claim of Allende's imitation of García Márquez and argue for taking both on their own terms.

Throughout this study, the term *magical feminism* has been suggested, evaluated, tried on for size, accepted in some cases, and rejected in others. In my application of the term, which I defined as, "magical realism used in a femino-centric novel, or to make an authentic observation about the behavior and condition of women in the sociohistoric conditions depicted in the novel," I went to great lengths to avoid divisive language that judges how "good" a feminist one woman is compared to another, and I also deliberately forged this definition from which male novelists would not be a priori excluded. It is my conclusion that García Márquez's most recent novel at the time of this writing, *El amor en los tiempos del cólera*, is a good example of magical feminism in many passages. I have spoken before of the monumental masochism of many of his earlier female characters—women who loved, yet guarded that love like a festering wound in their hearts until they could revenge it decades later, or women who found refuge in silence, endurance, or passivity. By contrast, the lover in this latest work who endures fifty-one years, nine months, and four days of separation is the male poet, Florentino Ariza, while the pragmatic character who forgets the youthful passion and goes on to make a practical marriage is the heroine, Fermina Daza. The magic of clairvoyance in the book is a trick that conceals Fermina's human changeability, and the delightfully exaggerated inability of Florentino to write even a commercial letter that does not speak of love also shows magic used to make insightful points about how men and women relate to each other. Moreover, the ending that García Márquez finds for his lovers, who reunite in old age and cruise on a South American "Love Boat" of infinite possibility, shows a compassion that the Colombian might well have learned from Isabel Allende.

Novelist Thomas Pynchon recognizes that the book marks a revolutionary change in the García Márquez canon:

> It is a daring step for any writer to decide to work in love's vernacular, to take it, with all its folly, imprecision, and lapses in taste, at all seriously—that is, as well worth those higher forms of play that we value in fiction. For García Márquez the step may also be revolutionary.[4]

He also recognizes the "magical" nature of seemingly "ordinary" events—in other words, that here "possible" or even "plausible" events may be considered "magical" when our heart tells us that they are nevertheless extremely unlikely:

> This novel is also revolutionary in daring to suggest that vows of love made under a presumption of immortality—youthful idiocy to some—may yet be honored, much later in life, when we ought to know better, in the face of the undeniable. . . . Through the ever-subversive medium of fiction, García Márquez shows us how it could all plausibly come about, even—wild hope—for somebody out here, outside a book, even as inevitably beaten at, bought and resold as we all must have become if only through years of simple residence in the injuring and corruptive world.[5]

Who is to say that the Colombian's decision to write so unashamedly about love was not motivated by Isabel Allende's fiction, or personal example? Who is to say that Allende did not ignite the Colombian's imagination with declarations like the following made to *El Periódico?*"

> Cualquier cosa sentimental, amorosa, o maternal es rechazada como cursilería por culpa de los valores impuestos por una cultura masculina, y yo, aunque vomite los críticos, seguiré por ese camino.[6]

Who is to say that García Márquez did not take up the gauntlet, respond to the challenge, and because of her influence, venture into the territory of magical feminism himself?

The question is, of course, impossible to answer, but for those obsessed with seeking influences, the objective datum remains that post-Allende, García Márquez has produced a novel that is much more "sentimental" (in a Flaubertian sense) than any previous, just as Allende produced magical realism after García Márquez. Ultimately, only a critic possessed of Clara del Valle's crystal ball could say for sure if one was under the other's spell at any given point. As a critic without the slightest trace of clairvoyance, I prefer instead to read *El amor en los tiempos del cólera* with gratitude that it *did* get written, whatever the influences and causes, and to anticipate the next nevel from Isabel Allende, happy that there is no earthly reason to choose between her work and that of García Márquez.

In conclusion, then, this study has examined the use of magic in Allende's fiction and found it to be specific to the events it describes. This is true especially in *La casa de los espíritus*, where I have shown the individual magical elements to have a direct relation to Chilean history of the time, and to Allende's particular story. All of this tends to negate the importance of the claim that she imitates García Márquez. In addition to this, I have found the term *magical feminism* to be applicable to much of her work. I think it could serve as a general description of *La casa de los espíritus*, and in *De amor y de sombra* it aptly describes the minor miracles performed by the unfortunate Evangelina Ranquileo. The strictly "magical" events in *Eva Luna* are few, but the sense of wonder, hyperbole, and the uncommon are strong enough to put the text into the "marvelous" category for me, just as the femino-centric descriptions of women finding new ways to live their lives and deal with their problems puts it into the feminist category, so that again, I find calling it "magically feminist" according to my definition both useful and apt.

I have demonstrated here how an author post–Isabel Allende

may be called magically feminist (García Márquez), but I think that much more value could come from the term if other scholars would like to evaluate its usefulness in terms of other writers, many of whom are previous or contemporary to Allende. I would welcome further discussion on the subject. New subdivisions might be coined, such as "hembrismo mágico," which would refer to a type of magical realism in which a reverse-machismo was used, often with the kind of absurd results that José Luis Coll demonstrates so succinctly in his *Diccionario de Coll*, by defining *Ano* as, "El masculino de Ana."[7] Such a term, however, would also invite a study on "machismo mágico," or magical realism in which the marvelous or magic was used to make sexist points. One suspects that this could be a monumental study, beginning with *Los pasos perdidos* and probably continuing through most of the accepted canon of magically real fiction.

For the moment, this discussion of narrative magic in the fiction of Isabel Allende must close, but even the closure is a kind of magical illusion, perhaps only temporary—the appearance of her next book may reopen the discussion of all these points and others again, or it may turn much of what I have said on its ear. Until then, I cannot help thinking of the lament that Erica Jong's Isadora makes about the lack of role models in literature for her:

> Where were the women who were *really* free? . . . We looked to our uncertain heroines for help, and lo and behold—Simone de Beauvoir never makes a move without wondering *what would Sartre think*? And Lillian Hellman wants to be as much of a man as Dashiell Hammett so he'll love her like he loves himself. And Doris Lessing's Anna Wulf can't come unless she's in love, which is seldom. And the rest—the women writers, the women painters—most of them were shy, shrinking, schizoid. Timid in their lives and brave only in their art. Emily Dickinson, the Brontës, Virginia Woolf, Carson McCullers . . . Flannery O'Connor raising peacocks and living with her mother. Sylvia Plath sticking her head into an oven of myth. Georgia O'Keeffe alone in the desert, apparently a survivor. What a group! Severe, suicidal, strange. Where was the female Chaucer? One lusty lady who had juice and joy and love and talent too?[8]

In 1973, this last was a wistful rhetorical question, but in 1988 there is at least one possible answer. There is Isabel Allende.

APPENDIX: *CIVILICE A SU TROGLODITA*

An early work of Isabel Allende that deserves mention is her comic book, *Civilice a su troglodita*, composed of brief pieces that first appeared in the magazine *Paula*. That in 1974 Allende was making her way as a writer, publishing, and earning her own living would be heralded by many as proof of her feminism. However, I did not want to include a discussion of the work in the text, because the level of the dialectics, intended for an old-fashioned "ladies' magazine" audience, is not representative of the Isabel Allende who wrote the three novels that are the subject of this study. These pieces, accompanied by cartoons, reflect the old-fashioned notion that a wife's role is to deviously make her man over into a useful domestic beast after she has tricked him into captivity. For example, the first installment of the book is full of advice on how to "hacerse la tonta":

> Para que el tome confianza, usted debe parecer estúpida de nacimiento y así le da a él la oportunidad de sentirse superior, lo cual no es fácil. . . . Hay que ponerse a gritar cuando ve una abeja, desmayarse si queda atrapada en un ascensor, ponerse histérica con los incendios, los temblores y las aranas. Finja que no entiende los chistes, parezca inútil, gastadora, chismosa. Eso es lo que los hombres entienden por "feminidad" y es completamente inútil tratar de hacerles cambiar de opinión.[1]

Of course, some might interpret this humor as simply poking fun at a status quo that needed to be changed. In my opinion, however, the book so relentlessly argued male stupidity and baseness that I found it an example of what I would call "humor hembrista," in other words, humor derived from jokingly arguing the inferiority of men. In a much subtler way, some parts of *La casa de los espíritus* may be seen as arguing another kind of male inferiority—spiritual or magical, rather than intellectual—but within the context of the novel there is much that tempers that view. In *Civilice a su troglodita*, by contrast, the early writings unaccompanied by contextualization do not do justice to Allende's development at present, and to quote from them extensively would be misleading and unfair. For this reason I have chosen to simply make brief reference to the book in this appendix.

NOTES

CHAPTER 1. INTRODUCTION

1. *Diccionario Enciclopédico Salvat Universal*, 1973 ed., s.v. "realismo."
2. "Realism," in C. Hugh Holman, *A Handbook to Literature* (New York: Odyssey Press, 1972).
3. Ibid.
4. *Webster's Third New International Dictionary*, 1986 ed., s.v. "realism."
5. George Eliot, *Adam Bede* (New York: Grosset & Dunlap), 165–66.
6. Holman, "Realism."
7. José Donoso, *Historia personal del "Boom"* (Barcelona: Anagrama, 1972), 56–57.
8. *Diccionario Enciclopédico Espasa*, 1978 ed., s.v. "magia."
9. *Oxford English Dictionary*, 1971 ed., s.v. "magic."
10. *Diccionario Enciclopédico Salvat Universal*, 1973 ed., s.v. "magia."
11. *Webster's Third New International Dictionary*, 1986 ed., s.v. "magic."
12. *American Heritage Dictionary*, 1976 ed., s.v. "magic."
13. Ibid., s.v. "supernatural."
14. Henry Cornelius Agrippa von Nettesheim, *The Philosophy of Natural Magic* (1518; reprint, Secaucus, N.J.: University Books of Seacaucus, 1974), 39.
15. Sir James George Frazer, *The Golden Bough* (1890; reprint, New York: Macmillan, 1945), 11.
16. This certainty is heightened by the fact that I have seen Bryant Gumbel perform the feat at eight in the morning on the "Today Show," and that friends tell me it has to do with laws of physics relating to heat and its transfer through metal, combined with pressure.
17. Carlos Fuentes, *La nueva novela hispanoamericana* (Mexico: J. Mortiz, 1969), 9.
18. Ibid., 10.
19. Enrique Anderson Imbert in *Literatura Hispanoamericana* (New York: Holt, Rinehart and Winston, 1970), 517.
20. Alejo Carpentier, *El reino de este mundo* (Caracas: Festival del Libro Popular Venezolano, 1954), 7.
21. Ibid., 8.
22. Ibid., 9–10.
23. Ibid., 11.
24. Rodolfo Usigli, "Realismo moderno y realismo mágico," in *Itinerario del autor* (México: Fondo de Cultura Económica, 1940), 104.
25. Angel Flores, "Magical Realism in Spanish American Fiction," *Hispania* (May 1955): 192.
26. Ibid., 190–91.
27. Juan Barroso, *"Realismo mágico" y "lo real maravilloso"* (Miami: Ediciones Universal, 1977), 26.
28. Amaryll Beatrice Chanady, *Magical Realism and the Fantastic: Resolved vs. Unresolved Antimony* (New York: Garland Press, 1985), 161.

29. Ibid., 161.
30. Ibid., 163
31. Barroso, *Realismo mágico*, 165.
32. David Young and Keith Hagarman, *Magical Realist Fiction: A Reader* (New York: Longman, 1984), 1–2.
33. Ibid., 3.
34. Ibid., 7.
35. Angel Valbuena Briones, "Una cala en el realismo mágico," *Cuadernos Americanos* 166 (1969): 233–41.
36. Seymour Menton, *The Spanish American Short Story: A Critical Anthology*, (Berkeley and Los Angeles: University of California Press, 1980), 256.
37. Teresinha (Teresinka) Pereira, *El realismo mágico y otras herencias de Julio Cortázar* (Coimbra, Portugal and Bloomington, Indiana: Nova Era and Backstage Books, 1976), 7.
38. Ibid., 28.
39. Alfonso Grosso, *Los españoles y el "Boom"*, ed. Fernando Tola de Habich (Caracas: Tiempo Nuevo, 1971), 191.
40. Ibid., 189.
41. Chanady, *Magical Realism*, 160.
42. Valbuena Briones, "Una cala," 233.
43. *American Heritage Dictionary*, 1976 ed., s.v. "feminism."
44. Virginia Woolf, "A Room of One's Own," in *Feminism: The Essential Historical Writing*: ed. Miriam Schneir (New York: Vintage Books, 1972), 346.
45. Simone de Beauvoir, *The Second Sex*, trans. and ed. H. M. Parshley, (New York: Vintage Books, 1974), 814.
46. Catharine R. Stimpson, "Introduction," in *Feminist Issues in Literary Scholarship*, ed. Shari Benstock (Bloomington and Indianapolis: Indiana University Press, 1987), 2.
47. She expressed this theory to me in person on a visit to Duke University in the fall of 1986, insisting that her "Quiela" was an admirable example of love that did not give up and of a woman who has not been hardened and "masculinized."
48. Ellen Morgan, "*Humanbecoming: Forms and Focus in the Neo-Feminist Novel*," in *Feminist Criticism: Essays on Theory, Poetry, and Prose*, ed. Cheryl L. Brown and Karen Olson (Metuchen, N.J., and London: Scarecrow Press, 1978), 145.
49. Mario A. Rojas, "*La casa de los espíritus* de Isabel Allende: un caleidoscopio de espejos desordenados," *Revista Iberoamericana*, July–December 1985, 919.
50. Juan Manuel Marcos, "Isabel viendo llover en Barataria," *Revista de Estudios Hispánicos* 19, no. 2 (May 1985): 132.
51. Paul West, "*The House of the Spirits*," *Nation*, 20 July 1985, 52.
52. Marion Glastonbury, "Isabel Allende: *The House of the Spirits*," *The New Statesman*, 5 July 1985, 35.
53. D. A. N. Jones, "Magical Realism," *London Review of Books*, 1 August 1985, 26.
54. Jorge Edwards, "Dos escritores chilenos hablan," *El Mercurio*, 3–9 May 1986, 6.
55. José Donoso, "Dos escritores chilenos hablan," *El Mercurio* 3–9 May 1986, 7.
56. Javier Goñi, "Un noveciento chileno," *Informaciones*, 13 January 1985, 22.
57. Ibid.

58. Ibid.
59. Luis Suñén, "Una excelente novela chilena," *El País* (Madrid), 23 January 1983, "Libros," 3.
60. Juan José Armas Marcelo, "*La casa de los espíritus:* verso de mujer," *Diario 16*, 30 January 1983, "Disidencias," iii.
61. "Isabel Allende y *La casa de los espíritus*," *Comercio-Gijón*, 25 December 1982, sección "Letra Viva," 13.
62. Maruja Torres, "Isabel Allende recoge en su primera novela la tradición oral de su familia," *El País*, 24 November 1982, 19.
63. Juby Bustamante, "Isabel Allende: la gran sorprsa literaria del año," *Diario 16*, 28 November 1982, 22.
64. Rolando Camozzi, "*De amor y de sombra*," *ABC Literario* (Madrid), 19 January 1985, 16.
65. Helen Zubar and Swantije Strieder, "Ja, diese Wochen waren fürchterlich," *Der Spiegel*, no. 45 (1986): 182.
66. Marcos, "Isabel viendo llover en Barataria," 131.
67. Ibid., 133.

CHAPTER 2. CLARA/CLARIVIDENTE

1. *Diccionario Enciclopédico Salvat Universal*, 1973., s.v. "clarividencia".
2. *Diccionario Enciclopédico Espasa*, 1978 ed., s.v. "clarividencia."
3. *Grand Larousse Encyclopédique*, 1960 ed., s.v. "clairvoyance."
4. Ibid.
5. *Oxford English Dictionary*, 1970 ed., s.v. "clairvoyance."
6. *American Heritage Dictionary*, 1976 ed., s.v. "clairvoyance."
7. Isabel Allende, *La casa de los espíritus*, (Barcelona: Plaza y Janés 1982), 15. Subsequent quotations from this work are cited parenthetically within the text.
8. J. E. Zimmerman, "Cassandra," *A Dictionary of Classical Mythology* (New York: Harper and Row, 1964).
9. Marcos, "Isabel viendo," 132.
10. Ibid., 133.
11. Rojas, "*La casa de los espíritus*," 919.
12. Ibid.
13. Marcelo Intili, "Una historia de amor sobre el fondo trágico de Latinoamérica," *La Prensa* (Buenos Aires) 5 June 1985, 5.
14. "Isabel Allende recoge," 19.
15. Vera Jarach, "Recupera su Chile contándolo," *El Mundo* (San Juan), 5 March 1985, Sección Panorama, 1.
16. Zuber and Streider, "Ja, diese Wochen waren fürchterlich," 182.
17. William K. Wimsatt and Monroe C. Beardsley, "The Intentional Fallacy," in *Essays Modern Literary Criticism*, ed. Roy B. West (New York: Holt, Rinehart and Winston, 1965).

CHAPTER 3. VISIONS AND REVISIONS

1. West, "*The House of the Spirits*," 52–53.
2. Patricia Blake, "Isabel Allende and *The House of the Spirits*," *Time*, 20 May 1985, 79.

3. Christopher Lehmann-Haupt, "*The House of the Spirits*," *New York Times*, 24 July 1985, C-29.
4. Richard Eder, "*The House of the Spirits*," *Los Angeles Times*, 16 June 1985, "The Book Review," 3.
5. Claudia Rosetti, "Love and Revolution in the House of Trueba," *Wall Street Journal*, 19 June 1985, 35.
6. Jones, "Magical Realism," 26.
7. Zuber and Strieder, "Ja, diese Wochen waren fürchterlich," 182.
8. Víctor Claudín, "De Isabel Allende a Antoni Tapies," *Liberación* (Spain), 25 November 1984, 22.
9. Joe Kennedy, "From the Heart: Writer Allende Taps Experiences in Latin America," *Roanoke Times and World News*, 13 March 1986, C-3.

CHAPTER 5. CALLING SHAPES AND BECKONING SHADOWS: INVOKING THE SPIRITS

1. Blake, "Isabel Allende," 79.
2. *American Heritage Dictionary*, s.v. "spirit."
3. Jarach, "Recupera su Chile contándolo," 1.
4. Joan Jara, *An Unfinished Song: The Life of Víctor Jara* (New York: Ticknor & Fields, 1984), 98.
5. Vicente Chávez Lira, *Guerrilleros de cafe: o por qué no hubo guerra civil en Chile* (Santiago de Chile: Nueva Prensa Latinoamericana, 1974), 333–34.
6. Simón Bolívar, quoted in Chávez Lira, *Guerrilleros de cafe*, 333.

CHAPTER 6. THE LEGEND OF "EL CANTANTE"

1. Jarach, "Recupera su Chile contándolo," 1.
2. Michael Moody, "Entrevista con Isabel Allende," *Discurso Literario*. 4, no. 1 (1987): 44.
3. Samuel Chavkin, *Storm Over Chile* (Westport, Conn.: Lawrence Hill, 1985), 213.
4. Ibid., 217.
5. Joan Jara, *Unfinished Song*, 243.
6. Ibid., 249.
7. Ibid., 244.
8. Galvarino Plaza, *Víctor Jara* (Madrid: Ediciones Júcar, 1976), 38.
9. Ibid., 91–92.
10. Joan Jara, *Unfinished Song*, 213–14.
11. Ibid., 235.
12. Camilo Taufic, *Chile en la hoguera: crónica de la opresión militar* (Buenos Aires: Corregidor, 1974), 121–22.
13. Miguel Calabazas, quoted by José Jorge Letría, *O canto-arma de Victor Jara* (Lisbon: Documentos, n.d.), 94–95.
14. For example, Joyce Horman repeated a version of this myth to me at the University of North Carolina at Chapel Hill, where she had come to present the film, *Missing*, in the fall of 1986.
15. T. S. Eliot, "Hamlet and His Problems," *Selected Essays 1917–1932*, (New York: Harcourt Brace, 1932).

16. Joyce Horman, personal conversation, fall, 1986.
17. Plaza, *Victor Jara*, 112.
18. Joan Jara, *Unfinished Song*, 209.

CHAPTER 7. THE GIRL WITH GREEN HAIR

1. Jarach, "Recupera su Chile contándolo," 1.
2. David V. Tansley, *The Raiment of Light: A Study of the Human Aura*, (London: Routledge and Kegan Paul, 1984), 7–8.
3. Ibid., 7.
4. Ibid.
5. Ibid., 43–44.
6. Ibid., 105.
7. Ibid., 103.
8. Ibid., 95.
9. Ibid.
10. *Funk & Wagnalls Standard Dictionary*, 1977 ed., s.v. "white."
11. *Diccionario Enciclopédico Salvat Universal*, 1969 ed., s.v. "blanco."
12. *Funk & Wagnalls*, 1977 ed., s.v. "white."
13. Tansley, *Raiment*, 106.
14. *Salvat*, 1969 ed., s.v. "blanco."
15. Jones, "Magical Realism," 26.
16. *Salvat*, 1969 ed., s.v. "albo."
17. *Salvat*, 1969 ed., s.v. "alba."
18. Holman, *A Handbook to Literature*, 201.
19. Tansley, *Raiment*, 107.
20. Jarach, "Recupera su Chile contándolo," 1.
21. Tansley, *Raiment*, 104.

CHAPTER 8. THE INCREDIBLE SHRINKING MAN

1. Sigmund Freud, *The Problem of Anxiety* (New York: W. W. Norton, 1936), 117.
2. Ibid.
3. Ibid., 119.
4. Gabriel García Márquez, *Cien años de soledad* (Madrid: Espasa-Calpe, 1982), 315.
5. Ibid., 316.
6. It would be pointless to abuse the reader's patience with a lot of irrelevant scientific support, but for example, says M.D. Douglas B. Hart, "It is a popular myth that some of the tissues continue to grow after death, but this has been shown not to be true" (interview).
7. In the same spirit, says mortician Carl Berg:

> On death, the muscles contract, and then later when *rigor mortis* passes off, gasses are produced in the tissues, and the body will bloat, but not get taller. Most people measure the height of a person by standing next to him. In my experience, it is uncommon for anyone to prop a dead body up and stand next to it. Maybe when a body is lying down on a bed or in a coffin it appears longer to some people.

8. William Shakespeare, *Julius Caesar*, act 5, scene 3, line 944.

CHAPTER 9. *DE AMOR Y DE SOMBRA*: MAGIC ABJURED?

1. Miguel Angel Candelas Colodrón, "Isabel Allende: *De amor y de sombra*," *La Voz de Galicia* (Spain), 24 January 1985, 24.
2. J. M. G., "Isabel Allende tras el hachazo y para que no lo borre el viento," *Diario de Granada* (Spain), 7 December 1984, 19.
3. Ibid.
4. "Ja diese Wochen waren fürchterlich," 182.
5. Ibid.
6. Moody, "Entrevista," 46.
7. Isabel Allende, *De amor y sombra* (Barcelona: Plaza y Janés, 1984). Subsequent quotations from this work are cited parenthetically in the text.
8. Zuber and Strieder, "Ja diese Wochen waren fürchtelich," 182.
9. Moody, "Entrevista," 43.
10. Ibid.
11. Ibid., 45.
12. J. M. G., "Isabel Allende," 19.
13. Moody, "Entrevista," 44.
14. Ibid., 43.
15. Manuel Puig, *El beso de la mujer araña* (Barcelona: Seix Barral, 1976), 285.
16. Intili, "Una historia de amor," 5.
17. William Faulkner, *The Sound and the Fury* (New York: Random House, 1929–56).
18. "Casi una crónica política," *La Nueva España* (Spain), 20 January 1985, 23.
19. *"De Amor y de sombra," El Europeo,* 31 January 1985, 14.
20. J. L. Martín Nogales, "Manifiesto contra la represión política," *Diario de Navarra* (Spain), 9 January 1985, 54.
21. Edward Estlin Cummings, "Pity this Busy Monster Man Unkind Not," *Complete Poems* (New York: Harcourt, Brace, Jovanovich, 1972).
22. Perhaps this is an allusion to Valle-Inclán's actress wife, Josefina Blanco.
23. Gloria Bautista, *"De amor y de sombra," Discurso Literario* 5, no. 1 (1987): 214.
24. Juan Manuel Marcos, "El género popular como meta-estructura textual del post-boom latinoamericano," *Monographic Review/Revista Monográfica* 5, no. 1–2, (Spring 1988): 273.
25. Ibid.
26. Ibid.
27. J. M. G., "Isabel Allende," 19.

CHAPTER 10. THE ROLE OF MAGIC IN *LA GORDA DE PORCELANA*

1. Isabel Allende, *La gorda de porcelana* (Madrid: Alfaguara, 1983), 3. Subsequent quotations from this work are cited parenthetically within the text.

CHAPTER 11. *EVA LUNA*

1. Isabel Allende, *Eva Luna* (Barcelona: Plaza y Janés, 1987), 25. Subsequent quotations from this work are cited parenthetically within the text.

2. Luis Alonso Girgado, "Isabel Allende: La cuentera y sus andanzas," *El Correo Cultural* (Santiago de Compostela), 8 November 1987, 29.
3. Roberto Saladrigas, "*Eva Luna* desde Isabel Allende," *La Vanguardia* (Barcelona), 8 October 1987, 49.
4. Ibid.
5. Ignacio Valente, "*Eva Luna:* entre la calidad y el éxito," *El Mercurio* (Santiago de Chile), 25 October 1987, 6.
6. Ibid.
7. Jose García Nieto, "*Eva Luna,*" *ABC Literario* (Madrid), 26 September 1987, 26.
8. José A. Ponte Far, "La brillantez narrativa de una prosa épica," *La Voz de Galicia* (Spain), 12 November 1986, 26.
9. García Nieto, "*Eva Luna,*" 26.
10. Rosa María Piñol, "*Eva Luna* es la feminidad aceptada, dice Isabel Allende," *La Vanguardia* (Barcelona), 20 November 1987, 20.
11. García Nieto, "*Eva Luna,*" 26.
12. Ibid.
13. Juan Carlos Suñen, "La progresión del cangrejo," *El País* (Madrid), 8 October 1987, 19.
14. Jacinto Antón, "Isabel Allende: lo primero no es hacer literatura, sino tocar el corazón de la gente," *El País* (Madrid), 20 November 1987, 45.
15. Ibid.

CHAPTER 12. CONCLUSION: THE INFLUENCE OF ISABEL ALLENDE ON GABRIEL GARCÍA MÁRQUEZ

1. Thomas Stearns Eliot, "Hamlet and His Problems," in *Selected Essays 1917–1932* (New York: Harcourt Brace), 1932.
2. David Lodge, *Small World* (New York: Warner Books, 1984), 60.
3. Marcos, "Isabel," 133.
4. Thomas Pynchon, "The Heart's Eternal Vow," *New York Times Book Review,* 10 April 1988, 1.
5. Ibid., 47.
6. "Isabel Allende presenta en sociedad otra novela mágica," *El Periódico* (Madrid), 2 November 1987, 20.
7. Jose Luis Coll, *El diccionario de Coll* (Barcelona: Planeta, 1975), s.v. "Ano."
8. Erica Jong, *Fear of Flying* (New York: Holt, Rinehart & Winston, 1973), 100–101.

APPENDIX: *CIVILICE A SU TROGLODITA*

1. Isabel Allende, *Civilice a su troglodita* (Caracas?: Editorial Lord Cochrane, 1974), 10–11.

SELECT BIBLIOGRAPHY

Agosín, Marjorie. "Review of *La casa de los espíritus.*" *Revista Interamericana de Bibliografía* 35 (1985): 448–58.

Agrippa von Nettesheim, Henry Cornelius. *The Philosophy of Natural Magic.* 1518. Reprint. Secaucus, N.J.: University Books of Seacaucus, 1974.

Allende, Isabel. *La casa de los espíritus.* Barcelona: Plaza y Janés, 1982.

———. *Civilice a su troglodita.* (Caracas?: Editorial Lord Cochrane, 1974.

———. *De amor y de sombra.* Barcelona: Plaza y Janés, 1984.

———. *Eva Luna.* Barcelona: Plaza y Janés, 1987.

———. *La gorda de porcelana.* Madrid: Alfaguara, 1983.

Amado, Jorge. *Dona Flor e seus dois maridos.* Sao Paulo: Martins, 1969.

Anderson Imbert, Enrique. "El leve Pedro." In *Literatura Hispanoamericana.* New York: Holt, Rinehart and Winston, 1970.

Antón, Jacinto. "Isabel Allende: lo primero no es hacer literatura, sino tocar el corazón de la gente.[11] *El País* (Madrid), 20 November 1987, 45.

Armas Marcelo, J. J. "*La casa de los espíritus:* verso de mujer." *Diario 16,* 30 January 1983, "Disidencias," iii.

Arreola, Juan José. "El guardagujas." In *Cuentos.* La Habana: Casa de las Américas, 1969.

Asturias, Miguel Angel. *El Señor Presidente.* Buenos Aires: Losada, 1980.

Badosa, Enrique. "Isabel Allende: toda una historia mágica de Chile." *El Noticiero Universal,* 26 November 1982, Sección Cultura, 1.

Barroso, Juan. *"Realismo mágico" y "lo real maravilloso."* Miami: Ediciones Universal, 1977.

Bautista, Gloria. Review of *De amor y de sombra. Discurso Literario* 5, no. 1 (1987): 211–15.

Berg, Carl. Personal interview, 14 February 1987.

Beauvoir, Simone de. *The Second Sex.* Translated and edited by H. M. Parshley. New York: Vintage Books, 1974.

Blake, Patricia. "Isabel Allende and *The House of the Spirits.*" *Time,* 20 May 1985, 79.

"Books." *Ms.,* June 1985, 62.

Borges, Jorge Luis. *Historia universal de la infamia.* Buenos Aires: Tor, 1935.

———. "El milagro secreto." In *Cinco maestros.* Edited by Alexander Coleman New York: Harcourt Brace Jovanovich, 1969.

Boschetto, Sandra. "La narración de una historia escondida: escritura y dialéctica feminina-masculina en *La casa de los espíritus* de Isabel Allende." Session on *La casa de los espíritus.* CHISPA Convention. New Orleans, 26 February 1986.

Bustamante, Juby. "Isabel Allende: la gran sorpresa literaria del año." *Diario 16*, 28 November 1982, 22.

Calabazas, Miguel, quoted by José Jorge Letría. *O canto-arma de Víctor Jara*. Lisbon: Documentos, n.d.

Camozzi, Rolando. "*De Amor y de sombra*." *ABC Literario* (Madrid), 19 January 1985, 16.

Candelas Colodrón, Miguel Angel. "Isabel Allende: *De amor y de sombra*." *La Voz de Galicia* (Spain), 24 January 1985, 24.

Carpentier, Alejo. *Los pasos perdidos*. La Habana: Tercer Festival del Libro Cubano, 1961.

———. *El reino de este mundo*. Caracas: Festival del Libro Popular Venezolano, 1954.

"Casi una crónica política." *La Nueva España* (Spain), 20 January 1985, 23.

Cecilia. *Fui*. Madrid: Discos CBS, S.A., n.d.

Chanady, Amaryll Beatrice. *Magical Realism and the Fantastic: Resolved vs. Unresolved Antimony*. New York: Garland Press, 1985.

Chávez Lira, Vicente. *Guerrilleros de cafe: o por qué no hubo guerra civil en Chile*. Santiago de Chile: Nueva Prensa Latinoamericana, 1974.

Chavkin, Samuel. *Storm Over Chile*. Westport, Conn.: Lawrence Hill, 1985.

Christie, Agatha. "The Mystery of the Bagdad Chest." In *The Regatta Mystery*. New York: Dell, 1973.

Claudín, Víctor. "De Isabel Allende a Antoni Tapies." *Liberación* (Spain), 25 November 1984, 22.

Coll, José Luis. *El diccionario de Coll*. Barcelona: Planeta, 1975.

Cortázar, Julio. "La autopista del sur," "Señorita Cora," and "Todos los fuegos el fuego." In *Todos los fuegos el fuego*. Buenos Aires: Sudamericana, 1966.

———. "Axolotl," and "Casa tomada." In *Relatos*. Buenos Aires: Sudamericana, 1970.

Cummings, Edward Estlin. "Pity this Busy Monster Man Unkind Not." In *Complete Poems*. New York: Harcourt Brace Jovanovich, 1972.

"*De amor y de sombra*." *Dunia* (Spain), 25 June 1985, Sección Guía en la Jungla del Ocio y la Cultura, 27.

"*De amor y de sombra*." *El Europeo* (Spain), 31 January 1985, 14.

Delacre Capestany, Cecilia. "La experiencia Latinoamericana vista por la mujer." *Revista "Américas,"* September/October 1985, 58.

Donoso, José. *Casa de campo*. Barcelona: Seix Barral, 1978.

———. *Coronación*. Santiago de Chile: Zig-Zag, 1966.

———. *Historia personal del "Boom."* Barcelona: Anagrama, 1972.

———. *El jardín de al lado*. Barcelona: Seix Barral, 1981.

———. *El lugar sin límites*. México: J. Mortiz, 1966.

———. *La misteriosa desaparición de la marquesita de Loria*. Barcelona: Seix Barral, 1980.

———. *El obsceno pájaro de la noche*. Barcelona: Seix Barral, 1970.

———. "Dos escritores chilenos hablan." *El Mercurio*, 3–9 May 1986, 6.

———. "Paseo" and "Santelices." In *Cinco maestros*. Edited by Alexander Coleman New York: Harcourt Brace Jovanovich, 1969.

Eder, Richard. "*The House of the Spirits.*" *The Los Angeles Times,* 16 June 1985, "The Book Review," 3.

Edwards, Jorge. "Dos escritores chilenos hablan." *El Mercurio,* 3–9 May 1986, 7.

"Eres alta y delgada." In *Canciones populares.* Salamanca: Universidad de Salamanca, 1982.

Eliot, George. *Adam Bede.* New York: Grosset & Dunlap, 1950.

Eliot, Thomas Stearns. "Hamlet and His Problems." In *Selected Essays 1971–1932.* New York: Harcourt Brace, 1932.

———. *Murder in the Cathedral.* London: Faber and Faber, 1964.

Faulkner, William. *The Sound and the Fury.* 1929. Reprint. New York: Random House, 1956.

Flores, Angel. "Magical Realism in Spanish American Fiction." *Hispania,* May 1955, 187–92.

Frazer, Sir James George. *The Golden Bough.* 1890. Reprint. New York: Macmillan, 1945.

Freud, Sigmund. *The Problem of Anxiety.* New York: W. W. Norton, 1936.

Fuentes, Carlos. *Aura.* México: Era, 1966.

———. *La nueva novela hispanoamericana.* México: J. Mortiz, 1969.

García Márquez, Gabriel. "El ahogado más hermoso del mundo." In *La hojarasca y otros cuentos.* Buenos Aires: Sudamericana, 1969.

———. *Cien años de soledad.* Madrid: Espasa-Calpe, 1982.

———. *El coronel no tiene quien le escriba.* México: Era, 1969.

———. *El otoño del patriarca.* Barcelona: Plaza y Janés, 1975.

Girgado, Luis Alonso. "Isabel Allende: La cuentera y sus andanzas." *El Correo Cultural* (Santiago de Compostela) 8 November 1987, 29.

Glastonbury, Marion. "Isabel Allende: *The House of the Spirits.*" *The New Statesman,* 5 July 1985, 35.

Goñi, Javier. "Un noveciento chileno." *Informaciones,* 13 January 1985, 22.

Grosso, Alfonso. *Los españoles y el "Boom."* Edited by Fernando Tola de Habich. Caracas: Tiempo Nuevo, 1971.

Hart, Douglas, M.D. Personal interview, 14 February 1987.

Holman, C. Hugh. *A Handbook to Literature.* New York: Odyssey Press, 1972.

Intili, Marcelo. "Una historia de amor sobre el fondo trágico de Latinoamérica." *La Prensa* (Buenos Aires), 5 June 1985, 5.

"Isabel Allende: Lo primero no es hacer literatura, sino tocar el corazón de la gente." *El País* (Madrid), 20 November 1987, 45.

"Isabel Allende: 'Me siento influída por García Márquez, el padre del realismo mágico.' " *ABC* (Spain), 23 November 1982, cultura y sociedad, 31.

"Isabel Allende presenta en sociedad otra novela mágica." *El Periódico* (Spain), 2 November 1987; 20.

"Isabel Allende recoge en su primera novela la tradición oral de su familia." *El País* (Madrid), 24 November 1982, 19.

"Isabel Allende y *La casa de los espíritus.*" *Comercio-Gijón* (Spain), 25 December 1982, sección "Letra Viva," 13.

J. M. G. (only initials given)"Isabel Allende tras el hachazo y para que no lo borre el viento." *Diario de Granada* (Spain) 7 December 1984. 19.

"Ja, diese Wochen waren fürchterlich." *Der Spiegel* no. 45 (1986): 182–90.

Jara, Joan. *An Unfinished Song: The Life of Víctor Jara*. New York: Ticknor & Fields, 1984.

Jara, Víctor. "Te recuerdo Amanda." *Gracias a la vida*. Recorded by Joan Báez. Columbia Records, 1973.

Jarach, Vera. "Recupera su Chile contándolo." *El Mundo* (San Juan, Puerto Rico), 5 March 1985, Sección Panorama, 1.

Jones, D. A. N. "Magical Realism." *London Review of Books*, 1 August 1985, 26.

Jong, Erica. *Fear of Flying*. New York: Holt, Rinehart & Winston, 1973.

Kennedy, Joe. "From the Heart: Writer Allende Taps Experiences in Latin America." *Roanoke Times & World-News*, 13 March 1986, C-1–C-3.

Lehmann-Haupt, Christopher. "*The House of the Spirits*." *New York Times*, 24 July 1985, C-29.

Lodge, David. *Small World*. New York: Warner Books, 1984.

Losey, Joseph. *The Boy with Green Hair*. RKO, 1948.

Marcos, Juan Manuel. "El género popular como meta-estructura textual del post-boom latinoamericano." *Monographic Review/Revista Monográfica* 5, no. 1–2 (Spring 1988): 270–79.

———. "Isabel viendo llover en Barataria." *Revista de Estudios Hispánicos* 19, no. 2 (May 1985): 129–37.

Martín Nogales, J. L. "Manifiesto contra la represión política." *Diario de Navarra* (Spain), 9 January 1985, n.p.

Marx, Karl. *Capital: A Critique of Political Economy*. New York: Vintage Books, 1977.

Menton, Seymour. *The Spanish American Short Story: A Critical Anthology*. Berkeley and Los Angeles: University of California Press, 1980.

Moody, Michael. "Entrevista con Isabel Allende." *Discurso Literario* 4, no. 1 (1987): 41–53.

Morgan, Ellen. "Humanbecoming: Form and Focus in the Neo-Feminist Novel." In Criticism: Essays on Theory, Poetry and Prose. Edited by Cheryl L. Brown and Karen Olson. Metuchen, N.J., and London: Scarecrow Press, 1978.

Neruda, Pablo. "La barcarola" and "La verdad." In *Poesías escogidas*. Madrid: Aguilar, 1980.

Nieto, José García. "*Eva Luna*." *ABC Literario* (Madrid), 26 September, 1987.

Martín Nogales, T. L. "Manifiesto contra la represión política," *Diario de Navarra*, 11 January 1985, 54.

"Nueva novela de Isabel Allende." *La Tarde* (Puerto Rico), 8–14 October 1986, 26.

Parra, Violeta. "Gracias a la vida." *Gracias a la vida*. sung by Joan Báez. Columbia Records, 1973.

Pereira, Teresinha (Teresinka). *El realismo mágico y otras herencias de Julio Cortázar*. Coimbra, Portugal, and Bloomington, Ind.: Nova Era and Backstage Books, 1976.

Piñol, Rosa María. "Eva Luna es la feminidad aceptada, dice Isabel Allende." *La Vanguardia* (Barcelona), 20 November 1987, 20.

Plaza, Galvarino. *Víctor Jara*. Madrid: Ediciones Júcar, 1976.

Poniatowska, Elena. Personal conversation at Duke University, fall of 1986.

Ponte Far, José A. "La brillantez narrativa de una prosa épica." *La Voz de Galicia* (Spain), 12 November 1986, 26.

Pynchon, Thomas. "The Heart's Eternal Vow." *New York Times Book Review*, 10 April 1988.

Puig, Manuel. *El beso de la mujer araña*. Barcelona: Seix Barral, 1976.

"Reportaje a Isabel Allende." *El Clarín* (Buenos Aires) 30 May 1985, 3.

Rodó, José Enrique. *Ariel: liberalismo y jacobinismo*. Montevideo: Ministerio de Instrucción Pública y Revisión Social, 1964.

Rojas, Mario A. "*La casa de los espíritus* de Isabel Allende: un caleidoscopio de espejos desordenados." *Revista Iberoamericana* July–December 1985, 917–25.

Rosetti, Claudia. "Love and Revolution in the House of Trueba." *Wall Street Journal*, 19 June 1985, 35.

Rulfo, Juan. "Luvina." *El llano en llamas*. México: Fondo de Cultura Económica, 1980.

———. *Pedro Páramo*. México: Fondo de Cultura Económica, 1980.

Saladrigas, Roberto. "*Eva Luna* desde Isabel Allende." *La Vanguardia* (Barcelona), 8 October 1987, 49.

Savater, Fernando. *La infancia recuperada*. Madrid: Taurus, 1981.

Stimpson, Catharine R. "Introduction." In *Feminist Issues in Literary Scholarship*, edited by Shari Benstock. Bloomington and Indianapolis: Indiana University Press, 1987.

Storni, Alfonsina. "Hombre pequeñito." In *Literatura hispanoamericana*, edited by Enrique Anderson Imbert. New York: Holt, Rinehard and Winston, 1970.

Suñen, Juan Carlos. "La progresión de cangrejo." *El País* (Madrid), 8 October 1987, 19.

Suñen, Luis. "Una excelente novela chilena." *El País* (Madrid), 23 January 1983, "Libros," 3.

Tansley, David V. *The Raiment of Light: A Study of the Human Aura*. London: Routledge and Kegan Paul, 1984.

Taufic, Camilo. *Chile en la hoguera: crónica de la opresión militar*. Buenos Aires: Corregidor, 1974.

Tennyson, Alfred. "The Lady of Shallot." In *Works of Alfred Lord Tennyson*, vol. 1. New York: Macmillan, 1908.

Torres, Maruja. "Isabel Allende recoge en su primera novela la tradición oral de su familia." *El País*, 24 November 1982, 19.

Usigli, Rodolfo. "Realismo moderno y realismo mágico." In *Itinerario del autor*. México: Fondo de Cultura Económica, 1940.

Valbuena Briones, Angel. "Una cala en el realismo mágico." *Cuadernos Americanos* 166 (1969): 233–41.

Valente, Ignacio. "*Eva Luna: entre la calidad y el éxito*." *El Mercurio* (Santiago de Chile), 25 October 1987, 6.

Vargas Llosa, Mario. *Pantaleón y las visitadoras*. Barcelona: Seix Barral, 1973.

Vela, Francisco, trans. *Nach-Expressionismus, magischer Realismus; Probleme der neusten europäischen Malerei*, by Franz Roh. Leipzig: Klinkhardt und Biermann, 1925.

West, Paul. "*The House of the Spirits*." *Nation*, 20 July 1985, 52.

Woolf, Virginia. "A Room of One's Own." In *Feminism: The Essential Historical Writings*, edited by Miriam Schnier. New York: Vintage Books, 1972.

Wimsatt, William K., and Monroe C. Beardsley. "The Intentional Fallacy." In *Essays in Modern Literary Criticism*, edited by Ray B. West. New York: Holt, Rinehart and Winston, 1965.

Yeats, William Butler. "Sailing to Byzantium." In *The Poems: A New Edition*. London: Macmillan, 1983.

Young, David, and Keith Hagarman. *Magical Realist Fiction: A Reader*. New York: Longman, 1984.

Zimmerman, J. E. "Cassandra." In *A Dictionary of Classical Mythology*. New York: Harper and Row, 1964.

Zuber, Helen, and Swantje Strieder. "Ja, diese Wochen waren fürchterlich." *Der Spiegel* no. 45 (1986): 182–90.

INDEX